MW01487023

# LUKE

# BELIEF

*A Theological Commentary*
*on the Bible*

GENERAL EDITORS

*Amy Plantinga Pauw*
*William C. Placher*[†]

# LUKE

JUSTO L. GONZÁLEZ

WESTMINSTER
JOHN KNOX PRESS
LOUISVILLE · KENTUCKY

© 2010 Justo L. González

*First edition*
Published by Westminster John Knox Press
Louisville, Kentucky

10 11 12 13 14 15 16 17 18 19—10 9 8 7 6 5 4 3 2 1

*All rights reserved.* No part of this book may be reproduced or transmitted in any form
or by any means, electronic or mechanical, including photocopying, recording,
or by any information storage or retrieval system, without permission in writing
from the publisher. For information, address Westminster John Knox Press,
100 Witherspoon Street, Louisville, Kentucky 40202-1396.
Or contact us online at www.wjkbooks.com.

Scripture quotations from the New Revised Standard Version of the Bible
are copyright © 1989 by the Division of Christian Education of the National Council
of the Churches of Christ in the U.S.A. and are used by permission.

Excerpt from "Where There Is a Will, There Is a Way," *Journal for Preachers* 25, no. 4 (2002):
32–34. Used by permission. All rights reserved. Excerpt, with slight variations, from
Justo L. González and Pablo A. Jiménez, *Púlpito: An Introduction to Hispanic Preaching*
(Nashville: Abingdon, 2005), 95–100. Used by permission. All rights reserved.

*Book design by Drew Stevens*
*Cover design by Lisa Buckley*
*Cover art: David Chapman / Design Pics / CORBIS*

**Library of Congress Cataloging-in-Publication Data**

González, Justo L.
  Luke / Justo L. Gonzalez. — 1st ed.
     p. cm. — (Belief: a theological commentary on the Bible)
  Includes bibliographical references.
  ISBN 978-0-664-23201-6 (alk. paper)
  1. Bible. N. T. Luke—Commentaries.  I. Title.
  BS2595.53.G66 2010
  226.4'07—dc22

                                                       2010003747

PRINTED IN THE UNITED STATES OF AMERICA

∞ The paper used in this publication meets the minimum requirements of
the American National Standard for Information Sciences—
Permanence of Paper for Printed Library Materials, ANSI Z39.48-1992

Westminster John Knox Press advocates the responsible use of our natural resources.
The text paper of this book is made from 30% post-consumer waste.

# Contents

# *Publisher's Note*

William C. Placher worked with Amy Plantinga Pauw as a general editor for this series until his untimely death in November 2008. Bill brought great energy and vision to the series, and was instrumental in defining and articulating its distinctive approach and in securing theologians to write for it. Bill's own commentary for the series was the last thing he wrote, and Westminster John Knox Press dedicates the entire series to his memory with affection and gratitude.

William C. Placher, LaFollette Distinguished Professor in Humanities at Wabash College, spent thirty-four years as one of Wabash College's most popular teachers. A summa cum laude graduate of Wabash in 1970, he earned his master's degree in philosophy in 1974 and his Ph.D. in 1975, both from Yale University. In 2002 the American Academy of Religion honored him with the Excellence in Teaching Award. Placher was also the author of thirteen books, including *A History of Christian Theology, The Triune God, The Domestication of Transcendence, Jesus the Savior, Narratives of a Vulnerable God,* and *Unapologetic Theology.* He also edited the volume *Essentials of Christian Theology,* which was named as one of 2004's most outstanding books by both *The Christian Century* and *Christianity Today* magazines.

# Series Introduction

*Belief: A Theological Commentary on the Bible* is a series from West-minster John Knox Press, featuring biblical commentaries written by theologians. The writers of this series share Karl Barth's concern that, insofar as their usefulness to pastors goes, most modern commentaries are "no commentary at all, but merely the first step toward a commentary." Historical-critical approaches to Scripture rule out some readings and commend others, but such methods only begin to help theological reflection and the preaching of the Word. By themselves, they do not convey the powerful sense of God's merciful presence that calls Christians to repentance and praise; they do not bring the church fully forward in the life of discipleship. It is to such tasks that theologians are called.

For several generations, however, professional theologians in North America and Europe have not been writing commentaries on the Christian Scriptures. The specialization of professional disciplines and the expectations of theological academies about the kind of writing that theologians should do, as well as many of the directions in which contemporary theology itself has gone, have contributed to this dearth of theological commentaries. This is a relatively new phenomenon; until the last century or two, the church's great theologians also routinely saw themselves as biblical interpreters. The gap between the fields is a loss for both the church and the discipline of theology itself. By inviting forty-two contemporary theologians to wrestle deeply with particular texts of Scripture, the editors of this series hope not only to provide new theological resources for the church, but also to encourage all theologians to pay more attention to Scripture and the life of the church in their writings.

We are grateful to the Louisville Institute, which provided funding for a consultation in June 2007. We invited theologians, pastors, and biblical scholars to join us in a conversation about what this series could contribute to the life of the church. The time was provocative and the results were rich. Much of the series' shape owes to the insights of these skilled and faithful interpreters, who sought to describe a way to write a commentary that served the theological needs of the church and its pastors with relevance, historical accuracy, and theological depth. The passion of these participants guided us in creating this series and lives on in the volumes.

As theologians, the authors will be interested much less in the matters of form, authorship, historical setting, social context, and philology—the very issues that are often of primary concern to critical biblical scholars. Instead, this series' authors will seek to explain the theological importance of the texts for the church today, using biblical scholarship as needed for such explication but without any attempt to cover all of the topics of the usual modern biblical commentary. This thirty-six-volume series will provide passage-by-passage commentary on all the books of the Protestant biblical canon, with more extensive attention given to passages of particular theological significance. The authors' chief dialogue will be with the church's creeds, practices, and hymns; with the history of faithful interpretation and use of the Scriptures; with the categories and concepts of theology; and with contemporary culture in both "high" and popular forms. Each volume will begin with a discussion of *why* the church needs this book and why we need it *now*, in order to ground all of the commentary in contemporary relevance. Throughout each volume, textboxes will highlight the voices of ancient and modern interpreters from the global communities of faith, and occasional essays will allow deeper reflection on the key theological concepts of these biblical books.

The authors of this commentary series are theologians of the church who embrace a variety of confessional and theological perspectives. The group of authors assembled for this series represents more diversity of race, ethnicity, and gender than any other commentary series. They approach the larger Christian tradition with a critical respect, seeking to reclaim its riches and at the same time to acknowledge its shortcomings. The authors also aim to make available to readers a wide range of contemporary theological voices from many parts of the world. While it does recover an older genre of writing, this series is not an attempt to retrieve some idealized past. These commentaries have learned from tradition, but they are most importantly commentaries for today. The authors share the conviction that their work will be more contemporary, more faithful, and more radical, to the extent that it is more biblical, honestly wrestling with the texts of the Scriptures.

William C. Placher
Amy Plantinga Pauw

# *Preface*

Sending a book to press is very much like seeing a child grow up. For a while, you had the opportunity and the responsibility to shape the child's life. But now things are different. Now the child has a life of its own, chooses its own friends, and determines the rest of her or his life. As I send this manuscript off to press, I do so with a similar feeling: I had a chance to shape it—although at times, like a willful child, the Gospel text forced me to go in directions I would not have chosen to go. Now it has a life of its own. Whatever it says to its readers—or whatever it does not say—I can no longer determine. I simply pray and hope that, like a well-reared child, it will contribute something to those who encounter it. Fare you well, my book!

With such a note of farewell must also go a note of gratitude. Even in the privacy of my study, I never came to the text of Luke alone. With me were the countless believers—monastics, many of them—who revered, copied, and preserved the text itself over the centuries. With me were some fifty generations of biblical interpreters, many of them whispering in my ear. With me were more recent scholars, providing insights, raising questions, leading in new directions. With me was my wife Catherine, working at the same time on her own volume for this series, but also correcting and enriching my style and my theology just as every day she enriches—and corrects!—my life. And with me was, I trust, the Holy Spirit of God, to whom I now commend these pages and those who will eventually read them.

Justo L. González

# *Abbreviations*

NIV      New International Version
NRSV   New Revised Standard Version

# Introduction:
# Why Luke? Why Now?

Like the other Gospels, Luke sets out to tell the story of Jesus of Nazareth. And, also like the other Gospels—indeed, like any narrative—he has his own slant and emphases. Thus the question of Luke's relevance for us today has much to do with those emphases, and how they relate to the issues and concerns of our day. What does the Gospel of Luke bring to the table that is less noticeable—or absent—in the other Gospels?

## An Ongoing History

As we read the newspapers today, or watch the news on television, it is obvious that our generation is very much concerned about history. Yet what concerns us is a particular kind of history. It is not history as we studied it in school, as a retelling of past events. It is rather history as the context within which all of life is lived, and particularly as the ongoing narrative of life on our planet. Debates about social policy, health care, and international relations are most often shaped in terms of the future outcome of our decisions. What will be the consequences of the fiscal deficit for our children and grandchildren? How will the earth survive its mindless exploitation? For us and our generation, history is an open, unfinished process. We study the past, not as if it were all of reality, or even all that is important, but rather as people immersed in the continuation of that past, and in its way to the future. History is not closed. It is not just about our ancestors. It is also about us and the generations to come.

On this point, our concerns are similar to Luke's. Of all the Gospels, only Luke carries the story beyond the resurrection and the appearances of the risen Lord. His Gospel goes on to the ascension. Then he continues the narrative in the second part of his writing, the book of Acts.

Although we have no way of knowing how much time elapsed between the writing of the two books, the combination of Luke–Acts is a two-volume piece. There is a clear connection between the two that has led many scholars to the conclusion that Luke–Acts was conceived as a whole, as a continued narrative first restating what others had written about Jesus, and then describing the development of the early Christian community. Yet there has long been a tendency to separate the two. Already in the mid-second century, when Marcion proposed the first list of Christian canonical books—which he had to do, since he rejected the ancient Scriptures of Israel—this list included an expurgated and abbreviated version of the Gospel of Luke and the Epistles of Paul, but not Acts. Even in our present-day canon of the New Testament, the placement of the Gospel of John between Luke and Acts interrupts the narrative flow of these two books, originally intended to be read together.

Significantly, there are a number of parallelisms between Luke and Acts. Both begin with a prologue addressed to a certain "Theophilus." In both cases, after an historical introduction, there is a quotation from the Hebrew Scriptures that will set the pace for the rest of the book—in Luke 4, the passage from Isaiah, and in Acts 2, the passage from Joel. Then there are parallel stories showing that the life of the church is patterned after the life of Jesus—notably some miracles in Acts that remind the reader of similar miracles in Luke, the trial and death of Jesus paralleled by the trial and death of Stephen, and the sufferings of Jesus paralleled by the trials and tribulations of Paul.

All of this implies that Luke has a particular view of Christian history. He would certainly agree with the other Gospel writers that the culmination of all of history is the life, death, and resurrection of Jesus. Indeed, as we shall see as we look at his chronology, he carries this point beyond Mark and Matthew. But this does not mean that history has ended, that whatever happens from that point on is not significant. On the contrary, Luke is concerned with how history now unfolds, particularly among those who share the common Christian faith that Jesus Christ is the end of history, and with placing this in the context of all of human history.

Luke did not write his two volumes to be read piecemeal, as we do today in church, in private devotions, and even in our commentaries. They involve an overarching argument, a grand narrative that gives meaning to the whole. The chronological dimension of that narrative—as in any story well told—is obvious. Luke–Acts begins by grounding Jesus in a genealogy that goes back to Adam, then tells the story of the birth, ministry, death, resurrection, and ascension of Jesus, in order to move in the second volume to the continued work of Jesus through the Spirit in the life of the church. The geographic dimension, though not as obvious, is just as important. The story begins in Galilee; slowly winds its way to Jerusalem, where it settles for the last chapters of the Gospel and the first chapters of Acts; and then moves on to Antioch, Asia Minor, Greece, and eventually Rome. Yet neither chronologically nor geographically is the story finished. Chronologically, we are left with Paul under house arrest in Rome, and are told nothing about the final outcome of his appeal to Caesar. Geographically, though Acts 1:8 promises the disciples that they will be witnesses "to the ends of the earth," the narrative takes us only to Rome (hardly "the ends of the earth"!) and there it leaves us, with no hint as to how the promise of Acts 1:8 is fulfilled.

On that basis, it might be appropriate to call Luke–Acts "the unfinished Gospel." It is unfinished chronologically, for the narrative has no conclusion. Rather than ending, it simply quits when Paul is in Rome—precisely the point at which it is most engrossing and the reader would wish to know more, like a serial in television, where at the end of each episode we are left hanging, waiting for the next. And it is unfinished geographically, for it leaves us waiting for the story of how the disciples of Jesus became his witnesses "to the ends of the earth."

This is not a flaw in Luke's writing. Interpreters have often debated why Luke does not tell us about the outcome of Paul's trial, and some have suggested that it is because Luke wishes to present the Gospel to Roman eyes in its best possible light, and he therefore does not wish to tell that Paul was executed by Roman authorities. This is hardly convincing, for at the very heart of Luke's narrative is the story of Jesus, condemned to death by Roman authority. My own inclination is to think that Luke–Acts is unfinished because its author was seeking not only to inform but also to invite. Theophilus and all subsequent readers of Luke's two volumes would learn about the story of Jesus and of the early church; but they would also be invited to see themselves as the continuation of that story, and to become witnesses "to the ends of the earth." The grand narrative is thus an invitation, a reminder to readers of who they are; and within that grand narrative the various smaller narrative units must also be seen as a calling and an invitation.

On this point, Luke is very close to our own interest in history. We study and write history to invite. Those who see hope in the present, use history to invite others to hope. Those who see doom, to invite others to fear. Those who seek guidance and correction, to invite others to follow the guidance and correction of history. For us, as for Luke, history is ongoing, unfinished, an invitation to join what God is doing among us.

But still Luke would insist on the counterpoint to that: this unfinished history is not simply up for grabs. Its end has already been written. It has been written in the life, death, and resurrection of Jesus, and in his final reign. And, because the end has been written, Luke invites us today to join in the grand narrative that begins in his Gospel, continues in Acts, and leads to us.

## An Unfinished Church

An element in this unfinished history that is of particular concern for me and for many believers is that the church itself is unfinished. As an historian of Christian life and doctrine, I well remember the first books that I read on the general history of the church. They were all written by North Americans or by Western Europeans. Reading them, one received the impression that in the Protestantism of the North Atlantic, Christianity had come to its full fruition, and that all that remained to be done was taking that form of Christianity to the rest of the world. Today very few church historians, even in the North Atlantic, would write history in such a manner. There is no doubt that the North Atlantic is becoming less and less Christian, and that the centers of vitality in the church are moving to other lands. From the point of view of many Christians in the North Atlantic, this seems to be the sad end of the story. But others, both in the North Atlantic and elsewhere, see it as a new beginning.

On this point, Luke's narrative may provide significant guidance, for just as today we have to write about the passing of the centers of Christianity to Asia, Africa, and Latin America, so did Luke write about the passing of the center from Jerusalem to Antioch, and about Paul's passing over to Macedonia.

But there is more here than the mere geographical movement. Luke's two writings are a significant step in the movement of Christianity into new cultural environments. This is true both in their content and in their method. In their content, this crossing of boundaries is clear, for the narrative moves to ever-widening circles. But it is also clear in Luke's method, for in his writings he adopts many of the linguistic and historiographic canons of Hellenistic culture. In so doing, he provides us with a clue as to how Christians today are called to cross similar boundaries, and to explore ways to express and incarnate their faith in the various cultures of the world.

## *The Great Reversal*

Reversal is a central theme of Luke–Acts, and this too is of particular interest to us today. A grand reversal is part of Luke's geopolitical narrative. In a world where all power and all important decisions were expected to come from Rome, and within the context of a Judaism centered in Jerusalem, Luke tells a story that begins in Galilee—a marginal land by both Roman and Jewish standards—and then moves on to bring its message and its power first to Jerusalem, and then to Rome itself.

Within the context of that geopolitical reversal, Luke offers numerous instances of other reversals no less astonishing. Mary announces this at the very beginning of the Gospel: "He has scat-

tered the proud in the thoughts of their hearts. He has brought down
the powerful from their thrones, and lifted up the lowly; he has
filled the hungry with good things, and sent the rich away empty"
(1:51b–53). In the parable of the Prodigal, it is the supposedly good
son who is left out of the feast, while the prodigal has a banquet
celebrated in his honor. Jesus shows particular compassion for those
whom his society would consider the worst sinners, and has harsh
words for good religious people. The hungry will be filled, and those
who weep will laugh; but those who are now full will be hungry, and
those who now laugh will weep (6:21, 23; see also 16:19–31). The
first shall be last; and the last, first. Things hidden to the wise have
been revealed to babes. The greatest is the one who serves. While
this great reversal appears also in the other Gospels (for instance,
Matt. 21:31) it has particular power in Luke, as we shall see repeatedly in the pages that follow.[1]

Reversal is a theme that is familiar to all of us from the time when
we first heard some of the classic children's stories, such as "Cinder-
ella" and "The Ugly Duckling." There is much in those stories that
is wrong: the notions that a girl's highest purpose in life is to marry
a prince, that physical beauty is to be valued above all things, that
women do not love their stepchildren, and others. But there is one
point that still rings true: justice requires a reversal of conditions for
the excluded and the oppressed—and, if they insist on their privileges, also for the insiders and the oppressors. This is a theme we
sometimes like and sometimes detest, usually depending on whether
we are the wronged or the wrongdoers. If we feel wronged, we call
for reversal. But if others claim we have wronged then, and call for a
reversal, we reject their pleas as unjustified, ungrateful, inordinately
proud, or even violent. It is at this point that the Gospel of Luke
both encourages and confronts us. It encourages us if we seek a just
reversal, and it confronts us if we resist it. Luke's unfinished history
includes a grand reversal as a sign of the reign of God, and invites us
to consider the reversals that we encounter in our day as possible
signs of that reign.

---

1. On this subject, see Allen Verhey, *The Great Reversal: Ethics and the New Testament* (Grand
Rapids: Eerdmans, 1984), 93–97.

## *A Reversal for the Poor*

While the theme of poverty and responsibility toward the poor is central throughout Scripture, and particularly in the Gospels, the Gospel of Luke is noted for its particular emphasis on this theme. Jesus' calling, according to his reading in the synagogue, is to announce "good news to the poor." The word "poor"—*ptōchos*—appears repeatedly in Luke's Gospel (4:18; 6:20; 7:22; 14:13, 21; 18:22; 19:8; 21:3). Interestingly, however, it does not appear at all in Acts. This has led some to claim that the theme of the poor is not as central to Luke's theology as the Gospel would seem to indicate. But most likely Luke is trying to show that in the community of the Spirit, the church, the new order of God's reign prevails to such a point that "there was not a needy person among them" (Acts 4:34).

For Luke, the gospel is "good news to the poor" (4:18), and this is part of the great reversal. While this is a central theme throughout his Gospel, probably the best-known example is the parable of the Rich Man and Lazarus, whose conditions are radically reversed in the end.

Here too Luke speaks to our day. Throughout the world, people are coming to the conviction that poverty is in large measure the result of injustice. Those of us who are more affluent, who have never really known hunger, nakedness, and lack of medical services, and who consider ourselves producers of wealth, find it difficult to understand such an interpretation of reality. We look for people who are poor through their own fault, and then claim that we are willing to help "the worthy poor," but not the rest.

> The hope of the poor is not grounded on general human kindness, nor in the goodwill of the powerful, nor in the dynamics of development. The poor throughout the world know that all these, rather than providing an escape from their problems, generally have made them worse. The hope of the poor is grounded rather in the intolerability of the present situation. Their past history and their present leave them no other route than turning their eyes to the future.
>
> **—Ignacio Ellacuría**
>
> *Conversión de la iglesia al reino de Dios para anunciarlo y realizarlo en la historia* (San Salvador: UCA, 1985), 107.

Conveniently, we then conclude that the worthy poor are just a few, and that therefore no radical action is needed.

The poor in Luke are the supposedly unworthy poor. Quite frequently, "the poor and the sinners" were lumped together. After all, the poor could not offer proper sacrifices, could not keep themselves clean of ritual contamination, and had to deal with many things that the godly considered unclean. It is to these poor that the message is good news. It is to these poor that the great reversal is announced. Thus once again Luke comes into our present reality speaking a word that, though unwelcome by many, our age needs to heed.

## *Women*

Throughout the world, our age is characterized by the emergence of women claiming their right to be protagonists of their own lives. This takes many different forms in various cultures, but even so is a universal phenomenon, often resisted by those who would keep women "in their place." Unfortunately, in the face of this struggle many Christians claim the Bible as a source of opposition to the hopes and aspirations of women—in the church as well as in society at large.

Here again the Gospel of Luke is particularly relevant to our time. Women have a significant role both in Luke's Gospel and in Acts—which, given the conventions of the time, may well be seen as one more instance of the great reversal. In the Gospel, the first person to hear the good news of the birth of the Messiah is a woman; and the first people to hear the good news of his resurrection are also women. Luke is the only Gospel writer who informs us that the early Jesus movement was financed by women (8:1–3). In the first chapter of the Gospel, Mary and Elizabeth are much more important than Joseph and Zechariah. Acts begins with the story of Pentecost, in which women as well as men receive the Spirit and announce the gospel. In Acts Priscilla is normally named before her husband Aquila, and Lydia is one of Paul's main supporters. Throughout the Gospel, Luke often couples a story or a parable about a man with one about a woman. In 2:25–38 it is Simeon and Anna. In 4:31–39

Jesus heals first a man and then a woman (Peter's mother-in-law). In 8:26–56 once again Jesus heals a man and a woman. The parable of the Good Samaritan in chapter 10 is followed by the visit to Mary and Martha. In 13:18–21 someone (apparently a man) plants a mustard seed, and a woman adds some yeast to the dough. In 15:1–10 a shepherd loses a sheep, and a woman loses a coin. There are so many such pairings that it is difficult to imagine that they are not done on purpose.

## *Eating and Feasting*

I find Luke's Gospel particularly appealing because eating is one of my favorite occupations, and it also seems to be one of Luke's favorite themes. As in the other Synoptic Gospels, Jesus is criticized because he and his disciples eat with unworthy people (5:30; Matt. 9:11; Mark 2:16). But much more frequently than in those other stories, Jesus attends banquets—which has led some to suggest that Luke is following the Greek tradition of the philosopher who teaches at a feast or *symposium*. As in Matthew and Mark, a highlight of the narrative is the last supper of Jesus with his disciples, just before he is betrayed. But of the three only Luke has two postresurrection appearances in which eating plays a central role.

There seem to be at least three reasons why Luke repeatedly places Jesus at a meal. The first of these is to affirm the joyful character of his message and the physical reality of his resurrection. Jesus eats because eating was the most common way of expressing and sharing joy. Second, Luke frequently depicts Jesus as eating because meals were one of the clearest expressions of the social and religious order, and therefore meals provided one of the best opportunities to break convention and to illustrate the great reversal. Jesus eats and drinks not only with the worthy but also with the supposedly unworthy, making them heirs to the great feast of God. Jesus uses meals to announce a different order, and he does this to the point of criticizing the sitting conventions at a banquet to which a leader of the Pharisees has invited him (14:7–11), and then suggesting to his host that his guest list is wrong (14:12–14). Finally, Jesus eats

> We eat on the run and graze, infrequently sitting together as a family. . . . Jesus, Luke, and their contemporaries knew of and participated in symposium meals, at which they reclined on couches and that were long and festive, featuring food and drink and lengthy conversation. No gulping and galloping at those meals.
>
> —Robert J. Karris
>
> *Eating Your Way through Luke's Gospel,* Calvin's New Testament Commentaries, 12 vols. (Collegeville, MN: Liturgical Press, 2006), 4.

because Luke and his prospective readers belong to a community whose main act of worship includes a meal—a meal in remembrance both of Jesus' earthly ministry, death, and resurrection, and of the final banquet when the great reversal will be fulfilled.

The dinner table is one of the places where we most clearly manifest our values as well as our social conventions and prejudices. We usually invite to dinner only those whom we like, or those whom we must invite because of some social convention or obligation. Those whom no one likes, those who are most in need of it, seldom receive a dinner invitation. And what is true of the actual tables in our dining rooms is also true at the larger table of the earth and its produce. Luke leads us to consider that perhaps our "good manners" at the table—both in our homes and in the larger home that is the world—need to be corrected by the manners of Jesus.

## The Spirit

As we look at the worldwide church in the twenty-first century, there can be little doubt that the doctrine of the Holy Spirit will be a central issue in our century as it has never been before. While many of the more traditional churches are losing membership, and some even seem to have lost hope, vibrant and growing churches throughout the world stress the work of the Spirit in their midst. There is no doubt that this may lead to excesses, of which many could be cited. But there is also no doubt that all Christians throughout the world need to rediscover what Scripture says about the Spirit. Thus a theology for the twenty-first century will be largely a theology of the Spirit.

Luke–Acts stresses the role of the Holy Spirit, both in the life of Jesus and in the life of the early church. There are seventeen references to the Spirit in the Gospel of Luke, while there are six in Mark and twelve in Matthew. And the main protagonist of the book of Acts is not any of the apostles but the Spirit, who is mentioned no less than fifty-seven times. This has led some to declare that Acts is the Gospel of the Spirit. Significantly, early in Luke Jesus' mission is based on the scriptural declaration, "the Spirit of the Lord is upon me" (4:18), while Acts practically opens with Jesus' promise that the disciples would receive the power of the Holy Spirit, and the fulfillment of that promise at Pentecost. Thus one could say that in Luke we have the story of the work and presence of the Spirit in Jesus, and in Acts we have the story of the work and presence of Jesus through the Spirit.

Ultimately, this is the answer to our initial questions: Why Luke? Why today? Simply, because it is precisely the Spirit whose work Luke emphasizes that makes any Scripture—and certainly the Gospel of Luke—relevant to us today. We do not study Luke because he was a good writer—which he was. Nor do we study Luke because he tells us of the customs and political figures of his time—which he does. We study Luke because, through the agency of that same Holy Spirit whose work and power Luke emphasizes, his Gospel becomes God's Word to us, leading and accompanying us as we seek to join Jesus in the great reversal he announces and brings about.

## This Commentary

While taking into account current discussions among scholars on matters such as sources, genre, date, and so on, in this commentary I do not deal with them. The main question that I seek to address is, What does the text mean to us? This question is not as simple as it sounds, for meaning is to be found not only in a text but also in its readers. A text is always offering new meanings as it is read in changing circumstances, by a variety of people who come to the text with different backgrounds, concerns, and questions. While this may be threatening for those who wish to claim simply that "the Bible says . . . ," it is what makes the Bible itself essential. If meaning

All good interpretation of the Bible is contemporary. If it were not so, it would not be good. . . . The Bible is not on a par with the subsequent interpretation; it is above it, as the text is antecedent to the commentary. And the interpretation is always an interpretation for the time in which it is written or spoken.
—Gustaf Wingren

*Theology in Conflict: Nygren, Barth, Bultmann*, trans. Eric H. Wahlstrom (Philadelphia: Muhlenberg, 1958), 154–55.

were something we could extract from a text in a final and definitive way, we would eventually be able to dispose of the text itself. But this is not the case. The text is always out there, presenting new possibilities, raising new questions, offering new insights—which is a simplified way of saying that the text is polysemous.

The recognition of such polysemy makes it necessary for the author of a commentary such as this to lay bare at least some of his or her own perspectives, interests, and background of which he or she is aware when approaching a text. In my own case, several such items may be of interest to the reader. First of all, I grew up in Cuba, at that time a predominantly Roman Catholic country where as a Protestant I repeatedly experienced religious prejudice and discrimination. Second, most of my mature years have been spent in the United States, where I have witnessed and experienced both much goodness and generosity and frequent instances of racial, ethnic, and cultural prejudice and discrimination. Therefore, as I read any text issues of inclusion and exclusion are of special interest to me. This is particularly true since in my repeated dealings with others who are excluded I often find myself among the included who in various ways exclude them.

Then, my academic training and my entire professional career have centered on the history of Christian thought. From my first years of seminary study I became convinced that one cannot understand Christian theology apart from its history, that theology is not an abstract discipline that one can study and learn apart from its historical circumstances and development. This means that as I read Scripture, in this case the Gospel of Luke, I am very much aware that I read not only through my eyes but also through the eyes of a long history of interpretation—a history that I both respect and seek to continue and to correct. Soon another conviction was added to this interest in the historical development of theology: the conviction that, at its very core, Christianity is a story. It is the story of God's dealings with humankind and with all of creation, particularly through Jesus Christ, and since then, by the power of the Spirit, in the church and in the world in which it has been placed. In concrete terms, this means that as I read the gospel story, in this case the Gospel of Luke, I do not believe that one improves on that story by distilling from it abstract principles, theories, or doctrines. Thus a "theological commentary" on Scripture—particularly on those parts of Scripture that, like the Gospels, are narrative—must not seek to supersede the narrative, nor to turn it into abstract principles, but to relate it to the life and proclamation of the church and of its members. This is what I have tried to do in the pages that follow.

# 1:1–4:13

# *Preparation and Early Ministry*

## 1:1–80
### *The Setting*

#### 1:1–4–*The Prologue*

Although this section has traditionally been called the "prologue" to Luke's Gospel, it is much more than that. In it Luke tells us much about his methodology and about how he understands the task he has undertaken. His "prologue" is similar to many others in his time. In many ways, it is also similar to what one would write today in an introduction to any book on history. It acknowledges his predecessors, says something about his research, and sets forth the purpose of his writing—"so that you may know the truth concerning the things about which you have been instructed."

Note that Luke does not say that he is writing his Gospel because other accounts are inaccurate. We tend to read this into the text, because in our time it is customary to justify the writing of an historical monograph and other similar material on the basis that one's predecessors have been wrong. But there is nothing of the sort in Luke's prologue. Although his words in Greek are not exactly the same, the NRSV is justified in translating what "others" have set out to produce as "an orderly account," and then to use the same words for what Luke himself proposes to write. He is not correcting others; he is simply telling the same story from a different angle and using some different materials. In this sense, he is more like a sportswriter who sets out to tell the story of the same game about which many of her colleagues are also writing. Others have reported on the same game. This particular sportswriter might even look at what some of those other colleagues have written. She will also follow certain stylistic conventions for this sort of article. Still, her story will differ from theirs. She may not claim that it is better; but it is still different, and worth telling. Thus news reporting makes clear what historians know, but their readers often forget: that the telling of events always reflects the perspectives of both the eyewitnesses and the narrators themselves. News, like history, can always be told anew and differently, and still remain the same news or the same history! This is crucial for our understanding of Luke's Gospel and of our own task in proclaiming the "good news" of Jesus Christ.

That Luke is not writing on the basis that the others are wrong is crucial also for understanding the nature of the Bible as Word of God. Almost certainly one of those other writings to which Luke refers is the Gospel of Mark. Luke is not claiming that Mark is wrong—not even that his story is better than Mark's. He is simply telling the story as he sees it and wants Theophilus to hear it. Since we do not know much about Theophilus, it is impossible to tell to what degree Luke's presentation of the story is geared to a particular audience. Some years after Luke wrote, the church began putting together various books into what we now call the New Testament. People were well aware that the four Gospels that we now have did not agree on every detail, yet they put them all together in one canon of the New Testament! By that time, some other documents were circulating, each of them claiming that it was *the* true story of Jesus and his teachings. They presented Jesus as far more "spiritual" and less physical that did our present Gospels. (One of those was the *Gospel of Judas*, whose relatively recent publication made headlines.) Yet the church rejected all those other documents and their claims to be the sole and absolute truth. Instead, it formed a New Testament including four Gospels that, while agreeing on the essentials, were written from different perspectives and even disagreed on a number of points. What was important was to affirm that Jesus Christ was indeed born, that he suffered and died on the cross, that he was raised from the dead, that all this was done for our salvation, that it is the fulfillment of God's ancient promises to Israel. The rest—how many people Jesus fed, what were his exact words from the cross, and the like—was secondary. As with sportswriters, there might be differences in interpretation and on details; but still all would agree on what team won, by what score, and other essential items. And, as in the task of writing on sports there are certain canons that reporters follow, so does Luke follow the canon of historical writing in his time.

This may be a problem for absolute literalists, who would have to claim, for instance, that Jesus taught his disciples two different versions of the Lord's Prayer. But in truth it is a boon for all of us, for it forces us to focus our attention on the central tenets of the Christian faith, and it also means that we can read the same story from four different angles—and then tell it ourselves from our own angle!

The foregoing does not mean that we are free to make up the story as we please. Luke is not making up his story out of whole cloth. He is very clear that he is writing "after investigating everything carefully from the very first." This is not fiction. Luke is not telling us what he thinks Jesus should or could have done or said. He bases his writing on the testimony of "those who from the beginning were eyewitnesses and servants of the word."

This notion of "witnessing" will appear repeatedly in Luke's two books, the Gospel and Acts. Events can be known only through those who have witnessed them. We know of past events because there are witnesses who tell us about them. Others after us will know of the same events because we and other generations have witnessed to them. The knowledge of historical events is possible only through an unbroken chain of witnesses, some oral and some written. Luke knows that the story he is telling has come to him through witnesses. Now he is witnessing to Theophilus. The implication (seen more clearly in Acts) is that Theophilus and others like him will join the unbroken chain of witnesses.

As to who "Theophilus" might have been, the truth is that we simply do not know. The title Luke gives him, "most excellent," was usually reserved for certain fairly high echelons in Roman society. Most likely he was a believer, perhaps one who was undergoing preparation for baptism. The name itself means "friend of God," and for that reason after about the year 200 it was often said that "Theophilus" is anyone who loves God. This is probably not true historically, and there was a Theophilus to whom Luke addressed his two books. But in another sense it is true: the book is addressed to all of us who, like Theophilus, need to "know the truth concerning the things about which [we] have been instructed."

On the other hand, we must see our task as parallel not only to Theophilus but also to Luke, who seeks to provide "an orderly account" from his own perspective and experience. Just as Luke does not deny the validity of those who have written before him, our affirmation of our own perspective is part of our witnessing. I witness to Jesus Christ as who I am (an elderly Hispanic Protestant church historian, and many other things!) or my witness is not authentic. Witnessing is always contextual—as is theology. Rather than decrying the wide variety of contextual theologies that have emerged in our time, we should rejoice in it, as we rejoice in the grace of God that has provided us with four Gospels to witness to the eternal gospel.

### 1:5–25 *John the Baptist Is Announced*

The rest of chapter 1 tells the parallel stories of the annunciations of John the Baptist (1:5–25) and of Jesus (1:26–38), whose mothers then come together in the visitation (1:39–56). The chapter then ends with the birth of John (1:57–80), thus setting the stage for the birth of Jesus in chapter 2.

Unfortunately, there is a tendency in religion to make things sound strange and archaic. This is why we often speak of "the annunciation" and "the visitation," when we simply mean the announcement and the visit. What we have here are parallel announcements to Mary and to Elizabeth, who then come together when Mary visits Elizabeth.

Immediately after his prologue, Luke gives us the historical setting for the story he is about to tell: "In the days of King Herod of Judea." He will continue this practice throughout his two books, for instance telling us who reigned at the time of the birth of Jesus (2:1–2). This is important for him not only as an historian, but also as a theologian. There were circulating at the time many stories of the seasonal death and resurrection of gods. Such myths sought to explain the apparent death of nature in winter, and its rebirth in spring. Some of the religions based on these stories claimed that the god actually died—or was sorely weakened—at the beginning of every winter, and then came back to life in spring. Others saw these myths as ancient events, before the beginning of history, which then were reflected in the cycles of the seasons. Very soon after the time of Luke's writings, some people would seek to interpret Christianity in similar fashion: the death and resurrection of Jesus are an eternal myth that explains and is reflected in the cycles of life. Others, without going that far, would claim that what was important about Jesus was not who he was or what he did, but what he taught. For them, the story of Jesus was only the means whereby his teachings were offered to humankind—or, most often, to that small portion of humankind that was privy to his secret teachings.

Luke will have none of that. The story he is telling is not about recurring phenomena, nor about mythical explanations for the way the world functions, nor even about the great teachings of Jesus. The story he is telling is about this person Jesus, the Christ, whose power extends even over natural phenomena, and whose teachings are indeed great; but who is above all an historical figure, who was born during the time of Herod, Augustus, and Quirinius (2:1–2), who lived during the reign of Tiberius (3:1), and who was crucified and raised from the dead when Pontius Pilate was governor of Judea.

The significance of all this for today should be obvious. Once again, some would turn the story about Jesus into a mystical and mythical explanation of the nature of life, depriving it of its essential character as an historical event. Much more commonly, many—perhaps even the majority in many traditionally Christian nations and cultures—would reduce the significance of Jesus to his teachings. For such persons, to be a Christian is to follow the teachings of Jesus, teachings that are often watered down and turned into generally accepted principles for social life within the existing values of the culture. In contrast to such views, Luke's book is not primarily about the teachings of Jesus, but about the story of Jesus. The teachings of Jesus are important, not simply because they make sense or are useful, but rather because they are *his* teachings. At the very center of Luke's understanding of the gospel stands this historical figure, this man of flesh and blood, whose life is part of history and yet has marked all of history.

That history, however, did not begin with Jesus. Here again, there would soon be Christians who claimed that nothing that happened before the time of Jesus was of any significance. Some would reject what we now call the Old Testament as the Word of God. Some would say that it was the word of a lesser god, an ignorant or misguided deity who made this world and ruled it with an iron hand until Jesus came to free us from the tyranny of that god of creation and of history. This too Luke would reject. For him, the story of Jesus is the fulfillment of the long course of human history and of God's dealings with humankind, a history reflected in the Old Testament.

This is the significance of the story of the announcement of the birth of John the Baptist. Those of us who are not steeped in the religion of Israel may find the story about Zechariah and Elizabeth confusing, or even distracting or irrelevant. Some scholars tell us that one of the reasons why Luke introduces this story here is to make clear that John the Baptist and Jesus were not two competing figures, but rather that the former was the herald of the latter. This is true. But the story of the conception and birth of John the Baptist also has another function: it serves as a bridge between the story of Israel in Hebrew Scripture and the story of Jesus in Luke's Gospel. As one reads the story of the announcement of the birth of John, one is immediately reminded of the birth of Samuel. The theme of the barren woman appears repeatedly in the Scriptures of Israel. Among the matriarchs, Sarah, Rebekah, and Rachel were all sterile; yet by the grace of God the lineage of Abraham was preserved through them. Samson and Samuel were also born of barren women; indeed, the birth of Samson is announced to his mother in terms that remind us of the announcement of the birth of John (Judg. 13:1–5). The way Luke tells the story of the birth of Jesus makes clear that Jesus himself is part of that history. That Jesus is born of the sterile woman par excellence—a virgin—makes him the fulfillment of the entire history of Israel (to which we shall return when commenting on Luke 2).

Finally, one element we often

> It was a great relief to Zacharias to hear this, to know that the faithfulness of God is not made of no account by his short-coming, but indeed falls out all the greater at last. It happens sometimes, that the Lord offers and fulfils what He has promised to the unbelieving in spite of their resistance.
>
> **—John Calvin**
>
> *A Harmony of the Gospels: Matthew, Mark and Luke*, eds. David W. Torrance and Thomas P. Torrance, trans. A. W. Morrison, Calvin's New Testament Commentaries, 12 vols. (Grand Rapids: Eerdmans, 1972), 1:17.

miss when reading the Gospel of Luke is how he weaves subthemes that appear more than once. In this passage, for instance, Zechariah loses his speech; later (11:14) Jesus will cause the mute to speak. Note also that when Zechariah sees and hears the angel, he is overwhelmed with fear, but the angel tells him not to be afraid, for he is the bearer of good news—a detail that immediately reminds us of the reaction of the shepherds when the angel appears to them in 2:9, and the words of the angel in the next verse: "Do not be afraid; for see—I am bringing you good news of great joy."

### 1:26–38 *Jesus Is Announced*

The parallelism continues between John and Jesus. At the very beginning of this section, Luke again gives us a chronological reference, now linking the announcement to Mary with the announcement to Zechariah: "In the sixth month. . . ." Here too it is the angel Gabriel who is the bearer of the news of the unexpected birth. And once again the theme appears, of moving from fear—or in this case, perplexity—into joy. Just as Zechariah asked, "How will I know that this is so?" Mary asks, "How can this be, since I am a virgin?" And, just as he did with Zechariah, Gabriel now tells Mary about the greatness of her promised son.

Those parallelisms, however, make the contrasts starker. Zechariah asks for proof that what Gabriel says is true. Mary simply knows that it is impossible, and asks for an explanation. In her case, the miracle is even greater than in Zechariah's. John "will be great in the sight of the Lord." But Mary's child "will be called Son of God."

In this combination of parallelisms and contrasts, Luke is telling us that the Jesus whose story he is now telling is both the continu-

> The one who, being begotten of the Father, created all ages, consecrated this day by being born of a mother. In that [eternal] birth he could have no mother, and in this [temporal] birth he needed no father. One may say therefore that Christ was born from a father and a mother, and yet without father nor mother: as God, from the Father; as man, from a mother; as God, without a mother; and as man, without a father.
>
> —St. Augustine
>
> *Sermon 184, On the Birth of Our Lord Jesus Christ* 3, my trans.

ation of the history of Israel and much more than that. Like other great leaders of Israel, he too will be the son of a barren woman—but this one a virgin! His reign was foreshadowed by David and his kingdom; but, in contrast with David, "He will reign over the house of Jacob forever, and of his kingdom there will be no end."

Back to Mary, we should look again at her question, "How can this be, since I am a virgin?" Her question is not only an expression of amazement at what would seem impossible. It is also a word of alarm and perhaps also of protest. To understand it, we must remember the laws of Israel and the prevailing custom regarding unwed mothers. Mary will have to bear the stigma—and perhaps even the penalty—of that condition. (There is a hint of this in Matt. 1:18–25.) This is the beginning of a story of pain and humiliation that will lead to her son being condemned to death as a common criminal. To her protests, the angel responds that Mary's relative (the text does not say "cousin," although we often take that for granted) Elizabeth is already pregnant, and that this too is the result of God's action. Mary is not alone, even though her situation is unique. In the end, Mary acquiesces to God's will: "Here am I, the servant of the Lord; let it be with me according to your word."

Finally, one other detail in this passage that is particularly significant for the rest of the story that Luke tells is that this took place in Galilee. As we shall see later on, the theme of Galilee, and how it was regarded by Judeans, will be a significant though often overlooked element in the Gospel narrative.

> Jesus was born to be a marginal person. He was conceived by Mary when she was unwed. . . . Thus, while the birth of Jesus to Mary was divinely justified, it was nevertheless socially condemned. Jesus, as well as his parents, was marginalized from the time of his conception.
>
> —Jung Young Lee
>
> *Marginality: The Key to Multicultural Theology* (Minneapolis: Fortress, 1995), 79.

### 1:39–45 *The Visit*

These verses tell the story that is traditionally called "the visitation." Note that the angel had not told Mary to go visit Elizabeth, but only

> "Born of the Virgin Mary."
> Once again and now from the human standpoint, the male is excluded here. The male has nothing to do with this birth. What is involved here is, if you like, a divine act of judgment. ... Man is not simply excluded, for the Virgin is there. But the male, as the specific agent of human action and history ... must now retire into the background. ... here the woman stands absolutely in the foreground.
>
> —Karl Barth
>
> *Dogmatics in Outline*, trans. G. T. Thomson (London: SCM, 1949), 99.

that Elizabeth too is pregnant. So Mary goes to visit her relative. This may be seen as a quest for solidarity: here is another woman who is also unexpectedly pregnant. But there is also a sharp contrast in their situations: Elizabeth is married. She and her husband have long been wishing to have a child, and now that wish is about to be fulfilled. Mary is not married. To the eyes of the world, she will bear the stigma of an unwed mother. She is going to visit this relative, who has been "living blamelessly according to all the commandments and regulations of the Lord" (1:6). One who does not know the story, reading the Gospel of Luke for the first time, might expect this righteous and religious woman to speak harshly to her unwed relative. But this is not what happens. On the contrary, Elizabeth perceives the stirring of the child in her womb as a joyful greeting from her child to Mary's, and responds not only with a word of welcome, but even with a word of obeisance: "Why has this happened to me, that the mother of my Lord comes to me?"

Obviously, by telling this story Luke is making sure that his readers understand that Jesus is not just one more among the prophets, and that he and John the Baptist are not competitors. Rather, John will be the herald announcing the coming of Jesus. Quite likely, at the time of the writing of his Gospel, Luke still knew of some disciples of John who did not acknowledge Jesus, and thus he is trying to persuade them to join the Jesus movement, and also trying to make sure others do not decide to declare themselves disciples of John rather than of Jesus.

In our day, however, there is another important dimension to this story. There has always been the danger that good, faithful, and obedient Christians will turn into judgmental critics of those who do not live up to their standards. Indeed, throughout history one of the most common factors leading to divisions within the Christian church has been the notion on the part of a particular group that another sector in the church pollutes the whole, that it is not sufficiently holy, and must therefore be rejected. A similar judgmental attitude has also been one of the main obstacles in evangelism, for it leads to a proclamation that, instead of announcing good news of grace and salvation, focuses on the bad news of condemnation and eternal damnation.

The story of the visitation calls us to a different attitude. Elizabeth is filled with the Holy Spirit. Because she is so filled, she is able to recognize the work of God in what by traditional human standards would merit only criticism and judgment. Thus the true work of the Holy Spirit in the church today does not lead to a "holier than thou" attitude, in which all who do not live "blamelessly according to all the commandments and regulations of the Lord," or who do not seem to do so according to our understanding of those commandments and regulations, are to be despised and shunned.

### 1:46–55 *The Magnificat*

The Song of Mary is traditionally called the Magnificat, for this word—which means "magnifies" or "praises"—is the first word in the traditional Latin translation. The song is clearly patterned after the Song of Hannah (1 Sam. 2:1–10). But this is more than literary borrowing. There is a theological perspective behind such borrowing.

> In this way Mary's canticle tells us something important of the mystery of the incarnation which no metaphysical reflection on the nature of the Redeemer (one person, two natures, exchange of the idioms) could have told us. . . . that God chose what is weak in the world to shame the strong. . . . We must have the courage to openly admit that a too unilateral and sometimes even obsessive insistence on the metaphysical aspects and problems of the incarnation has . . . caused the true nature of the mystery to be lost from sight, reducing it (as happened with the Eucharistic transubstantiation) to a metaphysical mystery more than a religious one.
> —Raniero Cantalamessa
>
> *The Mystery of Christmas: A Commentary on the Magnificat, Gloria, Nunc Dimitis* (Collegeville, MN: Liturgical Press, 1988), 21.

> The great Charter of the social doctrine of the Church begins at the point where Mary sings: "He has deposed the mighty from their thrones and raised the lowly to high places. The hungry he has given every good thing, while the rich he has sent empty away." In the Gospel we find the highest and most irresistible revolution.
>
> —Chiara Lubish
>
> In René Coste, *The Magnificat: The Revolution of God* (Quezon City: Claretian Publications, 1988), 138–39.

The story of Jesus, as Luke and the other Gospel writers tell it, was already prefigured in earlier events in the history of Israel. This may seem strange to us, for when seeking to relate the Old Testament to the New we have traditionally looked for "prophecies"—for words that mysteriously announce future events, particularly in the life of Christ. But in this other manner of using the Hebrew Scriptures the focus is not on the words, but on the events that prefigure other events in the later history of Israel and in the life of the church, and most particularly in the life of Jesus. Under God's guidance, events prefigure other events, all leading to the central event of all history—the life, death, and resurrection of Jesus Christ. This understanding, in which some events prefigure others, is called "typology."

## FURTHER REFLECTIONS
### *Typology*

The theological foundation for typology was expressed quite clearly by Justin Martyr in the middle of the second century: "Sometimes, by action of the Holy Spirit, something took place that was clearly a type of the future. But at other times the Spirit spoke in words about what was to happen, as if it were present or past."[1]

In this brief passage, it is important to note the contrast that Justin makes between "words" (*logoi*) and "types" (*typoi*). The first refer to what we usually call "prophecy": there are words in the sacred text that refer to future events, particularly to the events of the life of Christ and the birth of the church. In the "types," by contrast, what

---

1. *Dialogue with Trypho* 114, my trans.

the Holy Spirit directs is not the actual words of the writer, but the events of which the writer speaks. Both point to the future; but in one case what points to the future is the text itself, and in the other it is the event of which the text speaks. To a modern reader such interpretations may seem as far-fetched as the most capricious of Origen's allegories. To the ancients, however, there was an important difference: while an allegorical interpretation does away with the historical meaning of the text, a typological interpretation sees the meaning in the earlier event itself, whose historicity it does not deny. This was stated quite clearly by Irenaeus, bishop of Lyons, late in the second century: "Jesus was not seen by the prophets only by means of visions, but also in events, so that by such events he would prefigure and show future events."[2]

While in the passage we are currently studying the main typology has to do with the barren women and their sons, another common typology connects Jesus with the temple itself, which prefigures the coming of Jesus. We shall encounter this typology later on in the Gospel of Luke.

What Luke is doing in borrowing from the Song of Hannah for the Magnificat is precisely this sort of typological interpretation. There are parallelisms between Hannah and Mary, and particularly between Samuel and Jesus, and Luke is presenting Samuel as one of many "types" pointing to Jesus. In this particular case, the "type" or theme is that of the barren women. This is a recurring theme in the Old Testament, where again and again there are women who apparently could not conceive, but eventually do by God's intervention; and the child who is born (Isaac, Jacob, Joseph, Samson, Samuel) plays an important role in God's saving acts. We tend to read the story of their barren mothers, and their eventually conceiving, as a mere story of vindication, where a woman who suffered, and sometimes was treated with contempt, because of her barrenness is vindicated by God. But these stories are much more than that. The significance of the story of these barren women is also in the child who is born to them. Their barrenness makes clear that the child they produce is

---

2. *Against Heresies* 4.14.3, my trans.

not simply one of the millions of human children born in the course of history. Their barrenness is the sign that God has intervened in history to permit the birth of this child. And the child is an essential element in the continuation of the people of God. That is to say, if this child had not been born, then God's people might have ceased to exist, or their history would have been very different. Take for instance the case of Isaac, who carries forth the promise that a great nation would descend from Abraham. Abraham and Sarah had earlier decided that it was entirely too much to expect Sarah to have a child, so they agreed that Hagar would bear Abraham a son. But God insisted that it would be the child of a barren woman who would bear the promise.

Now Luke picks up on that theme. He has already presented John as the child of a previously barren woman. John is the continuation of that long history of children born by divine intervention through whom God acted in history. His very conception is a sign that something important is about to happen. But then comes Mary, the barren woman par excellence, since she is a virgin. The child born of her will be in the same line of Isaac, Jacob, Joseph, Samson, and Samuel. But he is more than they. His mother has no reason to conceive. She is a virgin! In the child born of her the long history of agents of God born of barren women comes to its culmination. Its meaning has been fulfilled.

The content of the Magnificat is also worthy of attention. Since it is based on the Song of Hannah, it too is a song of vindication. Hannah saw in her act of conceiving a divine vindication of her sorrow and humiliation. Mary sees in her own act of conceiving, and in the child who is to be born out of that act, a sign of the way in which God

> Just as God in the beginning of creation made the world out of nothing, . . . so His manner of working continues unchanged. Even now and to the end of the world, all His works are such that out of that which is nothing, worthless, despised, wretched, and dead, He makes that which is something, precious, honorable, blessed, and living. On the other hand, whatever is something, precious, honorable, blessed, and living, He makes to be nothing, worthless, despised, wretched, and dying.
>
> —Martin Luther
>
> The Magnificat, trans. A. T. W. Steinhauser, Luther's Works 21 (Saint Louis: Concordia, 1956), 299.

works. Her song is not like many of the "praise" songs of today, proclaiming how great God is. It is a hard-hitting proclamation of a God who overturns the common order of society. Mary begins by declaring how God has done this in her: "he has looked with favor on the lowliness of his servant," and as a result "all generations will call me blessed." But in this again what is happening to Mary is a sign of how God works in history: "He has brought down the powerful from their thrones, and lifted up the lowly; he has filled the hungry with good things, and sent the rich away empty."

In placing these words on the lips of Mary, Luke is letting us know both that the story he is about to tell is the culmination of the history of Israel, and that this history—and certainly its culmination—is of a great reversal in which the lowly are made high, the high are brought low, the hungry are filled with good things while the rich are sent away empty, the last become first, and the least become the greatest.

### 1:56–80 *The Birth of John the Baptist*

Luke tells us that Mary remained with Elizabeth for "about three months." Since the angel had told Mary that Elizabeth was in her sixth month, Luke's chronology implies that Mary had left briefly before the birth of John. That birth causes rejoicing at first, then some conflict, and finally awe. In verse 58 the neighbors and relatives learn that Elizabeth has had a child, and they rejoice with her. But then in verses 59–63 there is dissension. "They" (we are not told who) wished to name the child after his father, but Elizabeth insisted that his name would be John. The dissension is not caused by her attempt to name the child, for in the Old Testament twenty-eight children are explicitly named by their mothers, and only fourteen by their fathers. Apparently the issue was whether the child should be named after his father. Elizabeth's refusal to give her child his father's name or the name of any other relative would give the impression that she did not want to honor her husband or their family. During all this time, Zechariah does not participate in the debate, for he cannot speak. He was literally "struck dumb" by the angel who announced the birth of John (v. 20), although not, as we use the phrase today, out of surprise or awe, but as the result of his incredulity when the angel came to him. Finally, those arguing decide to ask Zechariah's opinion. He asks for a writing tablet, and writes, "his name is John." Luke then tells us that "all were amazed," although he does not tell us why. What is important in the story is that Zechariah is being obedient to what he was told by the angel: "you will name him John" (v. 13). Significantly, Zechariah does not say that the child's name *will be* John, but that it *is* John. Zechariah is not making a decision; he is being obedient to what has already been decided. Immediately after this act of faithful obedience, he recovers the power of speech, which he had lost by his earlier attitude of disbelief.

> What is the meaning of Zachariah's silence, if not that until the preaching of Christ the prophecies were veiled and as closed and hidden, and now with the advent of the one of whom they spoke are open and illumined?
>
> —St. Augustine
>
> *Sermon 293, On the Nativity of John the Baptist 2*, my trans.

Now the mood shifts from dissension to awe ("fear" in the NRSV). Those present know that they have witnessed something important, but do not know exactly what it is, or what its consequences will be.

The entire episode reminds us of a situation in which many faithful believers often stand. They are called to do the unexpected, and perhaps the culturally unacceptable. The pressure of friends and neighbors—which in Elizabeth's and Zechariah's case also represents all kinds of cultural and traditional pressures—conflicts with what they know to be the will of God. We usually think of such conflicts in what were traditionally called "mission fields," where people from a variety of cultures and traditions are brought into the church. Thus we speak, for instance, of the experience of people whose culture practices ancestor worship, and how they have had to deal with issues of idolatry. But we probably ought to thinks also in terms of our own culture, many of whose values—individualism, success, economic power, popularity—may also clash with what we know to be the will of God.

As the neighbors and relatives are wondering about what has taken place, Zechariah breaks forth in a hymn of praise. As we proceed with our study of Luke, we will notice that he often pairs up a passage about a male with another about a female. This will become more apparent in other passages. For the present, it should suffice to note that the song of Zechariah is the counterpart of the song of Mary. (As in the case of Mary's Magnificat, this hymn is also known by the first word of its Latin translation, *Benedictus,* "blessed.") In this song, Luke depicts Zechariah as placing the story of John within the context of the entire history of God's actions among the people of Israel. There is continuity between that history and what Zechariah and his kindred are witnessing. Yet there is also something radically new, unparalleled. According to Zechariah's prophecy, John will be called "the prophet of the Most High." He will not be just one more among the prophets. He will be of singular significance, because he "will go before the Lord to prepare his ways." With these words on Zechariah's lips, Luke is stressing both the importance of John and his subservience to Jesus, whose herald he will be.

> John is born of a sterile and elderly woman; Christ, of a young virgin. John is the fruit of barrenness; Christ, of wholeness. . . . One is announced by the voice of an angel; and at the voice of the angel the other is conceived.
>
> —St. Augustine
>
> *Sermon 293, On the Nativity of John the Baptist 1, my trans.*

## FURTHER REFLECTIONS
### *Continuity and Discontinuity*

In the very first chapter of his story, Luke is walking a fine line that Christian theologians have often found difficult to walk. This is the line between continuity and discontinuity. On the one hand, absolute discontinuity between Jesus and what goes on before him or apart from him would lead us far astray. What Jesus does must not be new in the sense that before his advent God was not active, or that whatever God did before the time of Jesus is irrelevant. But on the other hand uninterrupted continuity between Jesus and the rest of history and of creation makes it difficult to see what is special about Jesus, turning him into little more than one more chapter in human history.

In the early church, and through the centuries, this debate has dealt with continuity and discontinuity in two different directions: vis-à-vis the history of Israel, and vis-à-vis non-Christian culture and philosophy. In the second century, radical discontinuity was the position of Marcion, who claimed that the God of Jesus was not the same as the minor god who had created the world and led the history of Israel; on the contrary, the God of Jesus is wholly other, unrelated to the world and its history, until Jesus comes to deliver us from the old. According to Marcion, what has happened in Jesus is so radically new that it was in no way prepared for by the history of Israel, or by anything in creation itself. To this Tertullian replied, in his typically ironic style, that Marcion's god did not seem to amount to much, being absent all those centuries, and not even producing a miserable vegetable!

When it came to the matter of continuity and discontinuity between Christianity and Greco-Roman culture and philosophy, opinions were also divided. Tertullian—the same one who criticized Marcion for his teaching of radical discontinuity between Israel and the church—affirmed a radical discontinuity between the prevailing culture and philosophy and the true message of Christianity. As he put it, "What relationship is there between Athens and Jerusalem? What agreement between the Academy and the Church?"[3] Over against Tertullian, others, such as Justin Martyr and many of the greatest theologians of the early centuries, claimed that there was indeed a measure of continuity between Greek philosophy and Christian truth. The way Justin and others put it was to say that the Word or Logos of God who was incarnate in Jesus is the same through whom all things were made, and who "was the light of all people" (John 1:4). Many, following Justin's lead, claimed that, just as God gave the Law to the Jews as a handmaiden to lead them to the gospel, so did God give philosophy to the Greeks, also to lead them to the gospel.

The debate has continued over the centuries, although taking different forms. In the twentieth century, Karl Barth criticized

---

3. *Prescription against Heretics* 7, my trans.

Thomas Aquinas and the entire Roman Catholic tradition for declaring that "grace, rather than destroying nature, perfects it," and insisted that vis-à-vis human nature, God is "wholly other." To this, Adolf Harnack replied with a caricature of Barth: "Marcion all over again!" The same issue was at the heart of Barth's debate with Emil Brunner, whom he accused of promoting "a theology of the *and*," as, for instance, "nature and grace."

In more recent times, the question of continuity and discontinuity has been posed anew, and with a different agenda, by many liberation theologians, who reject the distinction between world or secular history (*Weltgeschichte*) on the one hand, and sacred or salvation history (*Heilsgeschichte*) on the other. Although this distinction became common in Protestant circles in the nineteenth century, even before that in many Catholic schools different courses were taught on "history" and on "history of salvation" (*historia de la salvación*). This was a normal part of curricula in Latin America throughout the nineteenth and early twentieth centuries, and is still found in some conservative Catholic schools in the region. In theory, this distinction allows for the study of the biblical narrative and of church history parallel to the general study of history. But in practice it conveys the impression that there is a chasm between secular and sacred events, that God's concern in only or primarily for the latter, and that therefore the main concern of believers should be their salvation and that of others, and not what takes place in the general history of the world and of society—injustice, oppression, violence.

Thus in this case the issue of continuity and discontinuity has serious theological and sociopolitical implications. Since that continuity is such that there can be no distinction between *Heilsgeschichte* and *Weltgeschichte*, God's saving acts take place within the context of all of human history, and all of that history is leading to salvation, which is understood as the fulfillment of God's ultimate design for all of creation.

The question of continuity and discontinuity arises today also in discussions of the relationship between Christianity and culture. Those who would emphasize discontinuity lean in the direction of condemning all of culture as a mere human production—as if there were such a thing as a Christianity not embedded in culture, or a

> There are not two histories, one profane and one sacred, "juxtaposed" or "closely linked." Rather, there is only one human history, irreversibly assumed by Christ, the Lord of history. His redemptive work embraces all the dimensions of existence and brings them to their fullness. The history of salvation is the very heart of human history.
>
> —Gustavo Gutiérrez
>
> *A Theology of Liberation: History, Politics, and Salvation*, trans. and ed. Sister Caridad Inda and John Eagleson (Maryknoll, NY: Orbis, 1973), 153.

culture that is particularly Christian. Those who would emphasize continuity make it difficult to see how Christianity differs from the surrounding culture—as if Christianity were little more than the best of human culture.

In such a debate, Luke would seem to take the side of those who emphasize continuity. Certainly, he is quite clear that he is writing about unprecedented good news, about a person and a series of events that have changed history forever. But he does this following the canons of historical writing in Greco-Roman culture, and insists on the continuity between Jesus and the earlier history of the Israel into which he was born. By giving names of rulers and political leaders, he repeatedly places his narrative in the context of Roman and Jewish political history. Furthermore, as we shall see, the genealogy of Jesus that he includes early in his Gospel implies that all of human history—not just in Israel, but throughout the world—is the context and the preparation for the events he will be narrating.

## 2:1–52
### *Birth and Childhood*

### 2:1–20 *The Birth of Jesus*

This is one of the better-known passages in the entire Gospel of Luke. It is characteristic of Luke, for it does not appear in any of the other Gospels. Although the mention of both Augustus and Quirinius poses some problems of chronology, there is no doubt that it indicates Luke's interest in placing his story within the context of world history. The theological significance of this has already been discussed above in the comments on 1:5.

The story about the inn, the manger, and the shepherds has been told so often that it is difficult for us to see its full poignancy. This is not a mellow, bucolic story about some shepherds tending their sheep with little or no care beyond the possibility of a wandering wolf. That is not the setting in which Luke presents the story. The setting is rather that of people living under an oppressive regime. The mention of Augustus and Quirinius—as earlier the mention of Herod—is politically charged. For a period before the advent of the Roman Empire, the Jews had been struggling against Syrian domination. Now their land was ruled from Syria by a governor appointed by Rome. Whatever the actual chronology may have been, the political structure is clear: the Jews have a puppet government under Syrian and Roman power. As usual, oppression is not a merely political matter, the concern only of those directly involved in politics. It also reaches the everyday lives of people, as is seen in the very fact that Joseph and Mary have to travel to Bethlehem even though she is about to give birth.

A census had sinister implications. It was not just counting people in order to see how many they were, and what population trends were. In ancient times, and long thereafter, a census was in fact an inventory of all the wealth of a region—its people, its animals, and its crops— so that the government would be able to tax people to the maximum. A census usually announced greater poverty and exploitation. It was as welcome among subjects of the Roman Empire as undocumented immigrants in industrialized nations welcome a census today. For this reason, it is not surprising that the spark that ignited the rebellion of Judas the Galilean (Acts 5:37) was a census. This is also what gave its title to England's famous census report, the *Doomsday Book*.

Given those circumstances, the setting of the shepherds keeping their flocks at night is much less tranquil and romantic. They live out in the fields, suffer all kinds of deprivations and even dangers, in order to protect their flocks. But the census threatens a new danger, a wolf more dangerous than any four-legged beast, a wolf that will probably decimate their flocks, and whom they cannot fight, for it is too powerful. It is not difficult to imagine what would be the talk of such shepherds as they sought to remain awake through the night. In that sort of circumstances, people vent their anger, frustration, and fear in what is at once idle and dangerous talk—talk that does not necessarily lead to rebellion, but that in itself is subversive, and the authorities will consider it rebellious and punishable. If not precisely at the moment when the angel appeared, certainly at some point these shepherds would have expressed similar feelings. Even if they had not, the setting itself was one of fear and oppression.

It is in that scene, perhaps silent, but not as peaceful as we tend to depict it, that an angel suddenly appears before the shepherds, and they are terrified. Their fear is not surprising. Those of us who have lived under dictatorial regimes have often had similar experiences and reactions. We learned to shudder if someone knocked at our door in the wee hours of the morning. Such a knock could easily lead to your "disappearance." Imagine a group of peasants in a country devastated—as so many are today—by a combination of tyrannical government and economic exploitation. They do not have to be conspiring or having a subversive conversation. They just have to be there, and to know what has happened to other peasants who ran afoul of the government. Suddenly there is a bright light, and an unknown person stands before them. It is not surprising that they would be terrified.

> What can I give him, poor as I am?
> If I were a shepherd, I would bring a lamb;
> if I were a Wise Man, I would do my part;
> Yet, what can I give him? Give my heart.
> —Christina G. Rossetti (1872)

So, the shepherds are terrified, not just because they do not understand what is going on, but also because in their circumstances any such occurrence might well have dire consequences. One of the ways in which the "little people" manage to survive under oppressive regimes is not to call attention to themselves. They seek to go on with their lives unnoticed by the powerful, who could easily crush them. Now these shepherds are literally in the limelight, and an obviously powerful personage confronts them

Then the scene takes an unexpected turn. The angel tells them not to be afraid, for he is bringing them "news of great joy." This is parallel to what happens to Zechariah in 1:12–14, when we are told that he was terrified, but that the angel told him: "Do not be afraid . . . you will have joy and gladness." Similarly, in the annunciation, the angel tells Mary: "Do not be afraid, Mary, for you have found favor with God" (1:30). An encounter with God's power and might leads to awe and terror, but then God's gracious word produces joy and comfort.

The angel tells the shepherds that he is bringing them good news that will bring "joy for all the people." Luke often uses the phrase "the people" to refer to the common folk. In the first five chapters of Acts, for instance, "the people" are repeatedly contrasted with the elders, the priests, the Sadducees, and in general the Jewish elite. Thus "the people" has a double meaning: on the one hand, it does mean everybody, or Israel as the people of God. But on the other it also means the common folk, particularly the common folk of Israel. Here the angel brings good news that will be "joy for all the people." But as the Gospel of Luke unfolds we shall see that, as Mary already announced in the Magnificat, the good news may be for all, but it will bring joy and comfort to some and pain and discomfort to others—unless they repent.

> The one who was born of her was God made flesh, not merely a divinely inspired human. He was not a prophet anointed with power, but the full presence of the anointer. Therefore, the anointer became the anointed, not by a change of nature, but by the hypostatic union.
>
> —John of Damascus
>
> *On the Orthodox Faith* 4.14, my trans.

The good news that the angel announces is the birth of a child, "a Savior, who is the Messiah, the Lord." This is the only text in the entire New Testament where these three titles appear together. The title "Savior" (*sōtēr*) was employed in the Septuagint (the Greek version of the Hebrew Bible that Luke used) to refer both to God and to those whom God sends to liberate Israel. In the Hebrew Scriptures, the function of such liberators is neither purely religious nor purely political. Actually, this is a distinction that people in ancient times would find difficult to understand. It would certainly be rejected by liberation theologians and others who also object to the distinction between world history and salvation history. The "saviors" in the Hebrew Scriptures liberate Israel from its political oppressors so that the people may be free to serve and obey God. Moses leads the people out of Israel, not only that they may be freed from slavery, but also that they may worship God (Exod. 7:16; 8:1). But the title "Savior" was also used by rulers who claimed special powers over their subjects. In ancient times, one finds names such as "Antiochus I Soter" for a ruler of Syria, and "Ptolemy I Soter" for a ruler of Egypt. Thus when the angel announces Jesus as "Savior," his declaration has both political and religious overtones. The child who has been born will free the people from bondage—bondage both to their sins and to their oppressors.

> How could he quit his kingly state
> for such a world of greed and hate?
> What deep humiliation
> Secured the world's salvation!
> —Johann Rist (1641)

## FURTHER REFLECTIONS
### *"Savior" and "Salvation"*

The meaning of the word "salvation," both in the New Testament and in the common usage of the time, is much fuller than we often imagine. Salvation means healing, liberation, freedom from the bondage of sin, promise of eternal life, and several nuances of each of these themes. Thus to say that Jesus is "Savior" means that he frees the people from all evil, including sin, eternal death, disease, oppression, and exploitation. If we do not see all of this as yet, it is because the work of Jesus has not been completed—the reign of God has not yet come to its full fruition.

The manner in which this opens up new vistas in our understanding of the New Testament is seen most clearly in the miracle stories in the Gospels as well as in Acts. A typical and much debated passage is Acts 4:12, where Peter says, "There is salvation in no one else, for there is no other name under heaven given among mortals by which we must be saved." The contemporary debate is usually framed in terms of whether people may be "saved"—that is, avoid eternal damnation—apart from faith in Jesus. Some say, for instance, that a good Buddhist is just as able to be saved as is a good Christian. Others insist on taking the passage "literally," and thus declaring that those who do not believe in Jesus in this life are condemned to hell in the next.

What the entire debate misses is that what is being discussed in Acts 4 is not primarily the matter of eternal salvation or damnation, but rather an act of healing. Peter and John have healed a man at a temple gate, and have then begun to preach. They are arrested and brought before the council. They are asked: "By what power or by what name did you do this?" and Peter's response includes the famous words about "no other name . . . by which we must be saved." Peter is not being asked how one goes to heaven; the question is simply by what authority he healed a lame man. His response is that he did it in the name and by the authority of Jesus, for there is "salvation" in no other name.

> For Christian faith, "salvation" is a technical term, expressing the eschatological condition of the human being, risen and divinized, in the plenitude of the kingdom of God in eternity. . . . On the one hand this salvation totally surpasses the historical process and is thereby "transhistorical." On the other hand it is within the historical process that this salvation is situated. And because it is situated in the historical process, we may speak of this theological element present in economic, political, and social material.
> —**Leonardo Boff**
>
> In Leonardo and Clodovis Boff, *Salvation and Liberation: In Search of a Balance between Faith and Politics*, trans. Robert R. Barr (Maryknoll, NY: Orbis, 1984), 56.

When you stop to think about it, Peter's words are astounding. He is not merely claiming what some do today, that one can only be saved through Jesus. He is also claiming that all healing—as well all liberation, and all eternal salvation—is due to the power of Jesus! A truly literal interpretation of these words leads us to affirm not only, as some conservatives do, that there is no eternal salvation apart from Jesus, but also that there is no healing apart from Jesus.

Thus the current debate about the applicability of Peter's words, no matter whether one takes the "conservative" or the "liberal" position, falls far short of Luke's vision of the power of Jesus. What Peter is claiming in that passage, and what Luke will exemplify through-out his Gospel, is that all goodness, all healing, all salvation of what-ever kind comes from the same Jesus in whom the church believes and whom the church proclaims.

Could it be that in this passage Luke is telling us something about the power of Jesus that is similar to what John says in the pro-logue to the Fourth Gospel? Could it be that as we read the miracles and other narratives in the Gospel of Luke we miss the point unless we see them in their cosmic dimen-sion—as signs of the struggle and victory of Jesus over all powers of evil?

Many Christians confuse salva-tion with justification, and limit both to God's forgiveness and to admission into heaven. This has two negative consequences. The first is that such salvation has little to do with the struggles of daily life, particularly with the social, politi-cal, and economic issues that shape the lives of entire communities. In other words, such a view of salva-tion is the foundation for the much criticized theology of "pie in the sky, by and by." And it certainly leaves aside much of what Scripture includes in the notion of salvation.

The second consequence, closely related to the first, is that, since justification is by the grace of God, we are led to the conclusion that whatever we do—particu-larly in terms of justice—has little to do with salvation. In contrast, a fuller understanding of salvation as the fullness of the life that God

> Therefore, because faith receives Christ our righteousness and attributes everything to the grace of God in Christ, on that account justification is attributed to faith, chiefly because of Christ and not therefore because it is not our work.
> —**Second Helvetic Confession**
>
> In *Book of Confessions: Study Edition* (Louisville: Geneva Press, 1996), 5.109.

> We understand the absolute divine initiative as a biblical truth. The difficulty resides in the fact that this principle is almost always read from the opposite direction, as meaning that human beings have no role in their salvation. . . . At worst, the conclusion is drawn that what a person does with his or her life counts for nothing, or that human efforts in history are of no worth.
> —**Elsa Tamez**
>
> *The Amnesty of Grace: Justification by Faith from a Latin American Perspective,* trans. Sharon H. Ringe (Nashville: Abingdon, 1993), 22.

intends for us leads to an emphasis on sanctification—a sanctification that is not just a matter of personal holiness, but also of justice, love, and mercy.

The title "Messiah"—and its Greek equivalent, "Christ"—means "anointed." In ancient Israel, kings and priests were anointed as a sign of divine approval and of their authority. By the time of the New Testament, foreign oppression and inner social disorder had led many to expect an "anointed one," a "messiah," who would free Israel from its difficult situation. Slowly, this had developed into the expectation of a final Messiah, one anointed by God to bring in God's final reign, and Israel's final victory over all its enemies. Thus, by claiming this title for Jesus, Luke is declaring that he is the one who will fulfill all the promises made to Abraham and his descendants, that he will restore the throne of David and do away with all oppression and injustice.

But Luke is claiming much more than that. The angel declares that the child who is born is not only "Savior" and "Messiah" but also "Lord." This was the word with which the Septuagint often translated the name of God, particularly the sacred, unpronounceable name of God (YHWH). Luke's Savior and Messiah is not one more among the long line of saviors, liberators, and anointed ones whom Israel has known along its history; he is "the Lord"! Later on, as his Gospel unfolds, Luke will give us more indications of this; but it is already present in the very first announcement that Jesus is born.

This announcement, however, combines power and weakness in a strange way. The presence of the angel overwhelmed the shepherds with fear. Now they are told that the reason for the angel's presence—soon to be made even more astounding by the heavenly host that will join the angel—is the birth of a child who lies in a manger. This is no ruler born to a human throne, nor even a respected member of a priestly family, but a homeless child lying in a manger. This is one of many instances of reversal or "upsidedownness" to be found in the Gospel—the poor fed while the rich are sent empty away, the last becoming first and the least becoming greatest, the foreign queen who judges and condemns the people of Israel (11:31), and so forth.

Then the heavenly choir joins the angel and sings the hymn that we often call the *Gloria*—from the first word in the Latin translation: *Gloria in excelsis Deo.* There is an interesting textual problem in connection with the end of this hymn. Does the angel proclaim peace among those who are the recipients of God's goodwill, or peace and goodwill among people? The latter is the traditional rendering of the King James Version: "and on earth peace, good will toward men." The NRSV, following what appears to be a better manuscript tradition, says: "and on earth peace among those whom he favors." There are

Jesus, our brother, strong and good,
was humbly born in a stable rude,
and the friendly beasts around him stood,
Jesus our brother, strong and good.

"I," said the donkey, shaggy and brown,
"I carried his mother uphill and down,
I carried his mother to Bethlehem town;
I," said the donkey, shaggy and brown.

"I," said the cow, all white and red,
"I gave him my manger for his bed,
I gave him hay to pillow his head;
I," said the cow, all white and red.

"I," said the sheep, with curly horn,
"I gave him my wool for his blanket warm,
he wore my coat on Christmas morn,
I," said the sheep with curly horn.

"I," said the dove, from the rafters high,
"I cooed him to sleep that he should not cry,
we cooed him to sleep, my mate and I;
I," said the dove, from the rafters high.

Thus all the beasts, by some good spell,
in the stable dark were glad to tell
of the gifts they gave Emmanuel,
the gifts they gave Emmanuel.
—Twelfth-century French carol

ancient manuscripts supporting each of these two readings. There are also theological problems with both readings, for in the one case it would seem that peace—and salvation—depend on God's capricious act of favoring some and not others, while on the other hand it would seem that it is a reward God gives to those who practice goodwill. The debate (not primarily on this text, but on the issues it implies) has continued through the generations: Augustine against Pelagius, Gottschalk against Hincmar, Luther and Calvin against traditional Roman Catholicism, orthodox Calvinists against Arminians.

As a result of the angel's message, the shepherds hasten to Bethlehem, where they find exactly what the angel has told them. (Did they leave their flocks behind? Luke does not tell us.) The result is that they are amazed, as are also those who hear their story.

> He became an infant and a child, so that you might be a perfect person. He was wrapped in swaddling clothes so that you might be absolved from the bonds of death. He was in a manger, so that you might be at the altar. He was on earth, so that you might be in heaven. He had no room at the inn, so that you might have mansions in heaven.
> —Ambrose of Milan
>
> *Exposition of the Gospel According to Luke* 2:41, my trans.

## 2:21–39 *The Naming and Presentation at the Temple*

Throughout his Gospel, Luke presents Jesus as obedient to the Law and to the observances of Jewish religion. The one significant and repeated exception is when such observances, or the Law itself, are used to subvert God's main commandment of love, in which case Jesus refuses to allow the Law to be used in such a way. This great exception appears so repeatedly in the Gospels that we tend to forget that in them Jesus and his family are presented as good and faithful Jews. This is obvious in the particular case of his circumcision and presentation in the temple. Jewish law requires that every male child be circumcised on the eighth day after birth, and Jesus' family complies with that requirement. Then, when the time comes for the child to be presented at the temple, his family once again fulfills the requirements of the Law. In this particular case, the requirement was that every firstborn male child be redeemed—bought back—from God. This was based on the story of the Passover, when the angel of the Lord brought death to all the firstborn among the Egyptians, but "passed over" the houses of the children of Israel, whose doors were sealed with the blood of a lamb. As a result, God claimed possession of every firstborn male in Israel: "for all the firstborn are mine; when I killed all the firstborn in the land of Egypt, I consecrated for my own all the firstborn in Israel . . . they shall be mine" (Num. 3:13). It is in obedience to this commandment that Jesus' parents bring him to the temple to be presented, and to offer the prescribed sacrifice for his redemption—for buying him back from God.

Curiously, Luke tells us that the Redeemer has to be redeemed, has to be bought back. This is not because he has sinned, but simply because he is a firstborn, and all the firstborn in Israel belong to God. The theme of the Passover as a type of Jesus (see above, "Further Reflections: Typology") appears repeatedly throughout the New Testament, with several layers of meaning. The paschal lamb that was sacrificed is a type of Jesus. Jesus himself is the new Passover, for in him God shows mercy to us. According to Luke and the other Synoptic Gospels, the last meal of Jesus with his disciples before the crucifixion is a paschal meal. It is there that he instituted the Lord's Supper or Eucharist. Here, at the presentation in the temple, another Passover theme appears: Jesus the firstborn is to be redeemed by the sacrifice of two turtledoves, and he will then redeem all humankind by his own sacrifice.

When Jesus is presented at the temple, two people give witness to his greatness, and to the significance of what he will accomplish: Simeon and Anna. Characteristically, Luke balances a prophetic utterance from a man with another from a woman. Both are profoundly religious. Both are elderly, or at least seem to be, for the age of Simeon is not stated, and can only be inferred from his song. Both are prophets. Upon seeing the child, both praise God and make declarations about him, although Simeon's words are quoted in the text, and Anna's are not.

Simeon's song is traditionally known by the first two words of its Latin translation, *Nunc dimitis*, "Now you dismiss." In it he makes clear that the child he is seeing has a role vis-à-vis both Israel and the Gentiles. He will be "glory to your people Israel," and also "a light for the revelation to the Gentiles." Then Simeon's prophetic announcement to Mary, that her son will give rise to great controversy, that many will stumble and many will rise because of him, and that a sword will pierce her soul, lets the reader know that the opposition Jesus will encounter in the rest of the Gospel, and his eventual crucifixion, are not unexpected.

### 2:40–52  *A Further Visit to the Temple*

The temple plays an important role in the life of Jesus. It is there that he is first acknowledged publicly as the hope of Israel, in the utterances of Simeon and Anna. The devil takes him to the pinnacle of the temple in order to tempt him (4:9). Jesus also announces the destruction of the temple (21:5–6). Although not so much in Luke as in the rest of the gospel tradition, the temple figures prominently in the week of the passion. Carrying his narrative beyond the other Gospels, Luke ends the Jesus story by telling us that after the ascension the disciples "were continually in the temple blessing God."

The story about the visit to the temple in Luke 2 has no parallel in the other canonical Gospels. Indeed, only Luke recounts an episode in the life of Jesus—this one—between his birth and the beginning of his ministry. In this particular case, Luke is again connecting Jesus with Samuel—which he already did in Mary's song, taken mostly from the Song of Hannah—for the words in verse 52 are patterned after 1 Samuel 2:26: "Now the boy Samuel continued to grow both in stature and in favor with the LORD and with the people." Here again there are typological connections: Samuel would bring in the kingdom of David, which pointed to the kingdom of God that Jesus would bring in. Furthermore, Samuel's connection both with the temple and with Jesus hint at the typology that sees Jesus as the new and final temple of God. For this reason, a common theme in early Christian theology was that the destruction of the temple showed that it was no longer necessary, for the temple prefigured the one who had already come.

The connection of Jesus with the temple goes far beyond the stories in the Gospels about his prediction of its destruction. In the early church, the temple was often understood as a typological figure announcing the presence of God in Jesus. In his prayer dedicating the temple, Solomon had said:

> But will God indeed dwell on the earth? Even heaven and the highest heaven cannot contain you, how much less this house that I have built! Regard your servant's prayer and his plea, O LORD my God, heeding the cry and the prayer that your servant prays to you today; that your eyes may be open night and day toward this house, the place of which you have said, "My name shall be there." (1 Kgs. 8:27–29)

The temple is the sign of God's presence in the midst of the people. To Solomon's question, "Can God indeed dwell with mortals on earth?" the New Testament has the surprising answer, yes! and points to the incarnation. The temple, and the tabernacle before it, were types of the incarnation that was to come. Elsewhere in the New Testament (Matt. 26:61; 27:40; Mark 14:58; 15:29; John 2:19–22), Jesus refers to himself when he says that if the temple is destroyed he will raise it up in three days. God can dwell with mortals on earth—even though the cross shows what mortals do when God does dwell with us.

Significantly, in a recent conversation among Jewish and Christian theologians, when a Jewish theologian said that the incarnation is the main, insurmountable difference between the two religions, another very respected Jewish theologian corrected him, saying that the presence of God in the temple is perfectly compatible with the presence of God in a human being. There are many other important differences, he said, but to the question, Can God indeed dwell with mortals on earth? Jews and Christians can both answer, Yes!

# FURTHER REFLECTIONS
## *Christological Perspectives*

Throughout the ages some Christians have emphasized the divinity of Jesus to such a point that his humanity seems to be lost, and others have taken exactly the opposite route, emphasizing the humanity of Jesus to the detriment of his divinity. In patristic times, the former tended to center around Alexandria, and the latter around Antioch, so that it has become customary for historians of theology to speak of these two positions as "Alexandrine Christology" and "Antiochene Christology." The particular story about Jesus in the temple at the age of twelve has been used by theologians to make points in two opposite directions.

On the one hand, and at first glance, the story seems to favor the Alexandrine position, for it is about Jesus' exceptional and perhaps even superhuman wisdom. Here is a young boy, not yet a teenager, conversing with the sages in the temple, and doing so in such a manner that "all who heard him were astounded." Thus commentators, both ancient and more recent, have read this passage as an affirmation that Jesus was omniscient, knowing all things as God does.

On the other hand, the last verse of the passage soon became a favorite of theologians of Antiochene inclinations. To declare that "Jesus increased in wisdom" is to deny any claim to divine omniscience. Jesus did not know all things by nature, but only, as is the case with all humans, through growth and learning. The very connection of Jesus with the temple was also used by the early Antiochene theologians as a means to express the manner in which Jesus is divine. Divinity dwelt in him, they would say, "as in a temple."

> Christology is a peculiar discipline, because its subject is Christ himself, the Word, the Logos. Christology is the science of the Word of God. Christology is *logology*. . . . Were this Logos our own Logos, then christology would be a matter of the Logos reflecting upon itself. But this Logos is the Logos of God, whose transcendence makes christology the crown of learning and whose coming from outside makes it the centre of scholarship.
>
> —Dietrich Bonhoeffer
>
> *Christ the Center*, trans. John Bowden (New York: Harper & Row, 1966), 27–28

The debate did not end with the Definition of Faith of Chalcedon in 451, which was a compromise excluding both extremes and
allowing for some latitude between them. It led to the first permanent divisions in the Christian church. In the West, which generally accepted the Definition of Chalcedon, some theologians have
leaned toward the Alexandrine, and others toward the Antiochene
position. At the high point of the Middle Ages, the passage we are
studying was pivotal in the *Quaestiones disputatae de scientia Christi*
(debated issues on Christ's knowledge), in which many theologians,
notably St. Bonaventure, participated. The issues were: Did Jesus
know all things? If so, how could he grow in knowledge? If not, how
could he be God? Were there in him two levels of knowledge, one
divine and one human? If so, how could he still be a single person?

The debate carried on to the time of the Reformation, when
again some theologians reflected the Alexandrine position, and
others preferred the Antiochene. For instance, John Calvin inclined
toward the Antiochene position partly based on the principle that
the finite is not capable of the infinite. Martin Luther, on the other
hand, insisted on the unity of the Savior to such a point that he
has been accused of being a Monophysite, although it should be
noted that he understood that unity, not as limiting the humanity
of Christ, but rather in the opposite
direction, pointing to a God who
is best known in the cross and in
weakness, rather than in power and
glory.

In the modern age Chalcedonian orthodoxy was frequently
challenged, for modern rational-
ism could not accept the notion
that a concrete, historical human
being could be the incarnation
of the eternal. Søren Kierkegaard
referred to this as "the scandal of
particularity," which he affirmed in
the face of most other theologians
in his time. Thus in general modern

> The whole of liberal theology
> must be seen in the light
> of docetic christology.
> It understands Jesus as
> the support for or the
> embodiment of particular
> ideas, values and doctrines.
> As a result, the manhood of
> Jesus Christ is in the last resort
> not taken seriously, although
> it is this very theology which
> speaks so often of the man.
> . . . It confuses the real man
> with an ideal man and makes
> him a symbol.
> —Dietrich Bonhoeffer
>
> *Christ the Center*, 83–84.

liberalism sought to explain the uniqueness of Jesus in terms of his being an exceptional human being—a great moral teacher, a man of profound religious insight, a critic of traditional religion, a person of unique charisma. To all of this Dietrich Bonhoeffer objected that, while apparently making Jesus more human, in fact it denied his humanity by turning him into a superhuman individual.

Clearly, neither the extreme Alexandrine position nor its Antiochene counterpart does justice to the person of Jesus as Luke presents him. He is indeed exceptional by nature, but he grows and develops like any other human being. In this regard, the Chalcedonian Definition of 451 is to be commended for avoiding the pitfalls of both extremes. But it remained within the parameters set by the earlier discussion in that it turned Christology into a metaphysical issue of how two natures, each defined apart from Jesus himself, can be united in one. Elsewhere, I have stated this difficulty as follows:

> What made this question particularly difficult was that, following the lead of Greek philosophy, the church had come to think of God in terms that are incompatible with a human being. On the one hand, God is omnipotent, omniscient, omnipresent, immutable, and so on. Being human, on the other hand, implies the opposite. Humans are limited in their power and in their knowledge. Humans are also limited in that they cannot be in more than one place at a time. And, in contrast with the immutability of God, for a human being to live is to change. The incarnation of God in a human being, which in any case would have been a mystery, was turned into a logical contradiction. To ask someone to explain how it is that the divine can be human was like walking up to a soda fountain and asking for hot ice cream![4]

For this reason, most contemporary Christology, rather than beginning with definitions of who or what God is, and of who or what a human being is, tend to begin with the person of Jesus as presented in the Gospels and as known in faith, and from there move to what we can say about the nature of God, and about what it means to be fully human.

---

4. Justo L. González, *A Concise History of Christian Doctrine* (Nashville: Abingdon, 2005), 113–14.

> The theological categories adopted by early Christianity to define the doctrine of Christ—early Christology, in other words—would seem to be inclusive of women. And yet, of all Christian doctrine, it has been the doctrine of Christ that has been most frequently used to exclude women from full participation in the Christian Church. How is this possible?
>
> —Rosemary Radford Ruether
>
> "The Liberation of Christology from Patriarchy," in *Feminist Theology: A Reader*, ed. Ann Loades (London: SPCK, 1990), 138.

## 3:1–4:13

### *Preparation for Ministry*

### 3:1–14 *The Preaching of John the Baptist*

Once again, Luke places his story within the context of secular history. In this case, he gives us no less than eight references to date the events he is recounting. He begins with Roman authorities (Emperor Tiberius and Pontius Pilate), then moves to those that, while claiming some connection with the region, were also representatives of Roman rule (Herod Antipas and Philip, sons of Herod the Great, and Lysanias), and finally completes his list with the names of two high priests (Annas and Caiaphas), who also hold their positions thanks to Roman support. It is possible to date all of these except Lysanias, whose name was shared by several rulers. On this basis, we can tell that Luke is placing the preaching of John the Baptist in the years 28–29 CE. Theologically, however, what matters is not so much the exact date as Luke's insistence on placing the gospel story within a concrete historical setting, and taking into account the political circumstances in which the story unfolds. These were not happy circumstances, for all whom Luke mentions were representatives of foreign domination. Like so many people and nations today, the Jews in Jesus' time were not the protagonists of their own history.

It is under these circumstances that John begins his preaching. Luke introduces the ministry of John with words that are reminiscent of the calling of the ancient prophets of Israel: "the word of

God came to John son of Zechariah." He then reaffirms this connection with a quote from Isaiah 40: "The voice of one crying out in the wilderness. . . ."

The significance of these words tends to be lost by its common use in our cultural tradition. If someone's message is not heeded, we say that he or she is "a voice crying in the wilderness." As a result, we tend to think that when Luke introduces John's preaching with these words

> John received a prophetic "call." He found himself irresistibly caught up by the mighty current of divine activity in human affairs, appointed to tasks which he dared not refuse, furnished with a message which he must at all costs deliver.
> —T. W. Manson
>
> *The Servant Messiah* (Cambridge: Cambridge University Press, 1961), 38.

he is implying that his message will be in vain. But this is not what Luke means. The words in the context of Isaiah convey a message of hope. The people who are in exile are to be led back home through the wilderness, where the voice of one who cries announces that the Lord will prepare a highway over the desert. Thus, "every valley shall be filled, and every mountain and hill shall be made low, and the crooked shall be made straight, and the rough ways made smooth." The result of all this is that "all flesh shall see the salvation of God." Luke does not depict John as a failed or unheeded prophet, but rather as one who, like the prophet of old, announces the opening of the way to freedom and salvation. Indeed, his success is significant, for Luke speaks of "the crowds that came out to be baptized by him."

Earlier (v. 3) John's message has been summarized as "a baptism of repentance." His words are harsh, pointing to the sin of the people. He calls them a brood of vipers that is fleeing from the wrath to come. This image merits some explanation. When vipers are hatched, they remain together, perhaps under a rock, until they begin to mature. But if something threatens them, they spread out and flee. This is what is happening with these people who are fleeing into the wilderness to be baptized by John. Something has warned them of the wrath to come, and they are leaving the comfort and security of their daily lives.

But the very notion of a baptism of repentance is in itself a harsh word. The most common baptism among Jews at that time was the baptism of proselytes. When a Gentile converted to Judaism, a baptism was performed as an act of washing away pagan uncleanness. Therefore, when John tells his Jewish listeners that they must repent and be baptized he is telling them that they are no better than unclean Gentiles. This is reaffirmed by John's own words: "Do not begin to say to yourselves, 'We have Abraham as our ancestor'; for I tell you, God is able from these stones to raise up children to Abraham."

John's message is not only harsh; it is also urgent. It is as if an axe-man had temporarily laid the axe at the root of the tree. The tree may not know it; it is not even hurt yet; but it is about to be cut down.

John's message, harsh and urgent, is also concrete. The other Gospels speak in general about John's preaching, about his baptism, and about how John pointed to the coming of the Lord. Luke adds some very specific guidelines for obedience. These have to do with justice and the well ordering of society. Those who have food or clothing must share them with the needy. Greed must not rule even in tax collectors and soldiers, among whom extortion is customary. They are to be satisfied with what is rightfully theirs on the basis of their work. Repentance requires obedience, correction, and—in those cases where others have been wronged and compensation is possible—restitution.

This interest in social justice and sharing with the needy is typical of Luke–Acts, and will find its culmination in the way Luke describes the early church in Acts as a community in which people shared what they had, and therefore "there was not a needy person among them" (Acts 4:34).

### 3:15–22 *John and Jesus*

John's message, harsh, urgent and concrete as it is, does not point to himself, but to another who is coming after him. This is an important point for Luke, who apparently was writing at a time when there were still those who claimed to be followers of John but not of Jesus, and such views had spread beyond the confines of Judea to Diaspora Judaism (see Acts 19:1–5). In presenting the teaching of John, Luke deals with this matter head-on. He tells us that the preaching of John was such that there was a general suggestion that he might be the

Messiah. But John responds that it is not so. He is not the expected one, but his humble forerunner.

The contrast between John and Jesus is twofold. First, John is at best a humble servant of the one who comes after him. John is not even worthy to untie the thong of his sandals. Sandals were usually worn outdoors, so that when arriving indoors, particularly after a long journey, people would untie their sandals. Those who were sufficiently rich boasted of their wealth by having servants untie their lacings. A sign of welcome to an honored guest was to untie his sandals and then wash his feet, a practice reflected in the footwashing described in John 13. Thus what John is saying is that he is not even worthy to be counted among the lowest servants of the one whose coming he announces. Later, in Luke 7:28, Jesus would declare that John was great ("among those born of woman no one is greater than John"), but even so, the reversals of the kingdom are such that "the least in the kingdom of God is greater than he." In brief, Luke presents John as perhaps the greatest among the prophets and as the heir to the long line of leaders of Israel whose significance was announced in that they were born of barren women; but even so, John cannot even be compared with Jesus.

Second, John expresses the contrast between himself and Jesus by referring to two sorts of baptism. John baptizes with water; but Jesus will baptize "with the Holy Spirit and with fire." Both water and fire are purifying agents; but fire is much more potent than water. Water may wash away whatever is unclean; but fire burns it away. In Acts 19, there is a fuller discussion of the matter. Paul arrives at Ephesus and there finds some "disciples." Yet these people did not receive the Holy Spirit when they became believers. Paul then inquires about their baptism, and when they tell he that they were baptized "into John's baptism," Paul expresses the contrast between John's baptism and faith in Jesus in terms that are reminiscent of what John says in Luke. According to the explanation that Luke places on the lips of Paul, "John baptized with the baptism of repentance, telling the people to believe in the one who was to come after him, that is, in Jesus" (Acts 19:4). When these disciples are baptized "in the name of the Lord Jesus," the Holy Spirit comes upon them. Thus in Lukan theology there is a difference between a baptism of repentance, which is what John performed, and baptism in the name of Jesus, which is connected with receiving the Holy Spirit. John calls people to repent, and when they do this he baptizes them as a sign that they are cleansed of their former impurity. But Christian baptism, while still employing water, is "with the Holy Spirit and with fire." It is a cleansing (fire) and empowering (Holy Spirit). Furthermore, fire is a sign of impending judgment. John had declared that the axe was at the root of the tree, so that a fruitless tree would be cut down and burned. Now something similar is said about the coming of Jesus: he comes with a winnowing fork in order to separate the wheat from the chaff, saving the former and burning the latter.

Surprisingly, Luke then characterizes what John is saying as "the good news to the people." Good news, that the axe is at hand to cut down fruitless trees, that the Messiah comes with a winnowing fork, and the chaff will be cast into "unquenchable fire"? How can this be good news? It is not good news in the sense that it will make everybody happy. It is not good news in the sense that whatever evil and injustice people have committed and still commit is no longer important. It is good news in the sense that a new reality is dawning. Thanks to the one whose coming John announces, evil and injustice will be undone. This is "good news to the people," because in Luke's usage, "the people" most often refers to the common folk, in contrast to those who rule over them and exploit them (see for instance Acts 2:47; 3:11–12; 4:1–3). But it is not good news for those who thrive on injustice, whose power is oppressive and unjust. For them, the good news is first of all the possibility—and the need—of what may well be a costly repentance.

That not everybody likes such "good news," Luke makes clear in verses 19 and 20. These verses are introduced with the word "But," thus indicating that what was good news to the people was not good news to Herod. Luke does not give details about the story of Herod and Herodias, and how this led to John's imprisonment and death. These may be found in Mark 6:14–29. Luke is content with noting the gist of the events, indicating that Herod had John imprisoned, and giving a brief indication of the reason for this. Luke is not trying to tell the story of Herod, nor even of John, but simply setting the stage for the ministry and teachings of Jesus.

The contrasting reactions to John's preaching—the "people" for whom it is good news, and the ruler who has John imprisoned—foreshadow the contrasting reactions to Jesus in the rest of Luke's Gospel, and the contrasting reactions to the preaching of the disciples in Acts. As Simeon declared earlier, "the child [Jesus] is destined for the falling and the rising of many in Israel."

At this point Luke seems to be in a hurry to get on with his story. While the other Synoptic Gospels tell the story of the baptism of Jesus by John, all that Luke tells us is that he was in fact baptized. Why does Luke omit the details of the baptism, which he could read in Mark? It is impossible to tell. Perhaps his concern over the claims of the disciples of John who refused to accept Jesus leads him to downplay the baptism of Jesus. Or perhaps he is ready to go on with his story, and what is important for him is that at the very beginning of his ministry Jesus is empowered by the Spirit and commended by God—and this he does include in his narrative.

Sometime after Luke, some Christians whom others dubbed "adoptionists" declared that it was at his baptism, when the Spirit descended on him, that Jesus was adopted as Son of God. Some ancient manuscripts read, "You are my Son. Today I have begotten you," and this would seem to give credence to such an interpretation. However, this would run counter to all that Luke has said to this point.

A question frequently asked is, if Jesus was sinless, and John was baptizing people who repented of their sin, why was Jesus baptized? The most ancient answers to this question may surprise us.

Writing early in the second century, Ignatius of Antioch declares, "The reason why he was born and baptized, was that he would purify the water by means of his passion" (*Epistle to the Ephesians* 18.2, my trans.).

Maximus of Turin (fifth century) expresses a similar view. He reflects on the question John asked of Jesus in Matthew 3:14: "I need to be baptized by you, and do you come to me?" How is it that Jesus needs to be baptized, asks Maximus, "he who is not justified by justice, but rather sanctifies justice itself"? And his answer is that Jesus was not baptized for himself, but for us, for "Christ, entering into the Jordan, washed the waters of that river" (*Sermon 12, On Christ's Baptism*, my trans.).

### 3:23–38 *The Genealogy*

We come now to what is perhaps the least favorite passage in the entire Gospel of Luke, the genealogy of Jesus. Most of us see little value or importance in such genealogies, to the point that people sometimes refer to them pejoratively as the "begat" passages. But we cannot dismiss them so easily. The Gospel authors must have had good reason to include them in their narratives.

There are two genealogies of Jesus in the Gospels: this one, and Matthew's. They are different both in their context and in their scope. The differences in the names themselves are obvious, and need not detain us here. Suffice it to say that the claim often made by inerrantists, that one is the genealogy of Jesus on Joseph's side and the other is his genealogy on Mary's side, is clearly wrong. Both genealogies lead to Joseph (Matt. 1:16; Luke 3:23), and they do not agree on numerous names, even on the name of Joseph's father. More interesting is the difference in scope and content between the two genealogies. Matthew's genealogy often points to skeletons in the closet of Jesus' ancestry. Perhaps he wished to show Jesus within the context of the checkered history of Israel as the Hebrew Scriptures present it.

Luke does not seem to have any such agenda. He just lists the names along the male line. But perhaps his agenda becomes clear when we consider the scope of the genealogy he offers. Mark, which is probably the earliest of the four Gospels, makes no effort to place the story of Jesus in its historical setting. It simply opens: "The beginning of the good news of Jesus Christ, the Son of God," and then moves very quickly to John the Baptist and the baptism and ministry of Jesus. Apparently the author of Matthew felt that this made it appear that the life and ministry of Jesus had no relationship with what God had done before among the people of God, and therefore wrote a genealogy connecting Jesus with Abraham and his descendants. Jesus is then the fulfillment of the promises made to Abraham, and the culmination of God's saving work among the people of Israel. But this is not enough for Luke. He needs to connect the story of Jesus not just with the history of Israel but with all of human history. Jesus is the culmination of the history of Israel; but he is also the culmination of the history of all humankind. In order to show this, Luke offers a genealogy that does not stop at Abraham, but goes back to the very beginning of creation, Adam. Jesus is not disconnected from all that went before him (see pp. 29–32, "Further Reflections: Continuity and Discontinuity"). Luke establishes that connection both by repeatedly referring to historical and political circumstances surrounding the life of Jesus and by presenting a genealogy that connects Jesus with Adam.

Scholars generally agree that the chronological order of composition of the four canonical Gospels is first Mark, then Matthew and Luke, and finally John. It this is correct, it is interesting to note that as time passed Christians seem to have become increasingly aware of the far-reaching scope of the events they had witnessed in Jesus Christ, eventually leading to the first words of the Fourth Gospel, which connect Jesus with the very beginning of all things.

There is a final point to be noted in Luke's genealogy. At the very end of the genealogy, when he has gone back to the very beginning with Adam, Luke adds a final touch: "Adam, son of God." Significantly, just before the genealogy, Luke has reported on the voice from heaven proclaiming Jesus as "my Son, the Beloved." Thus there is a particular connection between Adam, who in a sense is also a sort of son of God, and Jesus, who is the Son of God. This immediately brings to mind the connection Paul makes between Adam and Jesus as the "second Adam." In 1 Corinthians 15:21–22 Paul declares that "since death came through a human being, the resurrection of the dead has also come through a human being; for as all die in Adam, so all will be made alive in Christ." Romans 5:14 presents a similar image, leading Paul to conclude that Adam "is a type of the one who was to come" (see pp. 24–25, "Further Reflections: Typology"). Adam is the beginning of the old creation, and Jesus is the beginning of the new. Along the same lines, it may well be that

> Luke . . . lists the genealogy of our Lord all the way back to Adam . . . so as to connect the end with the beginning, and also to show that our Lord has joined in himself all nations and generations throughout the earth from Adam on, and all languages, as well as Adam himself.
>
> —Irenaeus of Lyon
>
> *Against Heresies* 3.22, my trans.

by placing the genealogy of Jesus immediately after he is declared Son of God, and then ending that genealogy with "Adam, son of God," Luke is pointing in a similar direction. Adam, the son of God in the sense that he was the beginning of the human race, is a type of Jesus, the Son of God, who has come to provide a new beginning and restore the race that fell in Adam.

### 4:1–13  *The Temptation of Jesus*

As we look at this passage, it is helpful to place it in the context of the preceding one. By means of the words from heaven declaring that Jesus is the Son of God, followed by a genealogy that leads back to "Adam, son of God," Luke has established a typological connection between Adam and Jesus. This connection is now carried into the next pericope, in which Jesus is tempted in the wilderness much as Adam was tempted in the garden. This sets the stage for a double typology, in which the theme of Adam in the garden parallels the theme of Israel in the wilderness. Significantly, while the entire passage reminds us of the temptation of Adam in the garden, the string of quotes from Deuteronomy with which Jesus responds reminds us of the temptation of Israel in the wilderness. Thus the entire story of the exodus and the wanderings in the wilderness becomes a typological axis, showing that from ancient times God was beginning to undo the evil that was done in the fall.

> As thou with Satan didst contend, and didst the victory win,
> O give us strength in thee to fight, and close by thee to stay.
>
> As thou didst hunger bear, and thirst, so teach us, gracious Lord
> To die to self, and chiefly live by thy most holy Word.
> —Claudia F. Hernaman (1873)

Although the devil plays a central role in the story of the temptation of Jesus, it is ultimately God who is in control. The temptation of Jesus is not just one more attempt by the devil to hinder or undo God's work; it is an integral part of the mission of Jesus, who is to confront and destroy the powers of evil. Luke declares that it was the Spirit who led Jesus into the wilderness. On this point, all three Synoptic Gospels concur, even though they use different verbs. Even while the devil is tempting Jesus, it is God who is ultimately in control, and it is God who not only allows but causes Jesus to be tempted. Today this would lead us into the thorny and unsolvable questions of theodicy: Does God will evil? Does God merely allow evil? If so, is God not all-powerful? But these are not the matters Luke is addressing here. From Luke's perspective, the purpose of God is that Jesus will undo the harm that has ensued from the sin of Adam. In order to do this, Jesus has to confront the powers of evil and conquer them. Ultimately, he will do this in the cross and resurrection. But now that struggle begins with the story of the temptation in the wilderness. Just as Adam was tempted, so must Jesus be tempted; but while Adam succumbed to temptation, Jesus will stand firm. In the first round of the conflict, the devil won; but now the devil will be thoroughly defeated by the work of Jesus.

While the parallelisms between Adam and Jesus are many, there are also significant contrasts, for the purpose of the second story is to undo the consequences of the first. There is first of all the contrast between the wilderness and the garden. The story of Adam is set in a delightful surrounding; Jesus is tempted in the wilderness. In the common imagery of Luke's time, the wilderness was a place of beasts and of fear, inhabited by powers of evil, that was best to be avoided. Adam can eat of all the trees in the garden except one; Jesus fasts for forty days and is famished. Jesus will confront temptation just as Adam did, but even more forcefully. As a result, his victory will be much greater than Adam's defeat.

The wording of the first temptation strengthens the link between Adam and Jesus. In the preceding, Luke has applied the title of "son of God" both to Jesus and to Adam. Now the temptation begins at exactly that point: "If you are the Son of God. . . ." The theme of divine filiation runs through the passage and connects it with the foregoing, reaffirming the Adam/Jesus typology.

Just as Adam was tempted to eat, so is Jesus tempted to eat. The temptation is not simply to prove that he is the Son of God by turning a stone into bread; it is also to eat when he is not supposed to do so. Jesus has been led into the wilderness by the Spirit of God. His fasting there is also under the guidance and power of the Spirit. To

> The corruption of humankind that began in Paradise when humanity [in Adam and Eve] ate doubly of what they were not supposed to eat, was undone by Christ's hunger in this world.
>
> —Irenaeus of Lyon
>
> *Against Heresies* 5.21, my trans.

break this fast by eating is parallel to Adam's eating of the tree that is forbidden to him.

Typology is often more than a one-to-one relationship, for the patterns of God's action are repeated more than once. This is true of the typology of the barren women discussed above (see 1:5–25). In the case of the temptation of Jesus in the desert, Luke connects it not only with Adam, but also with Israel in the desert. The context of the OT words that Jesus cites—"one does not live by bread alone"—makes this clear. The quote is from Deuteronomy 8, and appears in a setting in which Israel is led by God into the wilderness to be tested, just as Jesus has been led by the Spirit into the wilderness:

> Remember the long way that the LORD your God has led you these forty years in the wilderness, in order to humble you, testing you to know what was in your heart, whether or not you would keep his commandments. He humbled you by letting you hunger, then by feeding you with manna, with which neither you nor your ancestors were acquainted, in order to make you understand that one does not live by bread alone, but by every word that comes from the mouth of the LORD. (Deut. 8:2–3)

Jesus refuses to use his power in order to eat by turning the stones into bread, and thus reverses the deed of Adam, who used his power to extend his hand and eat of the forbidden fruit. In the Genesis story, the serpent won the struggle. In the desert and throughout all its history, Israel confronted evil, sometimes defeating it and sometimes not. Here Jesus defeats the devil, thus undoing the history of Adam and bringing the history of Israel to its full fruition.

The second temptation has to do with power. In order to understand this passage, two points are important. The first is that Luke sees all the kingdoms of the world as somehow belonging to the devil. This does not mean that all that is in them is bad. But it does mean that as a consequence of sin the present world is ordered in satanic fashion. It is a world of injustice and oppression. Such oppression and injustice are not merely the result of the will of the oppressors, or of exploitation by the powerful; they are the result of evil's dominance over all of creation as a result of sin. The devil has the power to grant kingdoms.

While this may seem strange to us when couched in such terms, it is a fact that we see constantly in our day. In one country, someone rises to power by means of religious fanaticism, exploiting and exacerbating the prejudices of the people, and leading to an oppressive regime in which all who do not comply to the wishes of the ruler will suffer dire consequences. In another, a dictator comes to power by fanning the hatred of the people for the policies of another country, or by promising a freedom and justice he cannot deliver. In more democratic nations, people come to power by making concessions to special interest groups, by lying about themselves and about their rivals, by skewing statistics, by promising what they have no intention and no possibility to deliver, and in general by compromising principles and character. We may not think in terms of the devil ruling the rulers; but there is no doubt that there is a power of evil over all human power—an evil so great that human effort cannot undo it (see pp. 69–72, "Further Reflections: Demonic Powers and the Mystery of Evil"). When Luke and the other evangelists claim that the devil has the power to grant all the kingdoms of the earth, they are simply acknowledging what we can see by simply reading the newspapers.

The second point to be made about this temptation is crucial for understanding it. What the devil offers Jesus is what ultimately will be his. As the hymn says, "Jesus shall reign where'er the sun does its

> It is good to note how Adam was cast out into the desert at the beginning, so as to note also how the second Adam returned from the desert to Paradise. . . . Adam [was born] from virgin soil; Christ, from the Virgin. One was made after the image of God; the other is the image of God. . . . Through the woman, folly; through the Virgin, wisdom. Death through the tree; through the cross, life. . . . Adam into the desert; Christ from the desert.
>
> —Ambrose of Milan
>
> *Exposition on the Gospel according to Luke* 4.1, my trans.

successive journeys run." The temptation is not to claim all the kingdoms of the earth, but rather to claim them prematurely and by an easy concession to the power of evil. Here again the story of Adam's sin helps us understand the theology and typology that stand at the heart of the passage. When the serpent says, "You shall be like God," the temptation is not simply, as we often think, in Adam wanting to be more than he ought to be. According to Genesis 1:26 Adam and Eve were already like God! In the early church, the entire history of creation and the fall was understood in the sense that God created Adam and Eve after the divine image in the same way in which a child bears the image of its parents. Like children, Adam and Eve were intended to grow into greater communion with and likeness to God. When the serpent tells us, "You shall be like God," the temptation is not in the desire to be like God, but rather in preempting the process set by God. The temptation is not so much pride as it is lack of trust, an unwillingness to follow the path and the process set by God. What the serpent promises Adam in the garden will eventually be his. (In early Christian theology, it is often pointed out that the tree that is forbidden in Genesis is promised in Revelation.) What the devil now promises Jesus in the wilderness will eventually be his. Adam stretches his hand in eager—and therefore untrusting—anticipation. Jesus resists the devil by reaffirming his trust in God and in God alone.

The difference between these two ways of understanding sin and temptation is crucial. If the root of all sin is pride, as Augustine and many others after him have claimed, the best antidote against it is humility. This may well be true for those whose standing in society is such that they are tempted to think of themselves more highly than they should. But the greatest temptation for a vast portion of humankind is not pride, but rather a false humility that leads to acquiescence to the existing order. If an immigrant farm laborer is told that his greatest temptation is pride, when union organizers speak to him of defending his rights, he may well decide that the possibility of claiming such rights is a temptation to pride, and thus decline to join the union. If a woman is considering launching into a new career in a field where women are not numerous, and she is told that pride is at the root of sin, she may well decide to "stay in her place" and not trouble the waters. In both cases, what appears to be humility may well be an unwillingness to take the risk and pay the price of a new future. Just as the temptation "You will be like God" has power only if one forgets that one already bears the divine image, so does the invitation to claim one's rights and possibilities become a temptation only if one forgets that one bears the image of God.

This interpretation of the original temptation, and of how Jesus overcomes it, is crucial in our day, when so many Christians— women, minorities, poor and oppressed believers—are reading the Gospel and all of Scripture from a different perspective. For us, the most common temptation is not so much thinking too highly of ourselves, as it is accepting the low opinion that others have of us, their definition of our roles, and not trusting in the God after whose image we have been created, and who will save and vindicate the divine image in us. From the perspective of the powerful, the root of all sin may be pride; but "from below," it is false humility, acquiescing to injustice, not trusting God's definition of who we are.

The third temptation once again points to Adam's temptation. The issue is not simply, as we might think, that Jesus is tempted to show off his power. The temptation is couched, like the first one, in doubts about Jesus' identity: "If you are the Son of God. . . ." Just as Adam is tempted to affirm his own worth by eating of the forbidden fruit, the devil now tempts Jesus to show that he is indeed the Son of God. Although we often think of the temptation of jumping off the pinnacle of the temple as the temptation of a great stunt, catching the attention and respect of all, there is no mention here of other witnesses beyond the devil and Jesus himself. The devil seems to be saying: "I don't believe that you are the Son of God. In fact, I don't think you are too sure either. So prove it to me and to yourself by jumping off the pinnacle of the temple and having angels come to protect you." And the devil makes his argument by quoting Scripture!

An interesting detail in the story of this third temptation is Jesus' response, quoting Deuteronomy 6:16: "Do not put the LORD your God to the test." Significantly, at the very beginning the entire story of the struggle of Jesus with the devil in the wilderness is connected with God's testing Israel in the wilderness. Just as Israel was tested, so must Jesus be. Now, at the end of the story, the counterpart is also true: just as Israel must not tempt or test God in the wilderness (Deut. 6:16), Jesus must not put God to the test in his own wilderness.

This temptation foreshadows what will happen at the cross, when the leaders of Israel will mock Jesus, saying: "Let him save himself if he is the Messiah" (Luke 23:35), and the soldiers of Rome would echo the same sentiment: "If you are the King of the Jews, save yourself!" (23:37). Luke says that after the temptations in the wilderness the devil left Jesus "until an opportune time." In a sense, the most opportune time, which repeated the temptations of the wilderness, was the cross. But in this case too Jesus was able to resist and defeat the powers of temptation.

# 4:14–9:50

# *Ministry in Galilee*

## 4:14–44

### *Jesus Begins His Ministry*

#### 4:14–15 *An Opening Summary*

Luke does not tell us what Jesus said or did in his very early ministry. He tells us two things. The first is that Jesus began this ministry "filled with the power of the Spirit." In 3:22 we were told that "the Holy Spirit descended upon him in bodily form like a dove." In 4:1 the story of the temptation in the wilderness begins by declaring that Jesus was "full of the Holy Spirit." Now he begins his ministry "filled with the power of the Spirit." The text from Isaiah that he will read in Nazareth begins: "The Spirit of the Lord is upon me. . . ." Of all the Gospels, it is Luke that most stresses the power of the Spirit working in Jesus. Significantly, it is the second part of this two-volume work, Acts, that tells the story of Pentecost and of how the Spirit worked in the life of the early church. This relationship between Jesus and the Spirit—and later among Jesus, the Spirit, and the church—is central to Luke's theology.

The second thing Luke tells us is that the fame of Jesus spread throughout Galilee, and everyone praised him. No details are given as to what Jesus said or did in those early days of his ministry, or to which villages he went—although later, in 4:23, we shall learn that one of them was Capernaum. The emphasis is not on Jesus' deeds or teachings, but on the power of the Spirit, which made his fame spread. Later Luke will give more details about both the deeds and the teachings of Jesus. But he wants to begin by making clear that what makes those teachings and deeds significant is the power of the Spirit.

### 4:16–30 *Preaching in Nazareth*

While traveling through Galilee and visiting various villages, Jesus finally comes to Nazareth, his hometown. Since it is the Sabbath, he attends the service in the synagogue. Luke's comment, "as was his custom," may be a way of reaffirming that Jesus was a faithful Jew. Later on in his Gospel, Luke will tell several stories of conflicts between Jesus and some of the Jewish religious leaders precisely on the subject of how to keep and sanctify the Sabbath. Luke's declaration at this point, that it was customary for Jesus to attend the synagogue on the Sabbath, serves to dispel any notion that Jesus was not a good, observant Jew. (Something similar happens to Paul in Luke's second volume, Acts. It is for this reason that, upon returning to Jerusalem after his travels, Paul is advised by the leaders of the church to present himself at the temple and partake in a series of rites designed to show that he is indeed a good Jew.)

In the Sabbath service in the synagogue it was customary to read the Shema (Deut. 6:4–9), and to follow this with a series of prayers, readings from the Law and the Prophets, and an exposition or instruction on the basis of such readings. As part of that service, Jesus is given the opportunity to read from the Prophets, and he selects and reads Isaiah 61:1–2. In its original setting, this passage referred to God's promise to bring Israel back from exile. Now Jesus interprets it as referring to himself and his ministry.

This passage plays an important role in the Gospel of Luke. It sets the tone for the entire book, much as the passage from Joel that Peter quotes in Acts 2 on the occasion of Pentecost sets the tone for that entire book.

The text from Isaiah is one of comfort and hope. As applied to Jesus, it means that his mission is to bring good news to the poor, to proclaim release to the captives and recovery of sight to the blind, to let the oppressed go free, and to proclaim the year of the Lord's favor. The last is a reference to the Year of Jubilee, when all debts were to be cancelled, the land was to be returned to its original owners, and in general whatever had gone wrong in the previous forty-nine years would be set aright. There is some debate as to the degree, manner, and frequency with which Israel observed the Year of Jubilee; but there is no doubt that by the first century it had come to be interpreted as an eschatological promise. It is in this sense that we should interpret Jesus' use of the passage: in him, the fulfillment of the ancient promises has come. This is clear in the words with which he begins his sermon: "Today this scripture has been fulfilled in your hearing."

According to Luke, the people who hear him are amazed at his wisdom. It is true that they recognize Jesus as a local boy, and show their surprise by asking, "Is this Joseph's son?" But up to this point the general reaction is one of surprise, and perhaps even pleasure at the "local boy who has made good." They have heard about what he has done in Capernaum and elsewhere, and are ready to listen to his words.

Jesus understands the situation. They are probably proud of him, or at least expect him to do for them what he has done for people in other villages. But Jesus confounds their expectations by quoting a proverb that they might think applies to the situation, and then indicating that the people in Nazareth have no special claim on him. The proverb is, "Doctor, cure yourself!" In other words, "you have been doing all these wonderful things out there in those other villages; now do them right here, for your own people." Jesus then goes on to tell them that prophets are not usually accepted as such in their own lands. (At this point one is reminded of Amos, who being from the kingdom of Judah is sent to the northern kingdom, Israel.) The implication is clear: his neighbors do not have an inside track into his favor or his wonderful powers. Then the examples that Jesus gives make this even clearer.

The first example (4:25–26) is the story of Elijah and the widow of Zarephath, told in 1 Kings 17:8–24. The point of the story, as Jesus

> But then the trouble begins. Jesus, not content to quit when he is ahead, points out that the gifts of God do not come automatically to those who attend the Temple. . . . And this is really too much! . . . The idea that the message is for worthless outsiders rather than us! The very notion that unbelievers will be the recipients of God's favor and we will not!
>
> —Robert McAfee Brown
>
> *Theology in a New Key* (Philadelphia: Westminster, 1978), 94–95.

summarizes it, is that in the midst of a terrible famine Elijah was not sent to relieve the needs of any of the many widows in Israel, as was to be expected, but rather to a Gentile woman, living in Zarephath of Sidon, a Phoenician or Philistine city. The second example (Luke 4:27) reinforces the first. It is the story of Naaman, which appears in 2 Kings 5. Naaman was a general in the armies of Aram (Syria), Israel's traditional enemy. Yet it was he whom Elisha healed, and not one of the many lepers in Israel. In the first case, the prophet went to the Gentile woman; in the second, the Gentile general came to the prophet. But in both cases a Gentile was favored above the children of Israel.

The point could not be clearer or more shocking. One can imagine, in our day, a young man who becomes a famous athlete and signs a contract for millions of dollars. He then returns to his hometown, and all come to receive him and hear what he has to say. The town band goes out to greet him. The local papers praise him. The town gathers at the stadium for a welcome ceremony. Everybody is excited. Some say: "It is difficult to believe that this is Joe, who grew up next door." When Joe finally comes to the speaker's stand, all are eager to hear what he has to say. They know that he has talked of the need for better schools and clinics, and that he has supported such institutions elsewhere. Now Joe stands up and says: "Do not think that because I grew up in Smallville you will receive any special favors from me. Actually, I have decided to support the school in Eastville, and the clinic in Northville." There will be a chilled silence. Soon shock will turn to anger, and anger to hostility. "Who does he think he is? We don't need him! Run him out of town!"

This is exactly what happens to Jesus in Nazareth. People are not angry because he claims to be the fulfillment of the prophecy. On the contrary, they are quite thrilled about it. It is when he tells them that they should expect no special favors—not even what he has done in places such as Capernaum—that they turn to him and seek to kill him.

Thus Luke depicts the public ministry of Jesus as beginning with one of the many reversals that will appear throughout his Gospel. What Jesus tells his audience is that they, who had every reason to believe that they were in, are out, just as the many widows in Israel in the time of Elijah, and the many lepers in the time of Elisha, were out, and the prophets ministered to a Phoenician widow and a Syrian leper. The reaction of the people of Nazareth reminds us of the prophecy of Simeon at the temple: "This child is destined for the falling and the rising of many in Israel" (2:34).

### 4:31–44  *Healing in Capernaum*

Luke now takes us to Capernaum, the same village to which Jesus referred in his speech in Nazareth. There he will show his power by healing two people: an unnamed man and Peter's mother-in-law. The setting of the first of these miracles is significant, for it takes place in the synagogue on a Sabbath. At this point, the general reaction is one of amazement, and we are not told of anyone reacting negatively to the actions of Jesus. But as the story progresses there will be repeated occurrences in similar settings in which some responses will not be as favorable as in this case.

The story itself is relatively simple: a man with an "unclean demon" is healed. Luke calls the demon "unclean," because at the time the word "demon" did not necessarily have the negative connotations it has for us today. Socrates' claim that a "demon" guided him is well known. So, by calling the demon "unclean," Luke makes clear that he means what today we would simply call a "demon."

We are not told what symptoms the man had. We tend to think of "demon possession" as necessarily related to madness; but that is not necessarily the case in NT usage. In Matthew 11:18, for instance, the refusal of John the Baptist to eat or drink is attributed to a demon. In Luke 11:14 a demon causes a man to be mute. The same notion appears in Matthew 12:22, where the man possessed by a demon is both blind and mute. Thus in general a demon is a personification of the power of evil.

This particular demon acknowledges the power and mission of Jesus: "Let us alone! What have you to do with us, Jesus of Nazareth? Have you come to destroy us? I know who you are, the Holy One of God." One notes that most of the demon's utterance is in the plural, thus implying that this particular demon is speaking not only for itself but for the entire demonic host. At the end of the utterance, now in the singular, the demon declares what others will learn much later in Luke's narrative, that Jesus is the Holy One of God, who has come to destroy the powers of evil. That the demon recognizes Jesus and the power of God is not surprising. In James 2:19 we read: "Even the demons believe—and shudder."

Significantly, although what the demon says is true, Jesus orders it to be silent. The powers of evil acknowledge the power of Jesus; but this is a witness Jesus does not want. (In Acts 16:16–18 Paul also rejects a true but evil witness.) As many liberation theologians tell us today, truth is not just a matter of correspondence with fact. Truth requires not only orthodoxy—right doctrine—but also orthopraxis—right action. A "truth" that limits itself to describing reality, no matter how exact its description, is not "the whole truth," and therefore is false. A false witness who tells the truth is still a false witness. Demons that declare that Jesus is the Holy One of God are still demons, and their witness, although true to fact, is demonic. Tyrants, dictators, and oppressors who support the preaching of Christianity are still tyrants, dictators, and oppressors, and their witness is false. Unfortunately, in our eagerness to spread "the truth," Christians have too often accepted and rejoiced in the support of such false—one could say "demonic"—witnesses.

Jesus rejects the testimony of the demon; but the rest of the story shows that what the demon says is a correct statement of who Jesus is: Jesus is the Holy One of God who has come to destroy the powers of evil. This notion is central to the NT view of Jesus and his work. We tend to think that in the New Testament the core of the saving work of Jesus is in paying for our sins. This view has indeed become normative in traditional Western theology. But the truth is that in the New Testament there is a different prevailing view of the work of Jesus: he is the one who conquers the powers of evil. This will reach its climax in the death and resurrection of Jesus; but it is apparent throughout the gospel story. Here, at the very beginning of the ministry of Jesus, Luke tells us that Jesus has come to destroy the powers of evil, and that those very powers acknowledge this and fear Jesus.

# FURTHER REFLECTIONS
## *Demonic Powers and the Mystery of Evil*

It is impossible to read the Gospels without having to face the question of demons. We who have been shaped by the modern age have difficulty with the very notion of demonic powers. We no longer believe that demons cause disease. We now know about viruses, and genes, and hormones, and chemical imbalances, and all the other causes of disease. Therefore, we can dispense with demons and other such supernatural explanations for disease.

But ultimately viruses, genes, and all our modern explanations do not do away with the mystery of evil and the suffering it causes. They simply push it one step back. We now know that if someone cannot speak, this is not caused by demon possession, but rather by a genetic or other condition. But we are no closer to knowing the ultimate cause of that genetic condition than were the ancients who would have recurred to the notion of demons. We may be able to move back along a chain of effect and cause; but we shall never be able to solve the mystery of evil.

Although we find it impossible to give a clear definition of evil, we know that some things should not be. People should not die in earthquakes. We know that the young boy next door should not have been run over by a car. We know that people should not starve

---

Finally, he got what he wanted: a Doctorate in Theology. . . . He was anxious to return home [to Africa] as soon as possible. . . . At home, relatives, neighbors, old friends, dancers, musicians, drums, dogs, cats, all gathered to welcome him back. . . . Suddenly there is a shriek. Someone has fallen to the ground. . . . The chief says to him, "You have been studying theology overseas for 10 years. Now help your sister. She is troubled by the spirit of her great aunt." He looks around. Slowly he goes to get Bultmann, looks at the index, finds what he wants, reads again about spirit possession in the New Testament. Of course he gets the answer: Bultmann has demythologized it.

—John S. Mbiti

"Theology in Context," in *Mission Trends No. 3: Third World Theologies*, ed. Gerald H. Anderson and Thomas F. Stransky (Grand Rapids: Eerdmans, 1976), 7–8.

to death. We know that all of this should not be, and therefore we call it "evil." But ultimately we can neither define nor explain evil.

This is so, because mystery is at the very heart of the notion of evil. If we could explain or understand evil, it would no longer be all that bad. If we say, as we often do, that something apparently evil happened so that a greater good might ensue, we are claiming that, even though it may be painful or unjust, it is not ultimately evil. But the truth is that evil does exist, that we cannot explain it, and that our power to overcome it is rather limited.

This we have learned through the tragedies and disappointments of late modernity. Some decades ago, the prevailing mood was one of trust in our ability to undo evil. If there was hunger in the world, we would fix it by means of education, irrigation, fertilization, and the like. If there was widespread disease, we could stop it by means of education, inoculation, better nutrition, and the like. If there was oppression and violence, these could be stopped by the development of democratic systems and better distribution of wealth. If some problems still seemed overwhelming, this was simply because we had not yet discovered the means to deal with them. In fact, we expected that many of them would be solved as soon as we found the proper technological fix.

But now things have changed. The high dreams of state socialism have resulted in tyranny, death, and gross inequalities. The equally high dreams of universal democracy have resulted in wars in which thousands of innocent civilians have died. International capitalism seems to rule the world unbridled, moving jobs and resources from one place to another according to its own interests, and with little attention to the suffering it may cause. Education, which many of us saw as the panacea that would solve the world's problems, is used by the educated to oppress and exploit the rest, to manipulate public opinion, and even to build weapons that can easily kill millions. Thousands of species are becoming extinct, many of which may play roles in their ecosystems unknown to us. In the midst of all this, we are learning that there are massive climatological changes taking place, and we seem unable to do much to reverse that trend.

What all of this means is that, surprisingly, we are beginning to regain a sense of what the Bible means when it speaks of demons.

Over the centuries, we had taken much of their sting away from demonic powers. First we turned them into mere powers of temptation, suggesting evil things to us as individuals. Then we made them subjects of humor, imagining little devils whispering into our ears. And now we discover that evil is indeed much more powerful than we had imagined; that it is overwhelming; that even though we can and must ameliorate evil conditions, we can do little to put an end to evil itself. The realities of domestic violence, world hunger, and the like are much more demonic than some little devil with a pitchfork and horns sitting on our shoulders and making evil suggestions.

We may glibly proclaim that modern science has done away with demons, and that we now know better. But is it that simple? Have we really explained evil? Perhaps a person's illness can be understood on the basis of genetic factors; but does that really do away with the evil of the disease? Does it make the disease less painful? Perhaps we can explain Hurricane Katrina on the basis of atmospheric conditions; but does that explain away its evil? Does it make it less tragic for those who were left homeless?

Theologians and philosophers have offered many responses to the question of evil—usually called the question of theodicy—often claiming to base their views on Scripture. But the truth is that the Bible does not explain evil, and does not even try to do so. (See more on this matter in the commentary on 13:1–9.) What Scripture does say is that evil exists, that there is true opposition to and rebellion against the will of God, and that in the end God will overcome all the powers of evil.

Thus in reading stories such as the exorcism in Capernaum or, later on in the Gospel, the calming of the storm or the healing of the Gerasene, even though we may—and should—insist on "natural" explanations for disease and for storms, we must take care not to forget the real power of evil, its real opposition to God and God's will, its ultimate irrationality—or, in the vocabulary of Luke, its demonic quality.

An important part of the gospel message is that Jesus has defeated the powers of evil, and that in the end his victory will become apparent to all of creation. When we dismiss such powers as little demons floating around and the product of a bygone age of superstition, we diminish the cosmic dimensions of the gospel. Evil is real. Evil is powerful. Evil is organized in its own mysterious ways. We can and must oppose evil, but overcome it we cannot. It is in Jesus, in his resurrection and his coming reign, that we trust as we today do battle against evil powers that we know are much greater than us.

The account of the healing of Peter's mother-in-law in Peter's home is brief. The one whom Luke here calls "Simon" will eventually be known as Peter. In years past this passage has fueled the controversy between those who insisted on clerical celibacy and their opponents. The latter claimed that the story about Peter's mother-in-law implies that he was married, and the former countered that he was widowed, and that this is the reason why in this story she seems to be the head of the household.

More significantly, here we have another story of Jesus casting out a power of evil. Although the word "demon" does not appear in the text, Jesus rebukes the fever—much as he will rebuke demons in a number of passages—and the fever leaves the woman.

The two miracles of healing are followed by a summary (4:40–44). Any historian knows that one cannot recount all the details of what took place in the past. Thus we often combine the narrative of a specific and illustrative event with more generalized statements that indicate that the particular story told is part of a larger story with many other instances. Luke does this both in the Gospel and in Acts. (See, for instance, Acts 2:42–47; 5:12–16; 6:7; 9:31; etc.)

These five verses are one of those summaries, indicating that what Jesus did in the synagogue in Capernaum and in Peter's home are examples of a sort of activity that was repeated elsewhere. As in the story in verses 31–36, demons know and proclaim that Jesus is the Messiah; but Jesus shows his power over them by casting them out. And, continuing what he had done in Peter's home, he also cures all sorts of diseases. Verse 42 seems to be speaking of a particular instance, but it actually serves to expand the scope of the summary itself. In verses 40–41 we were told that Jesus performed many miracles like the two just described. In verses 42–44 we learn that this was not limited to Capernaum, for Jesus went on to proclaim the message "in the synagogues of Judea." One may note that the first section of the passage speaks of Jesus primarily as a healer, while the end of the passage depicts him as preaching "the good news." In fact, these are not two separate activities, for the miracles of Jesus are acts of proclamation of good news, and the good news is precisely the defeat of the powers of evil and disease.

## 5:1–6:16

### *Calling and Controversy*

We now enter a section in which Jesus calls his first disciples, and also has his first controversies with the religious authorities.

### 5:1–11 *Jesus Calls the First Disciples*

Even though in his prologue Luke has spoken of writing "an orderly account," he is not always careful to tell us the chronological connection between one episode and another. Already in chapter 4 Luke has Jesus speaking of what he has done in Capernaum (v. 23), and it is later, beginning in verse 31, that we are told something of those activities of Jesus. Now we come to a series of passages that begin with phrases that are chronologically vague, such as "once" (5:1, 12), "one day" (5:17), "one sabbath" (6:1), "on another sabbath" (6:6). At other points, however, Luke does imply a chronological connection: "after this" (5:27), "then" (5:29, 33), "during those days" (6:12). Significantly Mark, whose Gospel is one of Luke's main sources, often gives more details on the chronological connection among various events. Perhaps it is precisely because he wishes to give "an orderly account" that Luke refrains from suggesting such connections when he is not altogether sure of them.

The story takes place on "the lake of Gennesaret," which is the same as "the Sea of Galilee." This is a medium-size lake, some eight miles wide and fourteen long. It plays an important role in the gospel story, where transitions are often marked by having the action move from one side of the lake to the other. The calling of these first three disciples appears also in Mark 1:16–20 and in Matthew 4:18–22.

In Luke's version, the context of the calling of the first disciples is the miraculous catch. Jesus has been using the boat owned in partnership by Peter (Simon), Andrew, and John as a sort of pulpit or platform from which to speak to the multitude—seated, as was customary for rabbis to do. (The text uses the word "partners" twice. It is not clear if the partnership owns the two boats, so that Peter is in one boat, and Andrew and John in another, or all three are in a single boat, and the "partners" whose help they request are simply other fishermen.) After his words (which Luke does not record) Jesus tells Simon, who apparently is the head of this small fishing corporation, to take the boat back into deeper water and let the nets out. Quite properly, Peter warns him of the futility of the attempt, for he and his companions are professional fishermen who have been fishing all night, and they should know whether there are fish to be caught. But he declares that he will nevertheless obey Jesus and put out the nets. This contrasts with another story Luke tells in Acts 27:9–11, also having to do with the sea. In that other story, Paul advises against sailing, but the centurion who is in charge pays more attention to the captain of the ship—as was to be expected, since the captain is a professional sailor and Paul is not. The result is great distress and eventual shipwreck.

Peter's trust and obedience are rewarded with an incredible catch of fish—so large that the nets threaten to tear, and others from another boat have to come to their aid, with the final result that both boats have so much fish that they are almost sinking.

Peter's response is one of terror. He prostrates himself before Jesus, begging him to depart, for he (Peter) is a sinful man. He calls Jesus "Lord," the term with which the Septuagint translated the sacred and unpronounceable name of God (YHWH). The entire episode reminds us of Isaiah's calling, where he declares: "Woe is me! I am lost, for I am a man of unclean lips, and live among a people of unclean lips; yet my eyes have seen the King, the LORD of hosts!" (Isa. 6:5). Peter is not confessing to any particular sin, but rather to his own essential sinfulness. His declaration may also have social connotations, for many among the Jewish elite called "sinners" all those who could not attend worship at the temple regularly, perform all the ritual sacrifices, and thus be ceremonially cleansed from their sin. Thus poor people—especially those living far from Jerusalem and in semipagan Galilee—were considered to be particularly sinful and unclean. In this case, Peter is reacting as many among the poor and marginalized today react when they meet face-to-face with a grand personage: he is overawed by the one before him, and confesses that he is nothing but a poor fisherman from Galilee of the Gentiles. At any rate, the passage includes Peter's first confession of Jesus as Lord. However, as we have repeatedly seen in Luke's Gospel (1:12–13, 30; 2:10), those who are fearful are called to joy and newness of life: "Do not be afraid; from now on you will be catching people."

When the three fishermen—Simon, Andrew, and John—return to shore, they leave everything and follow Jesus, who has invited them to follow him and to catch people rather than fish—or rather, has turned them from fishermen to fishers of people, for Jesus' words are not just an invitation, but a declaration: "From now on. . . ."

It is common, and proper, to use this passage as an example of the demands of radical discipleship. These three fishermen leave everything—their boats, their nets, their catch, their families—in order to follow Jesus. In this sense, the passage is a call to renunciation. What we often do not realize is that these three leave everything at what would have been the height of their career. Their trust and obedience have led them to an unimaginable catch. The "gospel of prosperity" has come true! Because they believed, they prospered. But such prosperity is short-lived. Because they believe—because their success is a sign of God's power—they abandon their prosperity and their success. They do not take their

> *Only he who believes is obedient, and only he who is obedient believes. . . . The first step of obedience makes Peter leave his nets, and later get out of the ship; it calls upon the young man to leave his riches. Only this new existence, created through obedience, can make faith possible.*
> —Dietrich Bonhoeffer
>
> *The Cost of Discipleship*, trans. R. H. Fuller (New York: Macmillan, 1955), 56.

prosperity as a sign of divine intervention and leave it at that. Rather, their unexpected prosperity itself is a sign that, as Peter declares, they are sinners, that they need a different life. And when Jesus invites them to such a life their prosperity and their success are left behind for a life of wandering and hardship.

### 5:12–16 *The Cleansing of a Leper*

Now follow two miracle stories that are set in undetermined times and places: "Once, when he was in one of the cities . . . " (5:12), and "One day, while he was teaching . . . " (5:17). The two stories are about healing: the first, of a leper, and the second, of a paralytic.

Leprosy was a very feared disease in ancient times. According to the law of Moses, it rendered a person unclean until such a time as a priest, after following certain clearly defined procedures, would declare that the disease was gone and the person was clean (see Lev. 13–14). Since what was then considered leprosy was a wide variety of skin diseases, people were occasionally declared healed and clean; but until then, they lived as outcasts.

In the particular event that Luke tells, the man is seriously afflicted—his entire body is "covered with leprosy." The man asks to be made "clean." The greatest suffering of those so afflicted was often not so much the disease itself as their condition of uncleanness, which kept them away from most human contact. The leper expresses his faith in Jesus by affirming that his being cleansed depends on Jesus' will. Jesus declares his will that the man be cleansed, touches him, and the man is healed.

Jesus' act of touching the leper is a significant part of the story. To touch an unclean person would render one unclean. The man's plight is that he is unclean. By touching him, Jesus not only shows compassion, as such a gesture would imply today; he is making himself part of the leper's uncleanness. He becomes unclean so that the leper may be cleansed. Thus in this story Luke is offering a sign of the work of Jesus, who came into a sinful and unclean world, and suffered from its sin and its uncleanness, in order to redeem it. Along the same lines, Paul declares that "for our sake he made him to be sin who knew no sin, so that in him we might become the righteousness of God" (2 Cor. 5:21). As 1 Peter 2:24 puts it, "He himself bore our sins in his body on the cross, so that, free from sins, we might live for righteousness."

At the beginning Jesus is in a city, where lepers were not allowed. At the end, he is in "deserted places." R. Alan Culpepper comments on the significance of the change of venue in this passage: "The turning point is the touch, which renders the man clean and at least by implication makes Jesus unclean. Ironically, Jesus then suffers the estrangement that the law imposed on lepers—he was exiled to desolate places."[1] (One must note, however, that in the text Jesus' solitude is self-imposed, and not the result of people considering him unclean.)

After cleansing the leper, Jesus tells him to go show himself to the priest. In this, he is simply telling him to follow the procedure prescribed by the Law. But Jesus also commands him not to tell anyone else. This is a theme that will appear repeatedly in the Gospel. It is commonly called "the messianic secret." Jesus is not eager to have his role as the Messiah universally known. On the contrary, he repeatedly tells those who see his wonders or who declare him to be the Messiah not to publish the news abroad. This becomes particularly clear at the point when Peter declares Jesus to be the Messiah, and Jesus "sternly ordered and commanded them not to tell anyone" (9:21). Obviously, Jesus is not performing miracles in order to gain followers or to increase his fame or popularity. (There is more on this subject in the section on pp. 120–21, "Further Reflections: The Messianic Secret.") In the case of the leper, as in many other such cases in the Gospel, this does not prevent the fame of Jesus from spreading, so that multitudes come to Jesus seeking to be healed. But Luke tells us that Jesus, who is clearly not looking for popularity, would leave such crowds and go to solitary places in order to pray.

---

1. R. Alan Culpepper, "The Gospel of Luke," in *The New Interpreter's Bible*, ed. Leander E. Keck (Nashville: Abingdon, 1995), 9:120.

## 5:17–26  *A Paralytic Is Brought*
## *in through the Roof*

Like the previous miracle, this one too takes place at an undetermined time and place.[2] We are told only that it happened "one day." The story, however, is quite detailed and dramatic, and has inspired many a sermon on the value of persevering faith—faith like that of the people carrying the paralytic. But many other details in the passage are worth considering.

First of all, Luke presents the story as a problematic situation. The problem is quite clear. On the one hand, the text tells us that "the power of the Lord was with him to heal." But on the other hand the text also tells us that this power was not available to some who were outside the house. Jesus had the power to heal. But that power was imprisoned, held in abeyance, by the multitude around him who kept others from approaching him. That is the first problem in the passage.

Verse 19 tells us that those who were bringing the paralyzed man could not get to Jesus "because of the crowd." Our immediate picture is that this crowd were the townspeople who had come to listen to Jesus, or to seek a miracle—after all, at the end of the previous passage Luke refers to such a crowd. But that is not what the text says. According to Luke those blocking the way were seated Pharisees and teachers of the law, who had "come from every village of Galilee and Judea and from Jerusalem." Nor does the text say that these teachers and Pharisees were bad people, or that they were hypocrites trying to catch Jesus in some slip from orthodoxy. Other passages speak of some such teachers and Pharisees. But not here. Indeed, in spite of all their bad press the teachers of the law and the Pharisees were those from among the entire population who took Scripture most seriously, and who studied it most assiduously. These particular Pharisees and teachers of the law are sufficiently interested in Jesus and his teachings to have sought him, some from fairly distant places.

---

2. Part of the commentary on this passage was published previously: "Where There Is a Will, There Is a Way," *Journal for Preachers* 25, no. 4 (2002): 32–34.

The problem is that, while these people sit around Jesus to listen to his teachings, and perhaps also to discuss them, outside the house there are others in need, people who cannot reach Jesus precisely because these people are sitting around him, listening to him.

Those who are outside are also fascinating. Among them we find the extremes of weakness and daring, of physical disability and liberating imagination. At the center of the group is a man in a bed. He is limited by his circumstance much more than people usually are. For this man his own body is a hindrance rather than a help.

But this lame man and his friends have imagination and daring. Perhaps the lame man himself, precisely because he has so long been tied to his bed, has learned to let his imagination fly free. The truth is that, if there is no way through the door, and if the windows offer no more than a glimpse, imagination finds its own way: through the roof.

It is thus that these excluded people, marginal ones who could not even break into the circle around Jesus, find a way in. Or rather, they make a way where there was not one. As Luke tells the story, "they went up on the roof and let him down with his bed through the tiles into the middle of the crowd in front of Jesus." The words "into the middle" are important. The paralytic is placed closer to the center than the teachers and the Pharisees.

When the paralytic is in front of him, Jesus declares his sins forgiven. This immediately draws the questioning and criticism of the scribes and Pharisees, who believe that Jesus is blaspheming, for only God can forgive sins. Knowing their thoughts, Jesus shows that he indeed has the power he claims by telling the man to stand up and go with his bed to his home. This is indeed what the man does, and Luke concludes the story by telling us, "Amazement seized all of them, and they glorified God and were filled with awe, saying, 'We have seen strange things today.'"

This story marks one more step in the progressive alienation of the religious Jewish leadership from Jesus. Here for the first time in the Gospel the scribes and Pharisees accuse Jesus of blasphemy, although these particular scribes and Pharisees apparently allow themselves to be convinced by events, and at the end are no longer accusing Jesus of blasphemy, but rather praising God for what they have seen. Since many of those reading this commentary (and the one writing it) may well be counted among the religious leadership of the church today (among its "scribes and Pharisees") we do well in considering the text within our own particular context.

Luke does not tell us exactly when this happened. He says simply: "One day. . . ." Yet what happened that day still happens today. Still today, like then, Jesus has power to heal and to save, to forgive sins and to free the lame from their beds. But still today, like then, there are circles and more circles around the Master. Today, like then, there are lame people who cannot reach Jesus, because access is blocked by the numerous and tight circles, circles of religious leaders and wise and profound theologians, circles of ecclesiastical, academic, and social structures—perhaps even circles of Bible commentators! We who sit in such circles are not particularly bad people, just as those Pharisees and doctors of the law were not bad people. We simply wish to come as close as possible to the truth of Jesus, as those teachers and Pharisees were seeking to hear him as closely as possible. Like those ancient teachers of the law, we have spent years studying Scripture, and theology, and history. We are eager to know, to discover, and to share truth. We are even eager to have others come and join in the circle and sit with us. Too often, however, sitting in the circle as if it were merely a matter of hearing something interesting, we do not realize that we may be blocking the way for the many lame ones who have urgent needs—or at least not making it any easier for them.

Thus for those of us who are part of the academic theological establishment, for those of us who are respected professors, for those of us who are religious authors, for those of us who are professional preachers of the gospel, the Word of God in this passage may well be: Take care. Take care lest in all your discussions about Jesus and about who he is, about Christian doctrine and its content, about the history of Christianity, or about how the Bible was formed, you do not turn your back on those needy ones for whom Jesus came, on those hurting ones who need his power to heal. Take care lest, in turning your back to them, you become an obstacle rather than a help along their way. Or, joining this with what was said above (4:34–35) regarding demons whose factually correct statements are

untrue, take care lest your truth become untruth—lest your orthodoxy not be confirmed by orthopraxis.

But then there are some who in many ways are not part of that
tight circle. Many must still struggle to be allowed into that circle.
Some are minorities, or women, some are Christians in "younger
churches," lacking in material and other resources—not the sort of
person who in our churches and in our society are expected to sit in
the inner circles. For whatever reason, there are many who, as they
peek in through the window, see a circle in which they wish they
could sit, where they would be rewarded with the joy of being closer
to truth, closer to the center of things.

For all such, the text also holds an important lesson: The people
who brought the paralyzed man could probably have elbowed their
way into the circle if they had been willing to leave behind the lame
man and his bed. If they had only been seeking *their* place in the
circle, it might have been easy. But they were not. Their commitment
was such that either they entered together or they would not enter.

Thus for those who for whatever reason stand at the edges, still
hoping to make a way into the center, there is also a Word of God
in this text: Take heed, lest in your eagerness to come into the circle
you leave behind those who need you and your support. Take heed
lest in your own theological and academic advancement, or in the
course of your pastoral career, you become all too willing to drop the
beds in which lie so many of your own suffering people. Take heed
lest you find yourselves sitting in the circle, in profound theological
discourse, but with your back turned to the needy who are still clamoring for the power of salvation. Or, again remembering the factual
but untruthful witness of the demon, take heed lest in your quest for
greater truth you lose the truth that comes to you in the least.

Finally, for all of us, there is a further word from God in this narrative. When through imagination and solidarity we manage to open
the way for those who would otherwise have remained forever outside, surprising things happen. First of all, the margin is brought to
the center. The lame man is placed at the very center, next to Jesus.
Second, the man who was captive to his bed is made free. Third,
even the tightly knit circle of the Pharisees and scribes is blessed, for
they are freed from their prejudices and are able to see the power of

Jesus in ways that they would never have seen had it not been for the lame man and his friends. Finally, no matter who we are or where we stand, the gulf between us will be bridged by the experience of the glory of God, as it was bridged in this story, where Luke tells us that the man who was healed glorified God, and that the teachers and Pharisees also glorified God.

# FURTHER REFLECTIONS
## *Miracles*

In the various and intermingling polytheistic systems of antiquity, events are explained on the basis of actions by higher and mysterious beings. Thus if it rains this is the result of an action on the part of a god; and if it snows this may be the doing of another god. Ultimately, the polytheistic world is capricious, depending on the whims of the gods. Within such a framework, the physical sciences as we now know them have very little possibility of developing.

In contrast, modernity leaves little room for miracles. The success of the physical sciences, and their application to technology, have fostered a view of the world as a closed system of causes and effects. When we moderns are asked to explain something, we usually look at its antecedents searching for a cause. If we do find the cause, we decide that we have found the explanation; and if we do not find such a cause, we decide that we simply have not been looking at the right place, or with the right instruments. Eventually, as we become more enlightened, the cause will be found, and thus we will have explained the phenomenon in question. Within such a framework, miracles are a claim that the system of causes and effects has somehow been interrupted; or rather, that a force from outside the system has intervened, and must be excluded by definition, for outside forces cannot intervene in the closed system that is the universe.

Such views have led to the advancement of the physical sciences and of their application to technology. But they have also led to a disconnect between thought and life, which must be lived as an open reality. It is this disconnect that is currently moving many beyond the worldview of modernity, and into what is often called postmodernity. Already Immanuel Kant, perhaps the high point of modern philosophical thought, showed that knowledge is never purely objective, and that even causality itself—the very foundation of the modern worldview—is at least as much in the mind as it is "out there." Then Karl Marx and Sigmund Freud opened our eyes to the degree to which social and economic interests, and atavistic dimensions of thought and motivation, impact our supposedly objective knowledge and ideas. In the physical sciences themselves, the development of random theory led many to the conclusion that, as Spanish philosopher José Ortega y Gasset put it, "reason is a narrow zone of analytical clarity between two unfathomable strata of irrationality,"[3] by which he meant that, at least from the human point of view, both the final results of analysis and its most far-reaching conclusions are in themselves irrational. In conclusion, the modern view of the world, which by definition excludes miracles, is not unassailable. The world is not as closed or as rational as modernity would have us think.

When Luke speaks of a miracle he is not implying, as many believed in ancient times, that this showed that a capricious power was at work. Nor is he implying, as we moderns tend to think, that the closed order of the universe has been broken, for neither he nor any of his contemporaries believed in such an order. A miracle is not an interruption of an order, but rather the irruption of the true order—the order of the creator God—into the demonic disorder of the present world. It is a sign of God's victory over the powers of evil. It is an announcement that the new order is at hand, that ultimately power belongs to the God of

> It is arbitrarily supposed that those levels of reality that our mind cannot penetrate are made of the same fabric as the small part that we do know, without considering the possibility that the very reason why it is known may be precisely that it is the only part of reality whose structures coincide with our reason.
>
> —José Ortega y Gasset
>
> "Ni vitalismo ni racionalismo," in *Obras completas*, vol. 3 (Madrid: Revista de Occidente, 1955), 279.

---

3. José Ortega y Gasset, "Ni vitalismo ni racionalismo," in *Obras completas*, vol. 3 (Madrid: Revista de Occidente, 1955), 277.

creation, of true order, freedom, and justice. The miracles of Jesus in the Gospel are not just a validation of his mission and his teaching. They embody and are part of the good news!

### 5:27–32 *Jesus Calls Levi*

Earlier in this chapter, Luke has told the story of the calling of the first disciples. Now, after two miracle stories, he tells us about another calling. This time the person being called is a tax collector. In the Roman system of taxation, taxes were farmed out to investors who paid a certain amount for the right to collect the taxes of a particular area. The government collected its taxes from those investors, who in turn kept most of what they raised. Often such tax collectors would sublet their rights to lesser collectors, who in turn sought to recover their investment by collecting taxes and keeping whatever they could. This led to much abuse and exploitation, for the investors' profit, as well as the income of those under them, depended on how much they could squeeze from the population. Most often the lesser echelons of the system were local folk who knew the assets of those to be taxed, and who therefore could levy as much as possible from them. As a result, throughout the empire the local population hated tax collectors not only because of their exploitation, but also because of their betrayal of their own people. In the case of Israel, such hatred and contempt were combined with the feeling that tax collectors, who were constantly in contact with Gentiles and with their idolatrous coins, were particularly unclean.

The publican in Luke's story is called Levi. Both "Levi" and "Matthew" (the name he is given in Matthew 9:9–13) are Hebrew names. Therefore, this tax collector is a Jew—one hated and despised both because he lives by exploiting his own people on behalf of Roman authorities and because he is ritually unclean. Thus this story brings together elements from the story of the calling of the first disciples—where Peter says, "I am a sinful man"—and the healing of the unclean leper. And, as in the case of Peter and his companions, Levi too "left everything, and followed him," although in this case it did not mean that he immediately gave up all he had, for he still had a home and the necessary resources to give "a great banquet." As we shall see as our story unfolds, banquets and feasts play an important role in the life of Jesus as Luke tells it. For the present, suffice it to say that this is the first of many such events in the Gospel narrative.

Those attending the banquet, apart from Jesus himself, are "a large crowd of tax collectors and others." These are both the "high society" in terms of financial resources and the least respected in terms of religious and political allegiance. To eat with them was religiously defiling and politically incorrect. Although not economically, in social and religious terms they were among the excluded.

Then there are the Pharisees. This is the second time Luke mentions them. The first time is in the story immediately preceding this one, where those gathered listening to Jesus included Pharisees who had come from a wide area. They criticize Jesus for claiming that the man's sins are forgiven, but in the end they too are among those who "glorified God and were filled with awe." In the present story, they criticize Jesus, and we are not told how they responded to his explanation. Later, as the narrative progresses, they will become increasingly hostile.

The term "Pharisee" has a bad connotation for many of us. We tend to think of it as synonymous with "hypocrite." This is in part because we look at the Pharisees through the lens of the Gospel stories, and in part because we do not wish to admit how much like those Pharisees we are. Among the various Jewish sects and groups, the Pharisees were the most worthy of respect. They were the people most concerned with making sure that the Law was applied and obeyed in every aspect of life. Others thought that temple sacrifices and obedience to the clear letter of the Law were sufficient. The Pharisees went beyond that, asking how the Law applied to cases not explicitly named in the Law. What is work, and what is rest? What is clean, and what is unclean? How do we make sure that we are a faithful people when we live in circumstances different from those when the Law was written? All of these are questions that faithful Christians have asked through the ages, and must continue to ask. As Christians, it is easy for us to look at others with disdain, or at least to question their standing before God. "He drinks . . . she flirts . . . they cheat . . . they blaspheme . . . they don't go to church . . . they practice immorality. . . ." In short, they are not as close to God as we are. In a way, we are justified in our attitude, and so were the Pharisees. But this is an attitude that prevents us from experiencing and accepting the grace of God. It is an attitude that, while claiming to serve the God of grace and love, denies God's love for others and God's grace for ourselves.

So the Pharisees are good, sincere, religious people. And they are disturbed that this man Jesus eats with unworthy, unclean people. That he does such a thing seems to invalidate his ministry and his authority. They have every right to criticize Jesus, who is certainly not acting as a good religious person ought to act.

But then comes one more of many reversals in the Gospel of Luke. Jesus has not come for the religious people (not for the Pharisees, nor for Christians), who do not need a physician. He has come for sinners like Peter and Levi, who are in need of repentance.

### 5:33-39 *The Issue of Fasting*

Luke presents this narrative within the context of the previous section, connecting it both chronologically—"then"—and thematically—by the reference to eating and drinking, by having the Pharisees be the challengers, and by centering the discussion on the disciples of Jesus. Reading the two stories together, the impression is that the Pharisees are criticizing Jesus and his disciples, first, for eating with unworthy people; and second, for being altogether too jovial, and not following the stricter customs of fasting and praying. (In some of the Latino churches I know, it would be said that they were "demasiado mundanales," "too worldly.") In verses 31 and 32 Jesus has responded to the first of these two criticisms, and he now turns to the second.

The first part of Jesus' answer would make sense to Luke's first readers, but probably not to his interlocutors at the time. It is both eschatological and christological. The phrase "the days will come" appears repeatedly in the Gospel as an announcement of the coming events in the life of Jesus and in the eschatological future (10:12; 19:43; 21:6; 23:29). This apparently dual usage points to the connection between Jesus himself and the drawing nigh of the reign of God. Early Christians reading the Gospel would understand Jesus as declaring that while he is with the disciples there is no reason to fast. It is not a time of mourning or longing, but rather of rejoicing—much as one rejoices at a wedding and mourns at a parting or a funeral. "The days will come when the bridegroom will be taken away from them, and then they will fast." Significantly, in Acts Luke affirms that the early disciples fasted.

Then Jesus turns to two sayings that may well be aphorisms already in existence. Both have to do not only with the incompatibility between the old and the new, but also with the negative consequences of trying to combine the two. In both cases, the new has a power that will destroy the old: the new patch will shrink and make a bigger rip in the old cloth, and the new wine will ferment and break the old wineskin. Without saying so explicitly, Jesus implies that the Pharisees have not recognized the radical newness of what is taking place before their eyes. They want to turn Jesus into one more of the many wise teachers of Israel—to patch him into the old cloth. But the power of the new will not allow such compromises. This does not mean that Jesus is claiming that there is no connection between him and God's work through the ages before him (see pp. 29–32, "Further Reflections: Continuity and Discontinuity"). But it does announce that Jesus is not just one more episode in the history of God's dealings with Israel. Jesus is the bridegroom for whom the ages have waited. Therefore, simply to add Jesus to the old social or religious practices and expectations would have disastrous consequences such as when one adds a patch of new cloth to a torn garment, or pours new wine into an old wineskin.

The last verse in the passage (v. 39, which does not appear in all manuscripts) would seem to indicate that the problem with the Pharisees is that they are drunk with their own "old" wine, and therefore do not wish to taste the

> As Christians in a privileged society, have we cultivated such a taste for the old wine that we despise the new? . . . The new wine has arrived bearing the date "the acceptable year of the Lord," and nothing in our relationships with others—especially the wretched, despised, and overlooked among us—can continue as it was.
>
> —R. Alan Culpepper
>
> "Luke," 132.

new. They are so invested in the present order of their religiosity that they cannot welcome God's action bringing about a new day.

The eschatological and christological direction of the entire passage would seem to indicate that we trivialize what Jesus is saying when we use the images of the new patch on old cloth or new wine in old wineskins as a way to deal with the inevitable tension in every ongoing institution between the need for change and the values of past practices. Luke's passage is much more than a commonplace comment about how change works. It is a radical christological and eschatological affirmation. To turn it into an illustration of how things always work is to miss the point, to forget the newness of the gospel, and therefore perhaps to side with the Pharisees in preferring the old and the given over the astounding newness of the gospel.

### 6:1–11  *Controversies over the Sabbath*

This section includes two stories connected by the theme of the Sabbath. The first takes place "one sabbath" (v. 1) and the other "on another sabbath" (v. 6). In both, Jesus is criticized for his activities on a Sabbath—in the first, by the Pharisees, and in the second, by both Pharisees and scribes. They both deal with activities that were forbidden on the Sabbath: one with harvesting and threshing, and the other with healing.

It is often said that in these two stories Jesus rejects the Jewish attitude toward the Sabbath. But this is not true. Several rabbis taught that in cases of life or death the Sabbath laws could be suspended; and the story of David eating from the "bread of the Presence" was interpreted as one such case. So in a way Jesus agrees with the best of rabbinic tradition. But not all concur. There are some for whom the Law is above all a way to preserve their own holiness, and who therefore tend to place obedience to rules above compassion for others.

In reading the first story, it is important to note that for travelers to gather fruit or grain from a field as they passed was not considered unlawful. There were rules prohibiting such travelers from carrying away food, which would be stealing; but a general principle in the law of Israel was that the hungry had a right to food. If passing by, they could take what they needed. If they were local residents, they had the right to glean the fields after the harvest, and the owner was not permitted to go once again over the field once it was harvested, for the gleanings belonged to the needy. So the Pharisees are not criticizing Jesus for taking what is not his, which would be our normal reaction today. They are criticizing him for doing on the Sabbath what it is lawful to do on any other day. The issue is not that his disciples have taken what is not theirs, but that they have reaped and threshed (albeit by rubbing the grain in their hands) on the Sabbath.

As Luke tells the story, it ends with what to those first listeners would have seemed a rather cryptic remark: "The Son of Man is lord of the sabbath." This could mean simply that humankind is above the Sabbath, or that Jesus is the eschatological figure known as the Son of Man, and that he is therefore lord of the Sabbath. Each of the other two Synoptic Gospels points in one of these directions. In Mark 2:27–28 the emphasis lies on humankind at large, for whom the Sabbath was made. In Matthew 12:6 the emphasis is on Jesus himself as "something greater than the temple." Luke's account, seeming to combine Mark's and Matthew's views, is purposively ambiguous, for in it Jesus refers both to what is the eternal purpose of God for all humankind and to himself as the fulfillment of that purpose. Jesus is not simply stating a commonly observable fact or a general principle. He is making a statement about himself and his mission as bringing creation to its intended order. What God intends for all human creation is fulfilled in Jesus.

In the first story, Luke says nothing about how the Pharisees responded to the words of Jesus, but that is not the case in the second story. The "scribes and Pharisees" are once again on the alert, trying to catch Jesus at fault. It is forbidden to heal on the Sabbath, and here is a man with a withered hand. Will Jesus break the Law and heal him? Jesus takes the initiative. Knowing what his enemies are thinking, he places the man next to himself, poses the question of whether it is lawful to heal on the Sabbath, and then goes ahead and does it. Rather than being convinced by the miracle, his enemies are enraged, and begin plotting against Jesus—"they were filled with fury and discussed with one another what they might do to Jesus." Significantly, miracles do not necessarily lead to belief. Here a miracle leads rather to fury and to plotting evil (see pp. 82–84, "Further Reflections: Miracles").

### 6:12–16 *The Twelve Apostles*

The passage begins with prayer. The naming of the Twelve is not a random event, nor a decision taken lightly. Before naming them the next day, Jesus spent the night in prayer. This is the only time Luke depicts Jesus as praying all night—which shows the importance of the decision about to be made. That decision is the selection of twelve among his disciples. In this and the following sections, Luke seems to be distinguishing among three concentric circles of followers of Jesus: the Twelve (who are also named "apostles"), the "disciples," and the "multitude" who come to listen to him and to be healed. While the list that Luke gives here coincides with the parallel one in Acts 1:13—except for the obvious omission of Judas in the latter list—it differs from those in Matthew and Mark, which also do not agree with one another. Thus we have three slightly different lists, one in each of the three Synoptic Gospels. John refers repeatedly to "the twelve" (John 6:67, 70–71; 20:24), apparently taking for granted that his readers know who they are.

While the exact names of the Twelve may not be important, their number is. On this all four Gospels, Paul (1 Cor. 15:5), and John of Patmos (Rev. 21:14) agree. That number is significant, for it corresponds to the number of the tribes of Israel. Luke himself makes the connection when he portrays Jesus as telling the Twelve: "you will sit on thrones judging the twelve tribes of Israel" (22:30). In many instances this has been interpreted as if the church were the new Israel, supplanting it as the chosen people of God. Indeed, in many medieval churches one finds parallel images of "the church" and "the synagogue," the latter blindfolded, and often holding a broken spear. But most probably this is not the way Luke would describe the situation. It is important to note that the Twelve are all Jews. For Luke it is not that Israel has been rejected and the church has taken its place, but rather that Israel has been expanded, so that now, as the book of Acts will amply show, Gentiles can be added to the people of God. As Karl Barth would put it, Christians are honorary Jews.

# 6:17–49

## *Jesus Teaches His Disciples:*
## *The Sermon on the Plain*

### 6:17–19 *Introduction*

The short sermon that occupies the rest of chapter 6 is parallel to, but much briefer than, the Sermon on the Mount in Matthew 5–7. Much of what Matthew includes, and Luke does not, has to do with the Law and its interpretation, thus suggesting that this would not have been a major concern for Luke's mostly Gentile audience.

Luke's introduction is a summary such as we have seen before. Jesus has been praying on a mountain, and there has chosen the Twelve. Now he comes down from the mountain to speak to the disciples in general and to a great crowd that has gathered. Thus while Matthew presents a parallelism between Jesus speaking on the mountain and God speaking to Moses on Mount Sinai, Luke's parallelism is with Moses coming down from the mountain and speaking to the people, a parallelism that immediately reminds us of the disobedience of the people, and places the sermon in a much harsher light.

The "great multitude" is described as coming from distances as far as a hundred miles. Their motivation is double: they have come both to hear and to be healed. Although we tend to think of those who come to be healed as people uninterested in Jesus himself and in his message, Luke makes no such distinction. Healing—defeating the powers of evil—is as much a part of Jesus' mission as is teaching. Those who come to be healed understand that something unique is present. Those who come to hear will be told that this unique presence requires a unique response.

Up to this point, Luke has told us little of the teachings of Jesus. We know that he clashed with the Pharisees and other religious people, and that his views on the Sabbath were not generally accepted by these opponents. We know that he taught in the villages and cities. But we know no more of the content of his teaching. So far, we have not even heard one of the parables of Jesus. Now, in this Sermon on the Plain, Luke's attention will begin to focus on the teachings of Jesus. Jesus will continue healing, clashing with religious leaders, and offering wondrous signs that in him something new is happening. But he will also teach.

### 6:20–26 *Blessings and Woes*

Luke's Sermon on the Plain begins like Matthew's Sermon on the Mount, with a series of blessings or "beatitudes." (The word "beatitude" comes from the Latin *beatus*, meaning happy or blessed, which is the word employed in the Latin Vulgate. Thus it has become customary to call this particular set of blessings the Beatitudes.) But while Matthew limits his account to a series of blessings, Luke includes a series of parallel woes.

In Luke's account the blessings are four, each with a parallel woe. Blessed are (1) the poor, (2) the hungry, (3) those who weep, and (4) those who are reviled and defamed. But there are also woes on (1) the rich, (2) the full, (3) those who laugh, and (4) those of whom all speak well. In all eight cases—the blessings and the woes—what is promised is a great reversal: (1) the poor, who have nothing, will have the kingdom of God; (2) the hungry will be filled; (3) those who weep will laugh; (4) those who are reviled will have a great reward in heaven; (5) the rich have already received their consolation, and should expect no more; (6) those who are full will be hungry; (7) those who now laugh will mourn and weep; and (8) those of whom all speak well will be shown to be no better than the false prophets of old. Thus the great reversal that we have already noted as one of Luke's major themes appears once again here, at the very beginning of the teachings of Jesus.

> Jesus has singled out the most miserable people of his society to pronounce happy, and has pronounced gloom and defeat on those whom his society takes not only to be happy but good. . . . Certainly the hearers of his own time and the readers of Luke's community must have been as bewildered at Jesus' opening of his Sermon as are those who sit in the pew and hear them in twenty-first-century America.
>
> —L. John Topel
>
> *Children of a Compassionate God: A Theological Exegesis of Luke 6:20–49* (Collegeville, MN: Liturgical Press, 2001), 126.

Nor will Luke allow us to avoid the poignancy of these blessings and woes by spiritualizing them, as does Matthew. Matthew says, "the poor in spirit"; Luke, simply "the poor." Matthew says, "those who hunger and thirst for righteousness"; Luke, simply "the hungry." Then Luke omits the blessings that Matthew lists that could be interpreted as merely a matter of attitude: the meek, the merciful, the pure in heart, the peacemakers.

As throughout Luke's entire book, what is presented here is a hard-hitting gospel. It is good news to the poor and the powerless. It is also good news to the rich and the mighty, but only if they follow a path of radical obedience, which in turn will affect their riches and their power.

> As Jesus uses the words, poverty and humility have their original meaning. The poor and those who mourn are those who have nothing to expect from the world, but who expect everything from God. . . . What unites those addressed in the beatitudes and pronounced blessed, is this, that they are driven to the very end of the world and its possibilities.
> —Günther Bornkamm
>
> *Jesus of Nazareth*, trans. Irene and Fraser McLuskey (New York: Harper & Row, 1960), 76.

In 6:22 Jesus refers to himself by a title that will appear repeatedly in the Gospel: the Son of Man. There has been much debate about this title, which according to the Gospels was the one Jesus preferred to apply to himself (see 7:34; 9:22, 26, 44, 56, 58; 11:30; etc.). Without entering into the debate as to the exact origins of this title, one must point out that its purpose is not simply to affirm Jesus' human nature or filiation, as it is, for instance, in the words of the hymn, "thou of God and man the son." It has eschatological connotations, and most often referred to a truly exceptional being who would do the work of God. But apparently its exact meaning was unclear even at the time when Jesus used it, and in the Gospels it often seems to be a way in which Jesus, while claiming an extraordinary mission, avoids many of the connotations of the title "Messiah" or "Christ." This is particularly true beginning in chapter 9, where immediately after Peter's declaration that Jesus is the Messiah, Jesus begins to speak about how the "Son of Man" is to suffer and die.

## 6:27–36 *Loving*

The Sermon on the Plain now turns to those who are ready to accept Jesus' call to a greater righteousness, and is therefore introduced with the words, "But I say to you that listen." This may also be read as a further explanation of the last beatitude and its parallel woe, which have to do with the hatred of others toward the disciples. Significantly, when one compares this section in Luke to its parallel in Matthew, it is clear that Luke emphasizes the use of possessions, and that he wants to make clear that Christian love is not just a sentiment or a feeling, but also an attitude leading to concrete action: "*do good* to those who hate you."

The passage may be divided in two. The first part, verses 27–31, bases the action of the disciples on the Golden Rule, expressed at the end of the section: "Do to others as you would have them do to you." The second part goes further, basing that action on God's very nature: "you will be children of the Most High; for he is kind to the ungrateful and the wicked. Be merciful, just as your Father is merciful." This is parallel to Matthew's "Be perfect, therefore, as your heavenly Father is perfect" (Matt. 5:48). While Matthew's words have often been taken out of context as the basis for a theological claim about God's ontological perfection, Luke's leave no room for such an interpretation. The divine perfection that the disciples are to imitate is the perfection of an all-embracing mercy. Furthermore, even though we often tend to think that the basis for the Christian ethics of love is the Golden Rule, in the final analysis the basis for Christian ethics is the very nature and action of God. As Luke Timothy Johnson declares, "The 'golden rule' of 'do as you would want done' is not the ultimate norm here, but rather, 'do as God would do.'"[4]

## 6:37–39 *Judging*

The previous verse, urging the disciples to be merciful just as God is merciful, could also be seen as the introduction to this section, urging the disciples to judge with a measure similar to God's. While

4. *The Gospel of Luke*, Sacra Pagina 3 (Collegeville, MN: Liturgical Press, 1991), 112.

the notion of "ask and you shall receive" is fairly common in the New Testament (Matt. 7:7; Luke 11:9; Jas. 1:5), here we find an interesting parallel: "give and it will be given to you." What will be given is "a good measure, pressed down, shaken together, running over." Here the image is of a measure of grain that has been shaken so that it can hold as much as possible. What will be given, even when thus shaken, will still run over—an image that brings to mind Psalm 23:5, "my cup overflows." In the context of giving and judging, it implies that the disciples are to judge with a liberality similar to God's, whose measure is full and even overabundant.

### 6:39–49 *Parables and Proverbs*

The sayings that follow, which Luke calls "a parable" but are more like a series of proverbs or wisdom utterances, reinforce the earlier points in the sermon. All of these (or very similar ones) appear also in Matthew (Matt. 7:3–17; 15:14) as well as in the *Gospel of Thomas* and in other early Christian literature, although not linked together in the same way as in Luke. Here they serve as reinforcements of what has been said before. In that context, the point of the blind leading the blind (6:39–40) seems to be that in order to be a teacher one must first be a disciple, and be like the original teacher. That teacher is the merciful Father of verse 36, whom the disciples are called to imitate so that they can in turn be teachers, and not be like the blind leading the blind. The reference to the speck in the neighbor's eye (6:41–42) means that true judgment begins with judging oneself. Unless one does this first, one is not able to judge others, for the log in one's eye does not allow one to see clearly. The image of the tree and its fruit (6:43–45) emphasizes the importance of inner goodness. Trees bear fruit according to what they themselves are, almost as if the fruit were already in the tree before it is produced. The same is true of people. Truly good deeds are those that emerge from a good person; and what evil people produce is evil. This is particularly true of speech (v. 45), for what the mouth utters expresses what is in the heart.

Finally, Luke closes his Sermon in the Plain with a parable (6:46–49) parallel to Matthew's closing of the Sermon on the Mount. As in

Matthew, the parable is connected to the manner in which various people respond to the sermon. The contrast is between one "who comes to me, hears my words, and acts on them," and another "who hears and does not act." Thus just as the Sermon on the Plain began with a series of beatitudes and woes, so it now ends with a promise and a warning—a beatitude for the one who listens and acts, and a woe for the one who hears but does not act.

# 7:1–8:56

## *Signs of Power*

Although at this point Luke has already given us several indications of the power and uniqueness of Jesus, this is the central theme of this long section. Here Jesus speaks mostly through his deeds, showing that he is greater than the prophets and John the Baptist. As the narrative advances, Jesus begins to indicate that his power and his greatness are different from power and greatness as the world understands them. He begins to announce his death—the ultimate sign of the true nature of his greatness—and he invites his disciples to follow the same path to greatness through service. All of this leads to the journey to Jerusalem, which begins in 9:51, and eventually to the cross and resurrection.

### 7:1–17 *Two Miracles*

The lordship of Jesus is manifested first of all in his power over disease and death, to which Luke points in telling the story of two miracles (see pp. 82–84, "Further Reflections: Miracles"). Significantly, one miracle has to do with the healing of a man's servant, and the other with the raising of a woman's son. Here, as elsewhere, Luke pairs a story about a man with another about a woman. The purpose of these two stories presented back-to-back is to stress the unique authority of Jesus.

The first of these two stories (7:1–10) has to do with a centurion, and therefore a Gentile. The way Luke describes him, he may well have been one of those "God-fearers" who will appear again in Acts—that is, Gentiles who, while not converting to Judaism, accepted much of its monotheism and its ethics. His servant is ill, and he wants Jesus to heal him. Much as today we ask for recommendations and letters of introduction, he asks some Jewish elders to appeal to Jesus in his name, apparently because he fears that Jesus will not respond to the request of a Gentile, and he wants Jesus to know that he is indeed a pious man who favors Jews. Jesus is willing to go to the man's house (even though a visit to a Gentile might render him ritually unclean) and starts on his way. But the man sends a message that stresses the power and authority of Jesus. Apparently, as he sees it, this is an authority given by another, for the centurion says that he too is "under authority," and that he also has "soldiers under me." On the basis of that authority he has received from above (presumably from Rome) he has the power to order people to come and to go. In comparing his own authority with that of Jesus, he is not stressing his own importance, but rather giving an indication that, if he receives his authority from Rome, Jesus receives his from God; and that, if he has the power to command people, Jesus has command over the powers of evil and disease.

Significantly, Jesus never meets the centurion. But even so he acknowledges the man's faith, which is greater than any he has found in Israel. Jesus seems to continue along his way, while those who had been sent by the centurion return and find that the servant has been healed.

The second miracle (7:11–17) takes place in Nain, a town approximately twenty-five miles from Capernaum. The story bears comparing with the preceding. The man in the first story sends a request to Jesus; the woman in the second is simply accompanying her son's funeral. Therefore, in the first story Jesus responds to an expressed need and hope; in the second he takes the initiative to meet the widow's grief and need without even being asked. In the first he does not even go to the man's house; in the second, he approaches the funeral procession and touches the bier—an act that would render him unclean. While the first is a miracle of healing, the second is a miracle of resurrection.

The juxtaposition of these stories shows that the common notion that miracles are necessarily connected to faith is not correct. The centurion has great faith, and his slave is healed. The woman has no expectation to see her son again, and does not even appeal to Jesus for help; and her son is returned to her. One miracle is based on the centurion's faith; the other on Jesus' compassion. Miracles or the lack thereof are not necessarily a measure of the faith of believers.

The geographical setting of the two stories is also significant. Both take place in Galilee—the first in Capernaum, and the second in Nain, near Nazareth. From Capernaum, which had for some time been a center of his activity, Jesus sends a message that announces his power even to far-away Rome. From Nain, his fame spreads "throughout Judea and all the surrounding country." These two, Rome and Judea, will be the powers that he will have to confront at the end, and that will bring about his crucifixion. Here, long before the crucifixion and resurrection of Jesus, Luke is giving us a hint of his far-reaching power. In these various geographical references and connections there is once again an element of reversal. From the point of view of Rome and its representatives, Galileans are Jews, and therefore not very important. From the point of view of Judea, Galileans are not quite as good Jews as those from Judea; indeed, they are almost as bad as Gentiles. But in these two stories the power of Jesus is made manifest to both Rome—in the person of the centurion—and Judea.

> The image of the Galilean to the Jerusalem Jews is comparable to the image of the Mexican-American to the Mexicans of Mexico. On the other hand, the image of the Galileans to the Greco-Romans is comparable to the image of the Mexican-Americans to the Anglo population of the United States. They were part of and despised by both.
>
> —Virgilio Elizondo
>
> *Galilean Journey: The Mexican-American Promise* (Maryknoll, NY: Orbis, 1983), 52.

### 7:18–35 *Jesus and John the Baptist*

At the end of the previous pericope, Luke told us that people were astounded at what Jesus was doing and began asking who he was, and that "this word about him spread throughout Judea and all the surrounding country." Now John hears these reports through his own disciples. In 3:20 Luke has already stated that John is in prison. Therefore, he cannot come to Jesus, nor does he hear directly of Jesus' doings. This is reported to John by his disciples, two of whom are then sent to inquire directly from Jesus himself.

The question John asks is prompted by what is being said about Jesus as a result of the raising of the widow's son. Essentially, John wants to know if Jesus is the long-awaited Messiah: "Are you the one who is to come, or are we to wait for another?" There has been much speculation among interpreters as to why John asks this question. Is he doubtful because Jesus has not turned out to be a harsh and vindictive Messiah? Is he simply hopeful that this may be the fulfillment of the promises made to Israel? Does he simply want Jesus to declare himself? All of this is mere speculation, for the text says nothing about John's motivation.

What is clear is that Jesus does not respond to John's question with a declaration or a claim as to who he is. He simply tells John's disciples to tell John what they themselves have seen and heard. (Seeing and hearing are a frequent combination in the New Testament, where people are often told to witness to what they have seen and heard.) There are essentially six things that characterize the work of God in the Old Testament, particularly in the stories about Elijah and Elisha: (1) the blind receive their sight, (2) the lame walk, (3) the lepers are cleansed, (4) the deaf hear, (5) the dead are raised (a reference to the story immediately preceding), and (6) the poor hear good news.

To this Jesus adds the strange comment: "blessed is anyone who takes no offense at me." In this context, this may be an invitation to John to accept Jesus as the promised one, and not to be derailed by the difference between what John expected the Messiah to be and who Jesus in fact is. It may also be Luke's way of warning that Christian faith and preaching would offend and even scandalize some, but that this was no reason to reject it.

After John's messengers depart, Jesus speaks about John to "the crowds." Luke is thus telling us that what Jesus says about John is public knowledge, and is probably responding to some even at the time of Luke's writing who saw Jesus and his disciples as competing with John and his.

> People today still judge Jesus by their expectations, instead of pausing and probing into the evidence to see what was really going on. They do the same . . . with Jesus' followers—criticizing some for being too strict, others for being too soft, some for being too intellectual, others for being too down-to-earth. . . . Following the Messiah who is different to what we imagined is always demanding; but this is the only way to the kingdom of God.
>
> —Tom Wright
>
> *Luke for Everyone* (London: SPCK, 2001), 88.

The general tenor of what Jesus says about John is paradoxical. On the one hand, he exalts John, whom he calls "more than a prophet," and declares that "among those born of women no one is greater than John." On the other, he says that "the least in the kingdom of God is greater than he." This is a stark reaffirmation of what Jesus will teach throughout the Gospel, that the kingdom of God is a radical reversal of the existing order. This is true not only of the social order, but also of the religious order itself. John was a great religious leader; yet even the least in the kingdom is greater than he. Luke then brings this home to Jewish society in his parenthetical comment in verses 29–30, to the effect that the tax collectors (considered the worst of sinners) acknowledged the justice of God, while the religious elite (the Pharisees and the lawyers) did not. In this context, the "justice of God" is shown to be different from human justice. According to human justice, the doctors of the Law and the Pharisees, being deeply religious, should be first, and the tax collectors should be last or even be excluded. But this is not what happens with the preaching of John the Baptist, nor later with the preaching of Jesus himself. In both cases those who acknowledged they were sinners had an advantage over those who thought their religiosity somehow put them right with God.

The passage then concludes with a comparison between "the people of this generation" and children at play in the marketplace. The words the children say may be part of a game known then but forgotten today. At any rate the point is clear: the reactions of those who hear John and Jesus are puerile. Like children, they are never satisfied. If you invite them to dance, they want to mourn; and if you invite them to mourn, they want to dance. Likewise, when John came preaching and practicing an ascetic austerity, people said that he was mad—"he has a demon." And now Jesus himself is accused of being a drunkard and a glutton, and of eating and feasting with unworthy sinners. (Today we would say that these people would not decide whether to fish or to cut bait.)

The last verse closes the entire section with a word of hope. Luke's rendering differs from its parallel in Matthew 11:19, where wisdom is vindicated "by her deeds." In Luke the reference to "all her children" harks back to the "children" playing in the marketplace, and seems to indicate that both those who play the flute (those who drink and eat) and those who wail (those of a more ascetic bent) are children of wisdom.

### 7:36–50 *The Pharisee and the Sinful Woman*

This is one of many meals that Jesus attends in the Gospel of Luke. It is closely connected with the foregoing, first, by the very theme of eating; second, by the invitation coming from a Pharisee. The other main character is "a woman in the city, who was a sinner." Interpreters often take for granted that she was a harlot, or that her sinfulness had something to do with her sex life. But the text says nothing of the sort. This episode is also often conflated with similar stories in Mark 14:3–9, Matthew 26:6–13, and John 12:1–8. But this particular story differs from those in many respects, including its setting in the narrative and the point it makes, for in those other Gospels the parallel event takes place shortly before the passion of Jesus and is an announcement of it, while in Luke it appears much earlier and has nothing to do with the passion.

As the story unfolds, it becomes apparent that the Pharisee, even though he had invited Jesus, did not extend to him some of the essential elements of hospitality and courtesy—water for his feet, a kiss of welcome, and oil for anointment. Apparently he thought that he was doing Jesus a favor by inviting him to dinner. The sinful woman, in contrast, bathed the feet of Jesus with her tears, kissed his feet, and anointed his feet. Still the Pharisee, whose name was Simon, was convinced that he was in the right, and that Jesus was wrong in accepting the woman's tears, kisses, and oil.

The story is inserted amid stories of pain and suffering that are fruits of injustice. The text opens up a space of light that allows something different to appear amid words heavy with death and deceit; it tells of a gratuitous, prophetic, revolutionary gesture. It is life opening up space within pain, within the patriarchal scheme of death.

—Silvia Regina de Lima Silva

"Dialogue of Memories: Ways toward a Black Feminist Christology from Latin America," in *Feminist Intercultural Theology: Latina Explorations for a Just World,* ed. María Pilar Aquino and María José Rosado-Nunes (Maryknoll, NY: Orbis, 1970), 171.

In an interesting turn of events, when Simon tells himself that if Jesus were really a prophet he would know who the woman was and would reject her ministrations, Jesus shows that he is indeed a prophet by being able to tell what Simon is thinking.

All of this sets the stage for a parable that makes the essential point of the contrast between the pious Pharisee and the sinful woman. If two debtors have their debts cancelled, and one's debt is ten times as great as the other's, who will be most grateful for the cancellation? Obviously, the one with the larger debt. Likewise, the Pharisee, being a pious and religious person, and thinking that his debt (if any) is quite small, is not able to offer the gratitude that the sinful woman is expressing with her tears, kisses, and oil. In response, Jesus says to the woman that her sins are forgiven (for which he is further criticized by the commensals) and that her faith has saved her.

This is one more passage in which Luke presents the radical reversal that Jesus preaches. The sinful woman is able to receive and accept grace in a way that the religious Pharisee cannot. Even though Jesus is a religious teacher, his teaching is not about religion. It is not about how to be more religious. It is not about how to gain God's acceptance. It is about a God whose acceptance of sinners the religious find jarring. It is about a God whose love cannot be bought even by great acts of praise or mighty deeds of justice. It is about sinners who rejoice at the great forgiveness they have received, and religious people who wish God were more religious—more amenable to being mollified by acts of worship, piety, and devotion.

### 8:1–3 *The Women Disciples*

Here we come to another of Luke's summaries, which depicts Jesus traveling and preaching. Significantly, among those who travel with him are not only the Twelve, but also a number of women. One of them is Mary Magdalene, often depicted as a reformed harlot, although the biblical narrative says nothing of the sort. Some of them, such as Joanna, wife of Herod's steward, must have been fairly well-to-do. The phrase "and many others" is in the feminine form in Greek, so these too are women. Significantly, it is these women who cover the expenses of Jesus and his party. Once again, Luke shows a particular interest in pointing out the role of women among the early disciples of Jesus.

> [Simon] now becomes her judge. . . . But the woman is on another plane: She is not the one "received," she is the one who *receives*. . . . Simon has not received her although he is the owner of the house. . . . He has tried to put on a pleasant dinner, but in fact he did not receive the guest. . . . She who receives Christ is not the owner of the house but an intruder.
>
> —Arturo Paoli
>
> *Meditations on Saint Luke,* trans. Bernard F. McWilliams (Maryknoll, NY: Orbis, 1977), 172.

The manner in which Mary Magdalene has been traditionally depicted merits some reflection. There is nothing in the text to suggest that the "seven demons" of which she had been cured had anything to do with sexual impurity or immorality. Nor is there any reason to think that the "sinful woman" of the previous section had any particular connection with Mary Magdalene. Yet the common notion, often depicted in art, is that Mary Magdalene was a prostitute. This may well be the result of a history of interpretation dominated by men—and by men who tended to see women almost exclusively as sexual objects, and their sins as mostly sexual in nature.

### 8:4–15 *The Parable of the Sower, the Seed, and the Soils*

We come now to one of the better-known parables of Jesus, usually called the "parable of the Sower." Like so many of the parables, this one is capable of different interpretations, and the history of its use in Christian theology and preaching is ample proof of it. Is the parable about the liberality of the divine sower, who scatters the seed with no regard for possible fruit? Is it about how the disciples are to view their own ministry, proclaiming the Word knowing full well that sometimes it will bear fruit, and sometimes it will not? Is it a call to the hearers, that they should be like the good soil, thus implying that the fruit depends on each one's response? Or is it an affirmation that some, like good soil, are predestined to bear fruit, and others are not? Contrary to his usual custom, Jesus explains the meaning of the parable to his disciples. Indeed, he explains its meaning in such detail that the parable seems to turn into an allegory in which each of the elements in the story has a metaphorical meaning (vv. 11–15). But even his rather detailed explanation still allows for the various interpretations just mentioned, as well as others.

Given that situation, we would do well paying particular attention to verses 9–10, where Jesus declares that the purpose of his teaching in parables is "so that looking they may not perceive, and listening they may not understand." In spite of what we have been told since childhood, the parables of Jesus are not always simple illustrations to make a point clearer. On the contrary, quite often they point beyond themselves. In particular, they often point to the disobedience of the supposedly obedient, and they do so in such a fashion that, if his hearers take exception to what he says, by that very response they are proving the point of the parable.

In this particular case, the parable should be read within the context in which Luke places it. Jesus has been going "through cities and villages, proclaiming and bringing the good news" (8:1). A "great crowd" has come to him. Apparently, they are all eager to listen to what he has to say. The theme of hearing and listening thus becomes central, and these verbs appear repeatedly in this passage. Jesus seems to be successful in gathering such a crowd of hearers. But he knows that their following, and even the following of his most trusted disciples, will be fickle. He tells them so; but he does not do this openly, in a confrontational manner. Rather, he offers a parable that concludes with the awesome warning, "Let anyone with ears to hear listen."

He then explains the parable to his disciples, telling them (and us) that they are privy to depths of understanding that casual hearers cannot attain. Apparently, they are content with this explanation, and they are as content with it as we are with our various explanations of the meaning of the parable. We know what Jesus is saying!

But then the rest of the story shows that the parable has a bite that neither the disciples nor any of us would expect. In Luke's Gospel, this parable appears shortly before Jesus "set his face to go to Jerusalem." Read in that wider frame, the parable is not just about the fickle crowd that hears and does nothing, or about those others who hear and follow for a while. The parable is about the disciples who would flee, and hide, and deny "in a time of testing." The parable is about the curious crowd; it is also about Peter and James, and about any who would claim to be hearers of the Word.

But then the parable is also about hope. It is about exuberant, extravagant, even ridiculous hope. Any Galilean farmer would react to most of the story as a simple statement of fact, based on the actual experience of farming. But then would come the astonishing line: a harvest of a hundredfold is the ancient equivalent to our own "if pigs could fly." (In ancient times, a harvest producing four or five times the seed planted was quite exceptional.) The parable is about the awesome power of the Word of God, capable of producing the unexpected, and even the apparently impossible. Like most of Jesus' parables, it is ultimately about the kingdom of God (a theme that appears in 8:1). The parable is a promise to all listeners—the curious, the enthusiastic, the fickle, and the stalwart—that God's harvest will come to fruition, and that neither rocks, nor the birds of the air, nor even the devil himself can prevent it.

When thus read, the parable goes far beyond our common explanation, that different people react in different ways, and that we should try to be like the good earth. It is a parable of hope, a parable that promises a final harvest that is inconceivable by our usual standard. Perhaps, at the risk of sounding disrespectful, one could even say that the parable is about a reign of God in which pigs will indeed fly!

> No matter how hard you try, you are not going to be able to bring order into mystery. You are not going to get rid of chaos. You are not creator. You are a sower of seed, that's all. . . . So do your best, and trust the rest to God.
>
> —Mark Trotter
>
> *What Are You Waiting For? Sermons on the Parables of Jesus* (Nashville: Abingdon, 1992), 19.

### 8:16–18 *"Floating" Sayings*

These sayings of Jesus, which appear elsewhere in both Matthew (5:15; 10:26; 25:29) and Luke (11:33; 12:2; 19:26), are loosely connected with the theme of hearing, obeying, and witnessing. However, it is difficult to know why they appear here, taken out of the contexts in which they are found in the other Gospels.

### 8:19–21 *A New Family*

The passage is self-explanatory. In times past, the reference to the brothers of Jesus was much debated between those who insisted on the perpetual virginity of Mary and those who did not. But the point is that those who hear and do the Word of God are a new family—the family of Jesus and of God. Note here again the reference to hearing the Word, a theme that was prevalent in the parable of the Sower.

The notion of this new family of which Jesus speaks is quite attractive today to many immigrants and other displaced people. For many of them, one of the sadder dimensions of their lives is the experience of being uprooted from the extended families that were the context of their earlier years. At best, all they have with them is their nuclear family. At worst—and most commonly—even that family has been left behind. When they join the church in their new places of residence, the church often becomes their new family. For this reason, Latino ecclesiology often stresses the particular image of the church as the family of God. While for many who have not experienced the loss of family the church is a conglomeration of families, and part of the task of the church is to

> How good, how indescribably good! What good news for me a woman, a woman born in India, among Brahmans who hold out no hope for me and the like of me! The Bible declares that Christ did not reserve this great salvation for a particular caste or sex. . . . I did not have to wait till after undergoing births and deaths for countless millions of times, when I should become a Brahman man.
>
> —Pandita Ramabai
>
> "A Testimony," in *In Her Words: Women's Writings in the History of Christian Thought*, ed. Amy Oden (Nashville: Abingdon, 1994), 325–26.

strengthen those families, for those who constantly experience and mourn such a loss the church is not a collection of families but their new family, the family of God! To them this story in Luke, which to others may seem callous, is a description of one of the ways in which they have been blessed by their hearing of the Word.

### 8:22–25 *Power over the Demons Let Loose in the Elements*

Luke now returns to the central theme of this entire section, which is the power of Jesus over demons. It is important for Luke's narrative to stress that power as a prelude to the entire section on the passion, in which that power seems to be brought to naught. Thus four miracle stories serve to remind us of who this is who will set his face to go to Jerusalem, and there suffer and die. The first of these stories shows the power of Jesus over the demons that wreak havoc through the elements.

In order to understand the passage about the calming of the storm in its historical context, we must remember that the notion of "nature" as an orderly system was alien to the ancient world. We must also remember the significance of water as representing chaos—images such as the parting of the waters in creation, the flood, and the monsters of the deep. Then we must keep in mind the parting of the waters in Exodus, which in the Old Testament represents the greatest expression of God's saving power. Finally, the story has overtones that remind us of Jonah and his disobedience—like Jonah, Jesus sleeps while the tempest rages.

When we put these various elements together, what emerges is a vision in which the storm at sea is an expression of the power of the demons of destruction—and a reminder of the corruption of all

> As a mother stills her child,
> thou canst hush the ocean wild;
> boisterous waves obey thy will,
> when thou sayest to them, "Be still!"
> Wondrous sovereign of the sea,
> Jesus, Savior, pilot me.
> —Edward Hopper (1871)

of creation as a result of sin and the fall. It is also an indication of the power of Jesus over the demons that threaten to sink the boat. But above all it points to the connection between God's saving work in Exodus and God's saving work in Jesus. The question at the end of the story, "Who then is this, that he commands even the winds and the waves, and they obey him?" points to the perplexity of the disciples; but the postresurrection community knows the answer: he is the one in whom God has done and is doing wonders such as were done by the same God at the parting of the waters in Exodus.

### 8:26–56 *Power over Disease and Death*

This section of the Gospel stressing the power of Jesus closes with the story of three miracles in which Jesus shows his power over disease and death: the restoration of the man living in the tombs, the healing of the woman suffering from hemorrhages, and the raising of Jairus's daughter. Jointly, the three narratives serve to announce that the one who will soon find himself in Jerusalem accused, mocked, and crucified is Lord over all powers of evil, including disease and death, and is yet loving and compassionate. Separately, they point to various aspects of the lordship and compassion of Jesus.

> She, too, who touched thee in the press
> and healing virtue stole.
> —William Cowper (1779)

The first miracle is the restoration of the man living among tombs. Although there are textual problems in this passage, so that it is impossible to tell exactly where the miracle is said to take place, it would seem that we are now in a Gentile area where large herds of swine were common. Thus one of the added dimensions of this story is that it is an early indication of the power of Jesus beyond the world of Judaism. Significantly, the demons know Jesus, declaring: "What have you to do with me, Jesus, Son of the Most High?" This reminds us of a similar statement by a demon in 4:34. That the powers of evil know of Jesus and his power is a theme that appears again in Luke–Acts (see Acts 16:17; 19:15), and in this context serves to underscore the general theme of the entire section.

Two other elements in this story merit particular attention. First, there is the irony of the fate of the demons. They are afraid to be cast into the abyss—which in the worldview of the time was the watery chaos—and they end up drowned in a lake. Then there is the matter of the reason why the people in the area wish Jesus to leave. The text mentions only "fear." Is it fear of the unknown and surprising power that has been manifested, or is it fear that Jesus will upset the economic well-being of the region, as he has already done by drowning the swine? If the latter, there is a parallelism here with the story of Paul's imprisonment in Philippi, which resulted from his having upset the livelihood of people who were exploiting a slave girl (Acts 16:16). Most likely it is both, for the power that Jesus has manifested will certainly affect the social and economic order.

The other two stories are closely connected, both to one another—one sandwiched within the other as they are—and to the preceding one. The contrasting geographical situation between the first story and these two merits attention. Jesus healed the man living among the tombs on one side of the Sea of Galilee; and he healed the woman and raised Jairus's daughter on the other side. One story takes place among Gentiles, the other among Jews. At the end of one story, Jesus orders the Gerasene to witness; at the end of the third story, he commands Jairus and his wife to remain silent and keep the secret (see pp. 120–21, "Further Reflections: The Messianic Secret"). But there is also a common theme in all three stories, even beyond the

> The people knew the locus of the evil, knew where the man lived, and devoted considerable time and expense trying to guard and to control him. A community thus learns to live with demonic forces, isolating and practically controlling them. . . . Even when it is for good, power that can neither be calculated nor managed is frightening.
>
> —**Fred Craddock**
>
> *Luke*, Interpretation (Louisville: John Knox Press, 1990), 117.

Today we [African women] are not to be satisfied simply with being healed. We are to join the disciples in being healers, in proclaiming that the reign of God has come, that we have touched that reign, become part of it, and have been empowered to become its heralds. We are in a unique position to help effect this wholeness of ourselves and of society, because like the woman with the flow of blood we have borne the weight of the illness, the alienation in society, and so should know better where it hurts and how it is to be healed.

—Teresa Okure

"Epilogue: The Will to Arise: Reflections on Luke 8:40–56," in *The Will to Arise: Women, Tradition, and the Church in Africa*, ed. Mercy Amba Oduyoye and Musimbi R. A. Kanyoro (Maryknoll, NY: Orbis, 1992), 230.

matter of Jesus' power over demons and death. It is the theme, so prevalent in Luke, of the outsider being brought back in, and of the restoration of community when this happens. The Gerasene who lived in the tombs is restored to his home and community. The woman who, because of her hemorrhages, was considered unclean and was therefore excluded from community is now cleansed and restored. The girl is restored to her family. In all three stories Jesus seems to go beyond the borders of propriety: he heals a Gentile; he commends an unclean woman who has touched him; he touches a corpse.

The demons that Jesus conquers are not only those of disease and death, but also those of isolation and exclusion.

The twelve years that the woman was ill correspond to the girl's twelve years of age. The girl would have come to bring joy to Jairus just as the woman was beginning her long struggle with disease and exclusion. One story speaks of twelve years of suffering, and the other of twelve years of joy in Jairus's house.

As a whole, the three stories warn us against being too systematic and dogmatic about the nature of the Christian mission. It is a mission to Gentiles, but also to those who should be part of the community but are excluded. At some points it is a mission inviting others to witness; and at other points it is a mission inviting some to be silent! It is a mission among crowds; but it is also a mission of personal touch. It is a mission of joy and restoration both to those who have long been oppressed by evil and to those who have suddenly discovered its demonic and life-destroying power.

# 9:1–50
## *The Beginning of a Movement*

This entire section prepares for the great transition that will begin in 9:51. At that point, Jesus will begin to make his way to Jerusalem, and to the events that will take place there. But throughout his two-volume work (Luke–Acts) Luke wishes to make clear that the mission of Jesus does not end with the end of his earthly presence. On the contrary, it begins through the work of his followers, as the book of Acts well shows. The mission of Jesus and the mission of his disciples—the church—are closely entwined. The mission of the church is not an afterthought, a later attempt to continue the work of Jesus. It is, on the contrary, something that began even during Jesus' earthly ministry, and that therefore is closely connected with Jesus and with his mission. For this reason, before embarking on the narrative of Jesus' march to the passion and resurrection, Luke tells us of the mission of the disciples. Here in chapter 9 Jesus sends his disciples; and here also Luke tells us much about the meaning of discipleship, and in particular about the connection of the Twelve with Jesus.

### 9:1–6 *The Sending of the Twelve*

Luke has told us earlier (6:13) that Jesus had called twelve "whom he also named apostles," that is, those who are sent. Now the apostles in name become apostles in fact. Jesus calls them together, gives them "power and authority over all demons and to cure diseases," and *sends* them out "to proclaim the kingdom of God and to heal." This is exactly what Jesus has been doing up to this point, and therefore Luke's point is clear: the mission of the apostles is the continuation of the mission of Jesus.

This becomes even clearer when we pay close attention to Jesus' act of giving the Twelve "power and authority." This is a phrase that Luke uses repeatedly to refer to Jesus and his deeds (see 4:36; 5:17; 6:19; 8:46). Jesus has been proclaiming the kingdom of God and casting out demons both because he has the power and authority to do so, and as a sign of that power and authority. Now this power is given to the Twelve, so that their proclamation of the kingdom and their healing ministry may be an extension and a continuation of Jesus' work.

But this presents a problem. It has been correctly said that power has the ability to corrupt those who wield it, and that absolute power corrupts absolutely. Having received "power and authority" like those of Jesus, the Twelve will be tempted—as later disciples will also be tempted—to use that power and authority in ways that are not consonant with the teachings and ministry of Jesus. Thus in much of the rest of chapter 9 Luke tells us a series of stories in which the Twelve (or some of them) play a major role, and in which both their power and their weaknesses are revealed.

In this particular passage, the sending is set within strict parameters. Those whom Jesus is sending are to take with them none of the things that would normally bring a sense of security: "no staff, nor bag, nor bread, nor money—not even an extra tunic."

The point of such instructions is not simple asceticism; the disciples are not to deprive themselves of such things because there is a particular virtue in not having them. The point is twofold: on the one hand, the disciples are to lay their security on none other than their Lord; on the other hand, they are not to exploit the power and authority that have been given to them. As to the first, one may note that Jesus lists all those things that travelers would normally carry for their own safety. A staff was not only an aid in walking, but also a potential weapon against beasts or thieves. A bag, bread, and money would provide for the traveler in time of need. These things are not bad in themselves. We have just been told that the women who accompanied Jesus in his Galilean ministry had funds with which they provided for the entire company. Jesus would also teach his disciples to pray for daily bread, and it has been pointed out quite correctly that in the Gospel of Luke Jesus seems to spend much of his time at meals and banquets. At the end of the Gospel, the paschal meal in Jerusalem and the breaking of bread with the disciples at Emmaus have particular significance for Luke. Thus in the passage that we are studying the problem is not with bread or with money in themselves, but rather in trusting on one's provision rather than on the support and guidance of the Lord.

As to the second point, we must read this particular passage in the context of a world in which (as in today's world) there was a proliferation of wandering charlatans who would arrive at a house or village, eat of their food, and when resources ran scarce, when their teachings were questioned, or when someone else offered more, would simply move on to live off another host. The disciples are not in mission for their own sustenance or their own comfort. They are to dwell in people's homes, as was customary in the hospitality of the time; but they are not to exploit them or to move on to greener pastures when they have the opportunity. From other documents of the late first and early second century, we know that this was one of the problems the early church had to resolve. Someone came declaring that he was preaching the gospel of Jesus. Should such a person receive hospitality and support? If so, for how long? How does one distinguish between the true and the false prophet? Here Luke seems to suggest that the true prophet does not abandon a field of work in quest of better conditions. The true prophet graciously accepts the hospitality of the audience, and is content with it. In Luke's time, this meant living within the means of the hosts, and not seeking more. In today's terms, one might say that ministry is not a "career" in which one seeks advancement; that "success" in ministry has little to do with the size or prestige of a congregation, with salary or with any other such measure, but must be understood primarily in terms of service. Thus, it is often unnoticed and unrewarded.

> As Jesus commissioned them to do, the Twelve go without the trappings of security, "just in case." Had they gone with money and extra provisions, their witness would have been undercut by such an evident lack of faith in God and trust in the hospitality of the people. (How many of the church's sermons are contradicted by budgets and programs of self-protection and security!)
> —Fred Craddock
>
> *Luke*, 122.

There will also be those who will not receive the gospel or its preachers. Jesus tells the apostles that in such cases they should simply leave and shake the dust of the town off their feet. This is a sign of rejection, much as when today we tell someone: "Do as you will; but from now on I am not responsible for you, and I owe you nothing." The disciples are to take nothing from the town; all of it is to be rejected—even its dust! If a town or village rejects the preaching of the gospel, it itself is rejected. It is rejected both now in the symbolic act of the disciples' shaking the dust off their feet, and in the final judgment.

In Acts 13:46–52 Luke offers a concrete instance of this symbolic shaking of the dust off one's feet. In Antioch of Pisidia Paul and his companions are at first well received in the synagogue, but eventually they are rejected. At this point, they shake the dust off their feet and declare that henceforth they will go primarily to the Gentiles (although, according to Acts itself, Paul continued his earlier practice of going first to the synagogue when arriving at a new city).

### 9:7–9 *The Perplexed Powerful*

At this point Luke introduces a commentary about Herod that seems to interrupt the narrative, but is an important contribution to it. Herod has heard "about all that had taken place," and begins to wonder who this Jesus is. Jesus is now becoming dangerous. He is no longer a solitary preacher followed by a band of disciples and attracting large crowds. He is giving birth to a movement. His disciples seem to be endowed with the same "power and authority" that Jesus has been showing. A solitary preacher Herod could afford to ignore, hoping that the man and his preaching would go away. But a nascent movement is another thing altogether. The authorities must look into this! And Herod does. Thus the conflict with the Jewish religious authorities, which has been escalating for some time, now involves also the political authorities who, although supposedly Jewish, are in the service of the empire.

> One may well admit that the death of Jesus and the crucifixion of the people are necessary, but only if it is a matter of historical necessity, and not a natural necessity. It is precisely its being an historical necessity that clarifies the depth of what happens in history, while also opening the way for its transformation, which would not be the case were it merely a matter of natural necessity.
> —Ignacio Ellacuría
>
> *Conversión de la iglesia al reino de Dios para anunciarlo y realizarlo en la historia* (San Salvador: UCA, 1985), 36.

In telling this story at this point, and relating Herod's concern with the Jesus movement to his earlier execution of John the Baptist, Luke is announcing that the Jerusalem to which Jesus will soon set his face is both a religious center and the puppet of wider political concerns, and that in Jerusalem these two will conspire to undo Jesus and his movement. He is also hinting at something that will become clear as we read through his entire Gospel: the powerful, by the very fact of judging all things from the perspective of their power, have great difficulty in hearing the gospel of Jesus Christ.

Throughout history, some of the most glorious episodes in the life of the church have taken place when it has been opposed not only by various religious leaders but also by established political authority. It is not that Jesus set out to provoke those authorities, nor that the church should set out to seek martyrdom. It is rather that the very preaching of the gospel, and the movement ensuing from it—the church—is likely to provoke the opposition of leaders and powers that measure success by other standards. Later in this chapter, Luke will tell us that the various opinions that Herod considered about Jesus were also circulating among the people. The implication is that Herod has heard these various opinions, that he does not know which to believe or what to do about them, and that he is trying to decide what political course to take. But, in contrast with the people, Herod's opinions, perplexities, and fears will eventually lead to unjust political decisions—and Luke, more than the other Gospel writers, stresses Herod's role in the story of the passion of Jesus.

### 9:10–17 *Feeding the Multitude*

This story appears in all four Gospels; in some cases it is even repeated in the same Gospel with slight variations, thus resulting in

> Is the one who multiplied the loaves in the hands of the distributors not the same one who multiplies the seeds in the earth, and from a few grains can fill barns? However, since this miracle takes place every year we are not surprised by it. Yet the reason why we are not awed is not that it is not wonderful, but that it is repeated so often.
> —St. Augustine
>
> *Sermon 130, On the Multiplication of the Loaves 1,* my trans.

six different versions of the event. In the midst of this confusing variety of accounts, a similarity stands out even beyond the actual story about feeding. In all six cases, there is a sequence of verbs describing what Jesus does with the bread: he *takes* it, he *blesses* it (or gives thanks for it), he *breaks* it, and he *gives* it. This sequence of verbs certainly has eucharistic connotations. They are the same four verbs that describe the institution of the Lord's Supper, for instance, in Luke 22:19: "he *took* a loaf of bread, and when he had *given thanks*, he *broke* it and *gave* it to them"; and in 1 Corinthians 11:23–24: "on the night when he was betrayed [he] *took* a loaf of bread, and when he had *given thanks*, he *broke* it." (In this account, although the *giving* is not explicit, it is certainly implied in the narrative.)

Thus Luke 9:10–17 must have had a eucharistic reference in the mind of the early church as well as in the mind of the writer. For those reading it (as was usually done) in the context of the eucharistic service, it served as a reminder that the gospel message is one of plenty, and of the hungry being fed. This is why Paul was adamant in condemning the practices in Corinth, where some ate their fill and others went hungry. In the eucharistic service the faith community brings its gifts of bread and wine to the table of the Lord, who then multiplies them so that all may be fed. In the early church, in which Communion was a communal meal (much like today's church suppers), this meant that by sharing all were fed.

Through its connection with the Eucharist, the feeding of the multitude also has connections with the entire history of God's actions and God's promises. In Genesis God gave the human creatures good food to eat. In Exodus God provided food for the people in the desert—and significantly, Luke tells us that the feeding of the multitude took place "in a deserted place" (9:12). In every account of the institution of the Lord's Supper, there is an eschatological element, for instance, the promise that Jesus "will not drink of the fruit of the vine until the kingdom of God comes" (22:18).

While all the Gospels have frequent eucharistic references, none has more than Luke. As already remarked, Jesus appears to eat his way through the Gospel of Luke. He is repeatedly at a banquet or at a meal with the disciples. His comments and actions in such banquets can usually be interpreted as guidance for the behavior of the eucharistic community. This community, fed by its eucharistic celebration, is to behave as Jesus indicated in his many banquets and meals. And it is Luke, above any other Gospel, that points to the revelation of the risen Christ in a meal that has clear eucharistic connotations, for we are told that in the meal with the disciples at Emmaus, "he *took* bread, *blessed* and *broke* it, and *gave* it to them" (24:30).

We must take care, however, not to spiritualize the story of the feeding of the five thousand in such a way that it becomes a mere metaphor for what happens at Communion. This is a story about *feeding*, not just about rituals or religious practices. It is a story that connects the Eucharist with real, actual, physical hunger and need. Thus, if the feeding of the multitude illumined the significance of the Eucharist, the Eucharist points to the importance of real, physical feeding and caring. If the feeding of the multitude is a sign of the feeding that takes place at Communion and in the final banquet of the kingdom, then the feeding that takes place at Communion must be a sign of a faith community that actually feeds the hungry and responds to human need.

> Come, sinners, to the gospel feast;
> let every soul be Jesus' guest.
> Ye need not one be left behind,
> for God hath bid all humankind.
> —Charles Wesley (1747)

If we look at this story within its wider context in the Gospel of Luke, its significance is further illumined. This entire section is about the apostles and their role sharing in Jesus' power, authority, and mission. In the passage immediately preceding, the apostles have been sent on their first mission. Now they return and are about to report when the entire procedure is interrupted by the multitude that comes to see Jesus and eventually to be fed by him. The interruption is such that Luke apparently forgets to tell us what the apostles actually reported. In the next chapter Luke will record a parable in which Jesus speaks of people who seemed so religious that they had no time to spare for a fellow human being lying half dead by the roadside. Here the opposite is exemplified: the work of the apostles, and even the program for the mission, must be interrupted when human need cries for attention.

The context in which this account appears also helps us see the role of the apostles as agents of Jesus' mission. The apostles do not always understand what Jesus is about (we shall see a glaring example of this later in chap. 9). But under his guidance they become agents for his work. They are the ones who provide the fish and the loaves. They are the ones who organize the distribution as Jesus tells them to do. They are the ones who receive the fish and loaves back from Jesus, in order to distribute the food among the crowd.

Finally, there is a small difference in Luke's account that may be worthy of note. All the other stories say that Jesus "had compassion" on the multitude. Luke says that "he welcomed them." This reminds us of the passage immediately preceding, which deals with the apostles being welcomed by others, and in general with the theme of hospitality. It points to the eucharistic community as a welcoming community—much in contrast to the practice of many churches, where the Eucharist is employed as a barrier to keep out those who are considered not as faithful as the rest. Tragically, not only has this sacrament of Christian unity become one of the most divisive issues in the life of the church; this sacrament of welcoming has also become a barrier that Christians build around themselves, often as an excuse not to practice the hospitality for which the gospel calls.

### 9:18–27 *Redefinitions: Messiah and Discipleship*

The connection between this passage and the foregoing is not strictly chronological. Luke is rather vague on this point, saying simply that this took place "once when Jesus was praying alone, with only the disciples near him." There is, however, a connection in that in the previous passage Jesus finds himself in the middle of a multitude, and later, in 9:37, "a great crowd met him." Between those two scenes of public ministry, Luke places this story of Peter's confession and its sequel, and then the story of the transfiguration, both witnessed only by the close group of his disciples.

At this point, following roughly the same order as Matthew and Mark, Luke comes to the point when the disciples—particularly Peter—are ready to declare that Jesus is the Christ, the Messiah, the anointed One who will come to save Israel. Many interpreters see all the foregoing in the Gospel story as leading to this point, with Peter's momentous declaration.

As soon as Peter declares him to be the Messiah, however, Jesus begins to correct some of the common perceptions of what the Messiah would do. In ancient Israel, both kings and high priests were anointed as a sign of their office, and of having been chosen by God for their offices. Thus to declare Jesus the Messiah or the anointed One was at once to declare him king and high priest; it was a challenge to the political as well as the religious establishment. A few verses earlier (9:7–9) Luke told us that Herod was perplexed, and obviously concerned, about this Jesus who had begun a new movement and about whom he heard so much. Herod feared that what people were saying of Jesus might be true, that he might be Elijah or one of the prophets having come back, or even—horror of horrors!—that he might be John, whom Herod had ordered to be beheaded. Little does he know that the situation is much worse: Jesus is the Messiah, the anointed One, the King of Israel. His very existence contradicts Herod's claims to power, even legitimated as they were by the might of Rome. Similarly, throughout all his narrative, Luke has shown that the religious authorities of Israel regarded Jesus askance, increasingly criticized him, and tried to catch him in one of their many traps. And now Luke tells us that he is the anointed High Priest of Israel!

No wonder then that Jesus instructs his disciples not to tell anyone. Significantly, he does not even claim the title for himself. This would be left for the church to do later, declaring him to be the Christ to the point that the title itself soon came to be used a s part of his name: "Jesus Christ." He does not deny Peter's declaration; but in Luke he does not affirm and praise it, as he does in Matthew 16:17. Rather, his response is twofold: he orders them to keep the secret, and he gives himself a different title and a different definition.

# FURTHER REFLECTIONS
## *The Messianic Secret*

At this point, we come face-to-face with the "messianic secret." The Gospel is very clear on this point. Jesus "ordered and commanded" that the secret be kept. Neither he nor any of the Gospel writers tell us why. On this point, there are two possible assumptions. One is that he did not want to be given that title for fear of premature opposition. The other is that he feared the wrong sort of success. The basis for the first hypothesis should be obvious: if Jesus declares himself publicly to be the Messiah, the anointed King of Israel, this will immediately provoke a crushing response from the established authorities—particularly Herod and the Romans who uphold his power. There will be consequences, and Jesus will be killed as a rebel and as a pretender to the throne of Israel. This is certainly what would eventually happen: Jesus was executed by the Roman authorities, with a sign indicating that he had claimed to be the King of the Jews (23:38). But Jesus believes that the time for such events has not come yet; there are other things he must still do on his way to Jerusalem. Therefore he orders his disciples to be silent.

The other possibility is that Jesus wishes to keep the messianic secret because he fears the wrong kind of success. Crowds are flocking to him, both immediately before this account and shortly thereafter. He could easily declare himself to be the Messiah, and lead a revolt against the existing authorities—Jewish as well as Roman. This may end in defeat (in which case we are back to the first hypothesis) or it could end in victory. But such an apparent victory would in truth be a defeat. If Jesus accepts such a role, and manages to become king without the suffering on the cross, he will have succumbed to the very temptations that he earlier resisted in the desert (4:1–13). His way will not really be a new way, but a mere continuation of the old.

Throughout the Gospel, Jesus has been teaching a different way and a different measure of success: the last shall be first; the least are the greatest; the poor own the kingdom of God; the hungry will be fed; woe to the successful, to the rich and to the full. . . . Now he applies the same measure to his own ministry and messiahship, which he redefines in terms that are as contradictory of common wisdom as is the declaration that the poor are blessed. The Son of Man—himself—he declares, "must undergo great suffering, and be rejected by the elders, chief priests, and scribes, and be killed, and on the third day be raised." In other words, the road to true victory leads through the horrible defeat of the cross.

The redefinition of messiahship immediately leads to a redefinition of discipleship. Those who follow Jesus are following one who marches inexorably toward the cross. The only way to follow him is to take the same path. The saying of Jesus about his disciples taking up the cross has been turned into a call for accepting whatever evil or sufferings befall. Thus a parent whose teenager child is going astray will be heard to say: "This is my cross." And the same comment is made with reference to chronic diseases, grief, unrelenting enemies, and so on. There may be a place and times for resigned acceptance of unavoidable suffering, but this is not what Jesus is talking about. Although a cross certainly involved suffering, when Jesus spoke these words it was simply an instrument for applying the death penalty, very much like the electric chair, the firing squad, or the gibbet in later times. It was freely employed by Roman authorities to punish those who rebelled against them, and to deter others from following the same path. It was certainly a means of torture and death; but it was also a sign of resistance to established authority, and an instrument of shame, as one hung naked and pitiful for all to see.

> The false Messianism craves public notice; it wants to create attention; it lives by self-assertion. The way of Christ was different. During his earthly life the promised Messiah was present but incognito. . . . It belongs to the nature of the Son of Man that he remains incognito until the time that he will become known through his revelation.
> —Anders Nygren
>
> *Christ and His Church*, trans. Alan Carlsten (Philadelphia: Westminster, 1956), 63.

Jesus has just told his disciples that in Jerusalem he will "be rejected by the elders, chief priests, and scribes, and be killed." This is bad enough. He will die as a heretic, rejected by the religious

> If we do not continually deny ourselves, we do not learn of Him, but of other masters. If we do not take up our cross daily, we do not come after Him, but after the world, or the prince of the world, or our own fleshly mind. If we are not walking in the way of the cross, we are not following Him; we are not treading in his steps; but going back from, or at least wide of, Him.
> —John Wesley

"Sermon 48: Self-denial," in *The Works of John Wesley*, 3rd ed., vol. 6 (1872; repr. Peabody, MA: Hendrickson, 1984), 104.

> But how is the Christian to know what kind of cross is meant for him? He will find out as soon as he begins to follow his Lord and to share His life.
> —Dietrich Bonhoeffer

*Cost of Discipleship*, 74.

leaders of his own people. Now he adds that he will be crucified. For a Jew, this was a particularly accursed death, about which Paul would later write: "Christ redeemed us from the curse of the law by becoming a curse for us—for it is written, 'Cursed is everyone who hangs on a tree'" (Gal. 3:13; see Deut. 21:23). Thus Jesus will die rejected, shamed, and even accursed by the religious leaders of his own people.

But the cross was a *Roman* instrument of torture and death. The traditional means of execution in ancient Israel was stoning. Thus in announcing that he will die on a cross Jesus is also declaring that he will die as an enemy of the Roman Empire, as a rebel or at least a subversive figure. He will be executed as a criminal. He is embarking on a path that can only be construed by the authorities as one of subversion. Jesus will not take the road of the Zealots, who oppose Roman violence with their own violence. But he will still oppose suffering, evil, and exploitation in all its manifestations, and thus become subversive to the existing order.

It is to this path that Jesus calls his disciples in inviting them to take up their cross and follow him. It is certainly a path of self-denial, but not of meaningless, resigned, or passive suffering. It is a path of opposition to all that is evil, even though that evil may appear respectable and even legal. It is a path of solidarity with all those who suffer under the present order of the world, of suffering with them. One might even say that it is a path of taking up not only the cross of Jesus, but also all the crosses that people are made to bear by the existing order—in this case the Roman Empire—and thus relieving them of their suffering and oppression.

## FURTHER REFLECTIONS
### *Violence and Nonviolence*

Jesus' resistance to violence has often been interpreted as passive acceptance of violence, and thus we are often told that Christians ought to be "nonviolent." The problem is that we do not take enough time to reflect on what nonviolence actually means, partly because we have a very limited understanding of violence. For many of us, violence is limited to *acts* of violence—to strike or kill another, to take up arms against others. But we are less likely to recognize that there are also *states* of violence. This is particularly difficult to see for those of us who seldom suffer under such states. In a state of violence, people die not because someone kills them directly, but because the social order is such that it leads to death. Thus if a child is killed by a robber, we see the violence in that act; but if a child dies of hunger we do not see the violence in the order that has led to the child's death. Yet both are equally violent.

> This is the well-known theme of the cross . . . often interpreted as an invitation to passivity and resignation. But the meaning here is very different: the people are already "under the cross." . . . The suffering of the just does not begin with Jesus, but is a constant presence in the experience of Israel and of all human history. Here Jesus declares himself to be in solidarity with his people to the very end—as Paul would later say, "to the point of death, even death on a cross."
> —Giorgio Girardet
>
> *A los cautivos libertad: La misión de Jesús según San Lucas* (Buenos Aires: La Aurora, 1982), 92.

This means that true nonviolence involves opposition both to acts of violence and to states of violence. Mere passive abstention from acts of violence, while states of violence continue unchallenged, is not true nonviolence. Rather, it is a hidden participation in—and often a benefiting from—states of violence.

How are we to respond to such states of violence? A possible—and understandable—course of action is to respond to violence with counterviolence. In the time of Jesus, this was the way of the

The fight of faith is perfectly peaceable, for it is fought by applying the Lord's commandments. Humanly speaking, to fight thus is to fight nakedly and weakly, but it is precisely by fighting so that we strip bare and destroy the powers we are called to contend against.... Jesus overcame the powers—of the state, the authorities, the rulers, the law, etc.—not by being more powerful than they but by surrendering himself even unto death.

—Jacques Ellul

*Violence: Reflections from a Christian Perspective*, trans. Cecilia Gaul Kings (New York: Seabury, 1969), 165–66.

Zealots—perhaps of those two others who were crucified with him as bandits, who may well have been Zealot rebels. One may well imagine that the Zealots were people who felt deeply the pain of Roman states of violence and oppression, and therefore responded with armed rebellion. In more recent times, nations that feel oppressed by others frequently respond by armed insurrection that eventually leads to independence. Significantly, in such cases the initial armed rebellion is celebrated as a great act of patriotism, but others who at a later time or in other countries follow the same route are considered unjustifiably violent. Consider, for instance, the manner in which the American Revolution and its violence are commonly justified and even glorified by people who bemoan similar movements in Africa or in Latin America today.

A more common response is to accept the state of violence and continue living as if there were no violence. Sometimes this implies active support of the violent order, as was most often the case with the Sadducees and the high religious authorities in Israel; and sometimes it implies simply ignoring the existing violence, and trying to live as if it did not exist, which seems to have been the attitude of most Pharisees. Such options still exist today. If, for instance, people in a particular country are being dispossessed of the land that their ancestors tilled for centuries, some (particularly those who benefit from the entire process) argue that this is the price of modernization and globalization, and that such people should not stand in the way of progress, while others (usually the majority) choose to ignore the issue altogether, as if it had nothing to do with them.

The way of Jesus is different from all these options. Jesus refused to respond to acts of violence with further violence. He would not perpetuate the cycle of violence, in which violence begets and apparently justifies a violent response that in turn results in more violence. But he also refused to let violence continue unrecognized and unchallenged. He knowingly pursued a course of action that led to the cross. And he invited his disciples to follow the same course.

The cross may be said to be the ultimate act of violence against violence. A violent response to violence simply results in more violence. A lack of response to violence simply lets it continue unabated. What Jesus does is to take violence upon himself, to direct it at himself, and to respond to it in the one way that violence cannot abide: with love and forgiveness! This is so radical that violence is defanged, and does not know how to respond.

This is the way of the cross. The ancients used to say that in the cross and resurrection Jesus "killed death"; we can likewise say that in the cross Jesus did the ultimate violence to violence: he laid it bare, and still did not succumb to it.

This is true nonviolence. It is a costly alternative, for those who practice it—people like Jesus, Gandhi, and Martin Luther King—will themselves suffer violence. By having violence turn against them, and do so unjustly, they unmask it, and thereby begin to undo it. It is to this costly alternative that Jesus is inviting his disciples, both in ancient times and today.

### 9:28–36 *The Transfiguration*

Significantly, at various times and in different ecclesiastical traditions the Feast of the Transfiguration has been placed at different points in the church year. Is it to be celebrated after the resurrection and ascension, as indicative of Christ's glory? Should it be connected with the beginning of Lent, since it appears in the Gospel just before Jesus "sets his face" to go to Jerusalem? Should it be connected with the eschatological emphasis of Advent? These various possible placements reflect an equal number of possible emphases in the interpretation of the passage. Furthermore, in Christian

O wondrous sight! O vision fair
of glory that the church shall
    share,
which Christ upon the
    mountain shows,
where brighter than the sun
    he glows!

The law and prophets there
    have place,
two chosen witnesses of grace,
the Father's voice from out the
    cloud
proclaims his only Son aloud.

With shining face and bright
    array,
Christ deigns to manifest that
    day
what glory shall be theirs
    above
who joy in God with perfect
    love.

—*Sarum Breviary*

Trans. John Mason Neale (1851),
*United Methodist Hymnal*, 258.

preaching the story of the trans-figuration is most often used at the conclusion of a "mountaintop" experience (a retreat, a revival, a celebration of achievement), the point being that just as Peter was inclined to build booths and to remain on the mountaintop but had to return to the valley, true disciples have to be willing to descend from the mountaintop to the valley, there to communicate their mountaintop experience to others.

The problem with this last—and most common—line of interpretation is twofold. First, it trivializes what the gospel presents as an awesome and mysterious event, turning it into a pedestrian example of what should be little more than common wisdom. Second, it ignores the point, so clearly stated in Luke, that the disciples "kept silent" and told no one about their mountaintop experience.

There is little doubt that in the Gospel writer's mind this story is closely connected with Exodus 24:12–18 (Moses on Mount Sinai) and Luke 3:21–22 (the baptism of Jesus). On the latter, just as the baptism of Jesus marks the beginning of his public ministry, now the transfiguration marks the beginning of the journey to Jerusalem. In both cases, a voice from heaven (or from a cloud) affirms the unique relationship of Jesus with God, and thus endorses his ministry, actions, and teachings. On the former, there is a clear attempt in the choice of words of the passage to show that Jesus is no less a figure than Moses (and Elijah), and that his experience at the mountaintop is parallel to Moses' experience on Mount Sinai. (Note that in the Greek text the "departure" of Jesus that Moses and Elijah discuss is literally his "exodus," which probably refers to the rest of the gospel story, culminating in the ascension.)

The two figures of Moses and Elijah clearly represent the Law and the Prophets, a common way of referring to the totality of Scripture. At the point when the Gospel was written, this would serve to refute all who claimed that Jesus somehow contradicted Hebrew Scripture—on the one hand Jews who saw Christianity as an aberration or a heretical departure from the faith of the ancients, and on the other hand Gentiles who claimed that Judaism and its traditions were false and that the Jewish Scriptures had nothing to do with the true faith. Thus the text shows Jesus to be at least the equal of Moses and Elijah, and certainly invested with the authority of God so that his teachings are inspired: "This is my Son, my Chosen; listen to him!"

The place at which this narrative appears in the Gospel is also significant. This entire section, particularly after Peter declares Jesus to be the Messiah in 9:20, seems to be a roller-coaster ride for the disciples. Peter's momentous declaration is followed by an order not to tell anyone, and then by Jesus' announcement of his impending suffering and death. That ominous announcement, however, concludes with a mention of his coming glory and of the kingdom of God.

In the transfiguration, while the emphasis lies on the power and glory of Jesus, there is also a reminder of his death, as we are told that Moses and Elijah were discussing his "departure" (again, his "exodus"). Coming immediately after Jesus' announcement of his sufferings and death, the transfiguration is thus a reminder that in spite of all outward signs of defeat and powerlessness, Jesus is ultimately more powerful than death and than the political and religious authorities in Jerusalem. Then in the healing of the epileptic boy (9:37–43a) the text points both to the power of Jesus and to the frustration of the disciples, who cannot heal the boy. While people are still "amazed at all that he was doing," Jesus announces his death again. Even so, the disciples wrangle over rank and precedence, and Jesus turns the entire social and religious order upside down (9:46–48). He tells them that, even though they might be the apostles, they do not have control of who preaches the gospel (9:49–50).

The roller-coaster experience of the disciples is also ours. Are we the Easter people, or are we the people of the cross? Both! And neither is of any significance without the other. At the same time that we celebrate the victory of Jesus—and our own—we must never forget his cross—nor eschew our own. There are "transfiguration moments" in Christian experience and in the life of the church; but they neither abolish nor diminish the need for the cross.

### 9:37–43a *A Miracle of Healing*

On the mountaintop, God affirmed his Son; now a troubled father asks for help for his only son. The son is the silent victim throughout the story. He never speaks, cannot help himself, and depends on his father's intercession for help.
—R. Alan Culpepper

"Luke," 208.

Besides its many points of contact with other similar stories of healing in Luke, this one has the added note that it points to the disciples' powerlessness, and thus fits in this section where the disciples are at once privy to Jesus' words and even to his transfiguration, yet do not fully understand the words of Jesus nor share in his power. Why Jesus is angry, or at whom, is not clear.

### 9:43b–48 *True Greatness*

This passage is parallel to Luke 22:24–30. See the discussion at that point.

### 9:49–50 *An Uncontrollable Message*

The disciples' feeling that those who did not belong to their group did not have the right to use the name of Jesus is parallel to that of many in the church who appear to believe that those who do not belong to their particular denomination cannot claim the name of Jesus. At the time when Luke wrote his Gospel, the Christian movement was beginning to expand far and wide, and no one had control of that expansion. By the second century there were efforts—some justified and necessary, and some not—to decide who were the true followers of Jesus. Eventually, this came to be determined by membership in a particular organization whose hierarchy had the right to decide who belonged and who did not. Ever since, various churches and denominations have acted as if they had the authority to forbid others to use the name of Jesus or to call themselves Christian. Luke reminds us that it is not that easy. The disciples of Jesus are not sole owners of his power or his name, and must be ready to see his work beyond the confines of their own denominations, plans, or actions.

# 9:51–19:27

# *On the Way to Jerusalem*

It is clear that the words in 9:51 are intended to begin a new section in the Gospel narrative. They are unique to Luke among the four Gospels, as are many of the chapters that follow (up to 18:14). What is not clear is the route that Jesus follows on his way to Jerusalem. If one looks at it on a map, this route does not seem to be very direct. Indeed, at some points Jesus is at the very outskirts of Jerusalem, and in the next episode he has moved away from that city. Scholars have long debated about this. Is Luke simply ignorant of the geography of Palestine? Is this just a jumble of isolated incidents, with no particular order? Is there a hidden concentric structure (in technical terms, a chiasm), so that the beginning is parallel to the end? Is it patterned after the book of Deuteronomy, following an outline parallel to that book?

In its life of worship and devotion, the church has developed its own perspective and its own reading of this section—a perspective and a reading that illumine the text much more significantly than the various theories mentioned above. The words of 9:51, "he set his face to go to Jerusalem," have traditionally been connected with Ash Wednesday, thus making the entire section on the journey to Jerusalem the text for the parallel journey of the church and believers from Ash Wednesday, through Lent, to Holy Week. The path that Jesus follows to Jerusalem is not a straight path, nor is the discipleship journey of Christians, symbolized in the Lenten journey. Furthermore, the way to Jerusalem is not entirely one of sorrow and preparation for pain and death. It is also a journey of joy and promise, with many high points, even frequent banquets that provide occasions for Jesus both to feast and to teach. Similarly, the path of discipleship has both its high and its low points, its victories and its defeats, its moments of daring and obedience, and its times of shying away from the implications and consequences of faith and obedience.

If one were to compare the structure of this long section in Luke with another section in the Hebrew Scripture, it would be the story of the exodus and the journey to the land of promise. (Remember that in 9:31 there was already a reference to the "exodus" awaiting Jesus.) In the story of the exodus, the path is not straight. It should not take forty years to travel from the Red Sea to the river Jordan! In that ancient story, there are glorious moments of manna and water from the rock; but there is also a golden calf. For the children of Israel, it is not a straight shot from Egypt to Canaan. It is not a straight shot for Jesus from Galilee to Jerusalem. And it is not a straight shot for us from Ash Wednesday to Easter, or from justification to sanctification.

It is also important to realize that in setting his face to go to Jerusalem Jesus is making a decision that many Christians through the centuries would have to parallel. It is a decision to confront the powers of oppression. This is never an easy decision. I have called them "powers of oppression" rather than "powers of evil," because quite often these powers try to pass as good, and as opposing evil. The religious leaders that Jesus would be confronting in Jerusalem were basically good, religious people. They were not above conspiring against those who questioned their authority, or

> The glory of these forty days
> we celebrate with songs of
>   praise;
> for Christ, by whom all things
>   were made,
> himself has fasted and has
>   prayed.
>
> Alone and fasting Moses saw
> the loving God who gave the
>   law;
> and to Elijah, fasting, came
> the steeds and chariots of
>   flame.
>
> Then grant us, Lord, like them
>   to do
> such things as bring great
>   praise to you;
> our spirits strengthen with
>   your grace
> and give us joy to see your
>   face.
>
> —Gregory the Great

"The Glory of These Forty Days," trans. Mauice F. Bell, *The Presbyterian Hymnal* (Louisville, KY: Westminster John Knox Press, 1990), 87.

who would endanger their precarious support from Rome; but still, they did all this in defense of religion, and the text gives no indication that they thought they were doing evil. The political structure that Jesus and his disciples would be confronting was not necessarily bad. On the contrary, Roman authorities prided themselves on the Pax Romana and the civilization they had spread throughout the Mediterranean basin. They were not above practicing extreme cruelty against those who opposed or resisted their authority; but they justified this on the basis of the defense of the order and stability they had created.

# 9:51–10:24
## The Mission Widens

Jesus had "set his face" to go to Jerusalem, to challenge the authorities that held power of life and death over him and over his nation. Taking this into account, both moving into Samaria and sending a further contingent of missionaries was a direct challenge to those authorities, who would see Jesus as subverting the order. This entire section should not be read with the triumphalism that has often marred Christian missions. It is not just a matter of going to new places. It is also a matter of throwing down the gauntlet before those who would oppose the mission and facing the consequences. Earlier in chapter 9, Jesus had sent twelve disciples, and this had provoked the interest of Herod. Now he sends six times that many. The rest of the Gospel will show the far-reaching consequences of a mission that is not afraid of those whom it must oppose.

### 9:51–56 The Samaritan Village

Samaria stood between Galilee and Judea, and therefore it would be natural that Jesus, having "set his face" to go to Jerusalem, would go through Samaria. Not surprisingly, his party is not well received. After all, they are Jews traveling to the capital of Judea, and between Jews and Samaritans there is no love lost. The passage should be read as preparation for the parable of the Good Samaritan. Jesus himself has experienced the rejection of the Samaritans; and, over against the inclination of his own disciples, has refused to condemn the village that would not receive them.

The passage could also serve as a basis for reflection on the way in which Christians have often dealt with those they consider heretics. From the point of view of the Samaritans, Jews were heretics. From the Jewish perspective, the heretics were the Samaritans. In this episode the Samaritans behave as one would expect, rejecting those whom they consider unfaithful. Jesus, on the other hand, refuses to have his disciples call down fire upon the Samaritans as punishment for their rejection. The presumed orthodoxy of the Samaritans leads them to inhospitality for those who disagree with them. The higher orthodoxy of Jesus prevents his disciples from responding in kind. Not only that, but Jesus rebukes his disciples for their vengeful attitude. Unfortunately, throughout Christian history, this is not the way in which Christians who consider themselves "orthodox," "pure," or "faithful" have normally responded to those others whom they consider heterodox, sinful, or unfaithful. And that history continues to this day.

But do these Samaritans reject Jesus and his followers simply because they are Jews, or because they fear the possible consequences of sheltering what could well be seen as a subversive group? The answer depends on how much force one gives to the phrase, "his face was set toward Jerusalem." If this is simply a reference to where he was going, then what we have here is a mere instance of anti-Jewish Samaritan feeling, in which case it would have sufficed for Luke to say that they did not receive them because they were Jews. But if it is a reference to the attitude and message of Jesus confronting the authorities in Jerusalem, then the episode may be seen as one more case in which people refused to admit Jesus and his disciples, or to follow him, because they feared the consequences—in this case, the political consequences. The text would seem to suggest the latter, for the reason why the Samaritan village refuses to receive Jesus is "because his face was set toward Jerusalem."

The very fact that these two interpretations are possible shows the degree to which religious and political considerations are often combined, and how the latter can surreptitiously pass as the former. A few years ago, during a time of repression in Guatemala, a village that had become mostly Protestant refused to allow two Roman Catholic "delegates of the Word" (lay Bible teachers) to enter the village. They said that the delegates of the Word would not be welcome because they are heretics and idolaters. But there was also the consideration that delegates of the Word were generally suspected by the government as subversive, and the villagers were afraid of being painted with the same brush and bringing the paramilitary death squads upon them. The villagers may have convinced themselves that they were refusing hospitality to the delegates of the Word for religious reasons; but there was also a political dimension to their action. It is experiences such as these that have led many to call for a more political reading of Scripture and of theology—one that takes into account both the political setting of the text and the present political settings of the readers.

### 9:57–62  *Discipleship Is Not for All*

Having set his face to go to Jerusalem, Jesus finds many who want to follow him—at least in part, or at a later time, or if conditions are favorable. He will have none of it. His is a call that radically uproots those who heed it, a point that this brief text makes thrice. The cross that his disciples are to take so they can follow Jesus is not some magnificent final act of valor or obedience; it is a difficult walk that leads through denial and abandonment.

The placement of these words becomes particularly poignant if one reads the story of the Samaritan village as a rejection motivated by fear, rather than by mere prejudice. In that case, after experiencing the rejection of a village that seeks to avoid reprisals, Jesus addresses other reasons why people may decide not to follow him, or to postpone a decision. But the radical demands of obedience do not become clear until we realize, as verses 60 and 62 declare, that to postpone a decision is tantamount to rejecting him.

## 10:1–24 *The Mission of the Seventy*

Some manuscripts say "seventy," and others "seventy-two." The exact number is immaterial. What is important is that Jesus now sends a number of messengers that is substantially more than before. His instructions are essentially the same as were earlier given to the Twelve, although much expanded. The danger has also increased, for Jesus tells these new missioners that he is sending them "like lambs into the midst of wolves." Jesus is the sacrificial Lamb; but his followers and his messengers share in his "lambhood," just as they must share in his cross and will share in his resurrection. Jesus sends them "like lambs into the midst of wolves"; but he is also the Lamb to be attacked and killed by the wolves. For this reason, there is a connection between Jesus and those whom he sends that includes both joining in his suffering and representing his presence: "whoever rejects you rejects me, and whoever rejects me rejects the one who sent me." While the missioners will face great risk, those to whom they are sent face an even greater risk, perhaps even

---

A famous Spanish poet bemoaned his delay in responding to the call of the Lord:

> Lord, what am I, that, with unceasing care,
> thou didst seek after me—that thou didst wait,
> wet with unhealthy dews, before my gate,
> and pass the gloomy nights of winter there?
>
> O strange delusion!—that I did not greet
> thy blest approach, and O, to heaven how lost,
> if my ingratitude's unkindly frost
> has chilled the bleeding wounds upon thy feet.
>
> How oft my guardian angel cried,
> "Soul, from thy casement look, and thou shalt see
> how he persists to knock and wait for thee!"
>
> And, O! How often to that voice of sorrow,
> "Tomorrow we will open," I replied,
> and when the morrow came I answered still, "Tomorrow"!

—Félix Lope de Vega y Carpio
Trans. Henry Wadsworth Longfellow

unknowingly, as is seen in the woes against Chorazin, Bethsaida, and Capernaum.

It is significant to note the connections between this passage and Jesus' sermon in Capernaum. There people rejected him because he spoke of God's love for those whom his hearers considered unlovable infidels. Just as in chapter 4 there are references to people from Sidon and Syria, here there are references to Sidon and Tyre. This reflects Luke's repeated theme of social and religious reversal—the outsiders being brought in, the last becoming first, and the least becoming great.

The response of Jesus to the report of the seventy is surprising: "I watched Satan fall from heaven like a flash of lightning." Satan in heaven? Our common view is that earth is the place of conflict, and that heaven is far above any such conflict, and certainly beyond the reach of evil. But the conflict between good and evil is of cosmic proportions far beyond what we imagine. In Revelation 12:7–12 we are told of a war in heaven where Satan is defeated and "thrown down to the earth," with the result that the struggle on earth becomes even fiercer. Apparently, Luke agrees with Ephesians 6:12 that the Christian struggle is "not against enemies of blood and flesh, but against the rulers, against the authorities, against the cosmic powers of this present darkness, against the spiritual forces of evil in the heavenly places." He also asserts that the proclamation of the message of the kingdom of God dethrones all such powers: "I watched Satan fall from heaven like a flash of lightning." The coming of God's kingdom is something "that many prophets and kings desired to see," but did not.

Within the context of the entire story of the sending of the seventy, the declaration of Jesus that he has seen Satan fall down from heaven adds an unexpected dimension to Christian mission. In this passage, Satan is defeated not directly by Jesus himself but by the preaching of his disciples. The Christian message is not just that Jesus conquers all powers of evil and oppression, but also that, as lambs sent into the world by the Lamb of God, Christians have the mission and the power to gain victory over evil and oppression.

In typically Lukan fashion, however, this is a strange sort of victory. It is a victory of reversal. In this particular case, Jesus rejoices in the reversal of knowledge. Things that were hidden from the wise and the intelligent have been revealed to infants. Not only do the last become first, but the wise become ignorant, and those with no understanding come to know.

These words of Jesus may well be an indictment on much of our theological work. We do theology mostly in dialogue with other theologians. Our main companions are our books, many of them written by others whose main companions were also books. In a word, we seek for wisdom among the wise and the intelligent, forgetting that there are things that God has hidden from the wise and the intelligent, and revealed them to infants. The God about whom we Christian theologians claim to teach and to write is speaking to us in the infants, in the illiterate, in the common folk, in the experience of believers who have no idea what words like *eschatology* or *homoousios* mean, but who have a very clear experience as to what the gospel is. We refuse to listen to them at our own peril.

At a first glance, verse 22 would seem to fit better with the Gospel of John than with Luke, for it is John who is most concerned with the relationship between Father and Son. But as we look at it more closely we see how it fits in Luke's Gospel. Reading verse 22 jointly with verse 21, three antithetical themes appear: the hidden and the revealed, the wise and the infants, the Father and the Son. At this point Jesus has repeatedly announced that his is a ministry and a victory through weakness and suffering. Here he declares that the Father who has revealed secret things to the infants, and not to the wise, is the one who is only known through the visible, frail, accosted, and eventually crucified Son. Luther would say that this is a clear instance in which the "theology of the cross" corrects the "theology of glory."

> A theology of glory calls evil good and good evil. A theology of the cross calls the thing what it actually is.
>
> He who does not know Christ does not know God hidden in suffering. Therefore he prefers works to suffering, glory to the cross, strength to weakness, wisdom to folly, and, in general, good to evil. These are the people whom Paul calls "enemies of the cross of Christ."
>
> —Martin Luther
>
> *Heidelberg Disputation*, thesis 21, trans. Harold J. Grimm, *Luther's Works* 32 (Philadelphia: Muhlenberg, 1957), 53.

# 10:25–42

## *An Unexpected Order of Things*

The rest of chapter 10 consists of two familiar passages: a parable and a narrative about Jesus. They are usually read and interpreted independently of each other. Indeed, when we preachers feel that the congregation should be more active in works of charity, we preach on the good Samaritan; and when we feel that the congregation is too activist, and needs more prayer, study, and meditation, we preach on Mary and Martha. If we preach on both, we try to keep them as far apart as possible, so that neither the congregation nor we ourselves will see the contrast between the teaching we draw from each. Yet in the Gospel the two appear back-to-back! This should be an indication that these passages are not as simple as we might imagine. Therefore, after considering them separately we must reflect on them jointly, as they are found in the Gospel text.

### 10:25–37 *The Good Samaritan*

The setting of the parable is a warning on the misuse of theology. The lawyer who confronts Jesus is well aware of what the Lord requires, and asks about it not to understand it more fully but "wanting to justify himself." He uses theological debate as a means to avoid obedience. Just as it is possible for a church body to postpone decision by referring matters to committees, so is it possible for a church and for individuals to postpone obedience by seeking further clarification. Quite often, what the Lord requires is clear; but the cost is also clear, and so we ask more and more questions. Will Jesus come before or after the millennium? Is God's decree of election prior to the decree on the fall? Did God create the world in six days? Should we baptize in this particular manner, or in another? Then we criticize the Byzantine church for debating on angels while Constantinople was besieged by the Turks! The lawyer in the parable knows full well who the neighbor is, or at least knows it well enough to begin doing what is required of him. But instead of simply obeying, he asks more and more questions. Questions are good, and various characters in the Gospel learn much by asking questions; but it is altogether too easy to ask questions whose only purpose is to delay an obedience that is quite clear.

The rest of the passage is well known, and is often used to call people to actions of love and service to others—to the point that we often call people who do help others "good Samaritans." In situations of racial or ethnic discrimination, it is also used as a call to recognize the goodness of the excluded, and to be ready to receive and to learn from those who are considered outsiders. Such uses of the passage are proper; but there are at least two other points to be taken into con-

In Jesus' story there are thieves and victims, spectators and helpers. The people who will read what I have to say ... clearly do not belong among the victims. I cannot say whether they should count themselves among the thieves or not. . . . Jesus intended this story for people of the "spectator" or "passer-by" type.
—Dorothee Soelle

*The Strength of the Weak: Toward a Christian Feminist Identity*, trans. Robert and Rita Kimber (Philadelphia: Westminster, 1984), 142.

sideration, apart from the matter of the apparent tension between this parable and the story of Mary and Martha.

The first is that the exclusion of the Samaritan is not only racial or ethnic. It is also religious. From the point of view of the Jewish doctor of the law, the Samaritan was a heretic, one who did not serve God properly. Earlier (9:50) Jesus had told his disciples that those who were not part of their group, but were doing good in the name of Jesus, should be allowed to continue. He had also refused to allow his disciples to call fire down from heaven on a village that did not receive them (9:53–56). Now it is the Samaritan heretic who is the obedient servant of God. Thus the parable has much to say about recognizing the action of God in those whose theology we may find faulty—in itself a very valuable lesson in these times of theological and political polarization.

The second is that Jesus' question at the end is not, as one might expect, who realized that the man by the roadside was a neighbor, but rather which of the three who went by was a neighbor to the man by the roadside. If that is the question, Jesus' final injunction to the lawyer, "Go and do likewise," does not simply mean, go and act in love to your neighbor, but rather, go and become a neighbor to those

If, then, we take this word in the strictest sense, a man of a catholic spirit is
one who . . . gives his hand to all whose hearts are right with his heart: One
who knows how to value, and praise God for, all the advantages he enjoys,
with regard to the knowledge of the things of God, the true scriptural manner
of worshipping him, and, above all, his union with a congregation fearing
God and working righteousness: One who, retaining these blessings with the
strictest care, keeping them as the apple of his eye, at the same time loves,—
as friends, as brethren in the Lord, as members of Christ and children of God,
as joint-partakers now of the present kingdom of God, and fellow-heirs of
his eternal kingdom,—all, of whatever opinion, or worship, or congregation,
who believe in the Lord Jesus Christ; who love God and man; who, rejoicing to
please and fearing to offend God, are careful to abstain from evil, and zealous
of good works. He is the man of a truly catholic spirit, who bears all these
continually upon his heart; who, having an unspeakable tenderness for their
persons, and longing for their welfare, does not cease to commend them to
God in prayer, as well as to plead their cause before men.

—John Wesley

"Sermon 39: Catholic Spirit," in *Works of John Wesley*, 5:503.

in need, no matter how alien they may be. It is not just a matter of
loving and serving those who are near us (which is what "neighbor"
means) but also of drawing near to those who for whatever reason—
racial, ethnic, theological, political—may seem to be alien to us.

### 10:38–42 *Mary and Martha*

Immediately after the parable of the Good Samaritan, Luke tells us
of Jesus' visit to the home of Martha, and of the events that took
place there. It is important to note that the home is Martha's, and
that Mary is simply her sister. Although one might surmise that
Mary also lives there, it is not the home of Mary and Martha, but the
home of Martha, who has a sister named Mary. Martha does what
is expected of her when a guest comes to the house. Mary simply
listens to Jesus. When Martha becomes exasperated and asks Jesus
to tell Mary to come and help, Jesus answers that "Mary has chosen
the better part, which will not be taken away from her." Although
at various times in Christian history it has been said that these are

simply two equally acceptable ways to serve Jesus—the "Mary" way of devotion and contemplation, and the "Martha" way of service—this is not justified by the text. Here Jesus rebukes Martha for doing what is expected of her, and commends Mary, who is eschewing her traditional woman's role.

Since this episode follows immediately after the parable of the Good Samaritan, the reader cannot but ask: Wasn't Martha being the good Samaritan? If the point of the parable is that one should go and serve those in need, Martha is certainly doing that better than Mary. And if the problem with the priest and the Levite in the parable was that they were religious people whose religion did not lead them to serve the needy, is that not precisely what Mary is doing? Had Martha been present when Jesus told the parable, and the point of the parable was that one should serve those in need, she would have more than sufficient reason to be angry!

The juxtaposition of these two passages warns us that the first is not merely a piece of generally good advice about the importance of serving those in need, and that the second is not merely a pious reminder that the life of study and devotion is important. They must both be read within the context of Jesus' preaching about the kingdom and radical obedience. In the chapters immediately preceding, Jesus has been teaching about the demands of the kingdom and of discipleship. In the coming of Jesus, something radically new has happened, and this radically new thing demands an equally radical obedience (see, for instance, 9:57–62). The parable of the Good Samaritan calls for a radical obedience that breaks cultural, ethnic, and theological barriers. The story of Mary and Martha is equally radical. First of all, we often do not realize that the first one to break the rules is Jesus himself. He is the guest, and against all rules of hospitality he rebukes Martha, who is his host. And Mary too breaks the rules. Her role as (most probably) a younger sister, or as one living in the house of her sister, is to help her in her various chores. Instead, she just sits at the feet of Jesus and listens to him.

Like so much else in the Gospel of Luke, these two passages point to the radical obedience, and to the upsetting and even reversal of roles, that the kingdom demands.

## 11:1–13

### *On Prayer*

Although these two passages—the Lord's Prayer and the parable about the man with unexpected guests—are often read and interpreted independently, the parable is an explanation and commentary on the Lord's Prayer, and should be read as such.

### 11:1–4 *The Lord's Prayer*

As we read this passage, the first surprise for many of us should be the manner in which Jesus replies to his disciple's request: "Lord, teach us to pray." Books abound today telling people how to pray. Most of these books focus on attitudes and practices: sincerity, perseverance, discipline, openness, faith, and so on. But Jesus responds to a similar request with a formula! His immediate answer is not about attitude (some of which he will discuss after proposing the Lord's Prayer) but is rather about words. It is an actual prayer.

Part of the reason why this surprises us is that we have lost much of the sense of the role of rite and worship in the life of discipleship. We tend to think that the relationship between attitude and action, between belief and rite, is unidirectional: an attitude leads to an action, and a belief leads to a rite that expresses it. But the converse is also true. Action shapes attitude, and rite shapes belief. Historians often refer to this with the Latin phrase *lex credendi est lex orandi*, "the rule of worship (or prayer) is the rule of belief." John Wesley was once told by a wise counselor that as long as he did not have saving faith he should preach as if he had it, and that when he did have it he should preach because he had it. In our everyday experience we know that the simple action of smiling

> Teach me, if Thou wilt, to pray;
> If Thou wilt not, make me dry.
> Give me love abundantly
> Or unfruitful let me stay.
> Sov'reign Master, I obey.
> Peace I find not save with Thee.
> What wilt Thou have done with me?
>
> —St. Teresa

"Poems," E. Allison Peers, trans. and ed., *The Complete Works of Saint Teresa of Jesus*, 3 vols. (London: Sheed & Ward, 1946), 3:280.

often leads us to want to smile. In the life of faith, faith leads us to worship; but worship also leads us to faith.

At the time when Jesus taught this prayer, many other rabbis and teachers proposed certain prayers for their disciples to repeat. The disciple in our text is probably referring to this when he asks Jesus to teach them to pray "as John taught his disciples." Such prayers were also signs of identification among disciples of the same teacher. At a later time, Christians would develop creeds that would have some of the same functions. So the Lord's Prayer is also the prayer of the disciples of the Lord—the prayer by which these disciples are formed, and which serves as the mark of their identity.

Luke's version of the Lord's Prayer is shorter than Matthew's (Matt. 6:9–13). It does not include the clause "Your will be done, on earth as it is in heaven." But this is implied in "Your kingdom come." Nor does it include the petition "but rescue us from the evil one."

The word translated as "daily bread" could also be read as "bread for the morrow," or as "heavenly bread." Most likely, the entire prayer should be read in the light of a very similar prayer in Proverbs 30:8b–9: "give me neither poverty nor riches; feed me with the food that I need, or I shall be full, and deny you, and say, 'Who is the LORD?' or I shall be poor, and steal, and profane the name of my God." In that passage, as in the Lord's Prayer, the main consideration is the name of the Lord. The Lord's Prayer begins with, "hallowed be your name," and the prayer in Proverbs ends with the concern not to "profane the name of my God." What Proverbs says is that injustice and inequality that lead the poor to steal profane the name of the Lord, and that abundance that leads to self-sufficiency ignores that very name. Thus "daily bread" or "bread for the day" is probably the best translation, for it implies neither want nor excess. It may well relate to the daily ration of a soldier on campaign, and if so the "daily bread" is what those who serve the kingdom need to sustain them in the struggle. Thus the petitions "hallowed be your name" and "your kingdom come" are not independent from the one about daily bread. This is not a list of petitions. It is a single, ardent call for the kingdom in which God's name is hallowed, and in which all have what they need.

Is this about physical, edible bread, or about spiritual bread? The question itself reflects a dichotomy that is alien to the biblical text. Eating is a spiritual act, and discipleship is reflected in eating and in sharing food. Furthermore, the very ambiguity of the word translated as "daily bread" points to both the physical and the spiritual. If the word is taken as "heavenly bread," it immediately recalls the manna in the desert. The manna, bread from heaven, was physical nourishment to the children of Israel. It could not be kept from one day to another, hence the "daily bread" dimension of the phrase. Nor could it be hoarded by those who were able to gather more, for God saw that its distribution was just (Exod. 16:16–21). In the Lord's Prayer, we are asking for exactly that sort of bread—bread of justice and of trust in God.

The clause on forgiveness should also be read in this context. Significantly, in Luke's version it is for our *sins* that we ask for forgiveness, just as we forgive *debts*. (In our translations of Matthew's version, which is the one most commonly used, some say "trespasses" while others say "debts," thus leading some to quip that Methodists are trespassers, while Presbyterians are debtors!) The implication is that our sins are like unpaid debts—perhaps even unpayable debts—and that while we pray God not to collect on us, we also commit not to collect on others. Connecting this with what has been said above about the kingdom and bread, those who pray for the kingdom and serve it commit not to claim for themselves more than is due, and at the same time, recognizing that they are not always faithful to that promise, to forgive those who take more than is their due. Finally, the petition about "the time of trial" may be an eschatological reference to the final judgment, and also a reference to the temptation not to trust God for daily bread.

### 11:5–13 *Commentary on the Lord's Prayer*

In both Matthew and Luke the Lord's Prayer is followed by an explanation. In Matthew it is the words on the forgiveness of trespasses (Matt. 6:14–15). Here in Luke it is the story about the person asking a friend for bread for an unexpected guest. In this story, the theme of bread serves as a link with the Lord's Prayer. The story is not about "perseverance in prayer" as the NRSV titles it. Actually, the word that the NRSV translates as "persistence" in verse 8 can also be understood as "impudence" or "shamelessness." So the story is about a man who is sufficiently concerned about the friend who has arrived unexpectedly to dare wake another friend in the middle of the night. It is about one who asks on behalf of another. The one caught with no bread when the friend arrives is also caught between two principles of conduct: hospitality to the unexpected guest on the one hand, and respect for the friend who sleeps on the other. To him, there is no choice—he must call upon the friend who has bread in order to feed the one who has not. One could therefore say that the parable is about intercessory prayer. It is not about my asking God for what I want, but rather about asking God for what others need. When on that basis we ask, we are given; when on that basis we search, we shall find; when on that basis we knock, the door will be opened. Significantly, at the end of the passage Jesus does not promise his disciples "good things," as in Matthew (Matt. 7:11), but rather "the Holy Spirit." What Jesus promises his disciples who ask is that they will be given the Holy Spirit, who in turn will help them ask on behalf of others.

In the early church, this was expressed in what was called "the prayer of the faithful." Only those who were baptized took part in this prayer, which was seen as the work of the priestly people of God praying for the entire world. Within that context, the church, the priestly people, is the one who asks a friend (God) to provide bread for the other friend in need (the world).

# 11:14–16:31
## Further Controversies

### 11:14–32 *An Exorcism and the Ensuing Debate*

#### 11:14–20 *God and Beelzebul*
The passage begins with an act of exorcism (see pp. 69–72, "Further Reflections: Demonic Powers"), which then leads to a debate about the mission and authority of Jesus. The exorcism itself is not the

focus of the story, but simply provides the occasion for the debate that follows. Indeed, if one reads the story keeping in mind the person who was healed, it becomes apparent that attention immediately moves away from him or her, in order to focus on the issue of how people are to respond to what they see Jesus doing. This in itself provides a vivid illustration of the manner in which the interests and issues of theologians and religious leaders so easily lead us away from the real issues and from persons in need, turning them into subjects of debate or of intellectual discourse. Rather than rejoicing in what God is doing and seeking to join it, these religious leaders choose to ask questions about it and to enter into a theological debate, a debate that most assuredly is not devoid of hidden agendas and issues of personal and institutional authority.

> To first-century people, to look upon a woman as child-bearer was so common that it was not at all surprising for the woman to come to Jesus and praise his mother's breasts and uterus. What was surprising was that Jesus differed with her.
> —Rachel Conrad Wahlberg
>
> *Jesus according to a Woman* (New York: Paulist, 1975), 45.

The exorcism itself leads to three different responses. First, we are told that the crowds were amazed. This crowd then recedes into the background until a woman speaks for it in 11:27. Second, some are quite certain that what they are witnessing is evil: it is by the power of Beelzebul that Jesus casts out demons. Others test Jesus by demanding a sign from heaven. Jesus will respond to this latter group in 11:29–32. For the moment, therefore, the debate is particularly with those who claim that Jesus' power comes from Beelzebul. In the entire incident and the ensuing discussion, it is clear that religious opposition to Jesus and his message is increasing and becoming more virulent. Now the claim is not just that he is misguided, that he is a false prophet, or that he does not observe all the strictures of the law, but that he is an agent of Satan! Here (as in so many religious and political debates of our time) the goal is to demonize the opposition.

Jesus argues that if it is by Beelzebul that he casts out demons, then Beelzebul is acting against himself, and his rule will not stand long, just as a kingdom that is inwardly divided will fall into pieces.

His actions and their results are clearly opposed to those of Beelzebul. What is implied here is that God is a God of life and wholeness, and that death and disease—in this case, the specific illness of the one who has been cured—are the work of the forces that oppose God. Furthermore, says Jesus, if the wonders he performs are attributed to Satan, to whom should be attributed the wonders of the followers of those who criticize him ("your exorcists," or "your sons")? The fact that among those who accuse him of serving Beelzebul there are also some who do similar works would seem to indicate that, if Jesus serves Beelzebul, so do they. And if it is by the power ("the finger") of God that Jesus casts out demons, this is not only a miraculous curse or a sign that Jesus is powerful; it is above all a sign that the kingdom of God is breaking into the existing order (v. 20).

The unavoidable conclusion of this entire debate, and of the narrative that serves as its context, is that "signs," miracles, or the casting out of demons do not in themselves prove the truth of a teaching or the justice of a cause. Faced by the same wonder, the crowd is amazed, some still ask for "a sign from heaven," and some simply attribute what they have seen to evil forces. This was already true in the exodus narrative, where Aaron's staff turns into a serpent, and Pharaoh's magicians respond with a similar feat. It will also be a recurrent theme in the rest of the Gospel of Luke, where the wonders Jesus performs, while leading to belief in many, in others result in greater opposition, eventually leading to the passion and the cross. Any miracle is still subject to interpretation, and the direction of that interpretation depends on the bias, perspective, and interests of the interpreter. In brief, miracles do not necessarily lead to faith, for it is faith that allows those who witness an event to see it as a wondrous work of God, while those who choose not to believe will remain adamant in their unbelief. Later, in the well-known parable of the Rich Man and Lazarus, we will see a concrete illustration of this point.

### 11:21–26 *When Demons Return*
The subject of casting out demons leads to what at first seems to be a digression. Jesus declares that if a demon is cast out, it may still return with even greater power. The imagery is of a powerful lord entrenched in a castle where he also holds his wealth. Suppose that

a greater warrior takes the castle and divides the first man's armor (that "in which he trusted") as plunder, and then restores order to the fallen castle or house. If after a while the first master of the castle, finding no other place in which to dwell, returns to the castle and finds it clean and unguarded, he will not only retake the place but also bring more of his associates with him.

The obvious meaning of this illustration is that those from whom a demon has been cast out must take heed, lest the demon return with other demons and greater force, so that "the last state of the person is worse than the first." With these words, Jesus is speaking of perseverance in discipleship. If after the house or castle is voided of demonic powers it is not properly guarded, the powers of evil will return and be even more destructive. In today's terms, one might say that it is not enough to raise one's hand or to come to the altar at a revival meeting. While the conversion expressed in such actions may be necessary, the discipleship that should follow them is just as necessary. Otherwise, if the house is left empty and unguarded, evil will return and be even more powerful than before.

In its immediate context, the story is also a warning against "your exorcists," those among Jesus' critics who also cast out demons. It does not suffice to cast out demons. The "castle" must be occupied and fortified by a new reality—the coming of the kingdom of God and service to it. This is why the story leads to Jesus' warning that "whoever does not gather with me scatters." Gathering is good. Many are out there gathering. But only one sort of gathering is permanent: those who gather with Jesus for the kingdom of God.

### 11:27–28 *The Source of Blessing*

With narrative skill, Luke turns to a woman from among the crowd whose cry of praise momentarily interrupts Jesus' response to those who demand a sign. (Note here another example of Luke's use of parallel male and female characters and examples. Here it is a woman in the crowd who provides an occasion for teaching. In 12:13 it will be a man in the crowd.) This passage has often been used in anti-Catholic polemics, arguing that Jesus says that his mother is not any more blessed than those who follow him. The main point, however, is that Jesus is offering blessedness (happiness) to any who would hear and obey the Word of God. Thus the woman and the crowd around her are invited not to look at what is happening as mere spectators, but to join in it.

### 11:29–32 *The Sign of Jonah*

When we hear of the "sign of Jonah," we immediately think of the three days in the belly of the fish (not a whale), and of the parallelism with the time Jesus lay in the grave. This is what the Gospel of Matthew says. But there is more than this to the sign of Jonah. Both Matthew and Luke offer more clarification as to the meaning of this sign of Jonah. The sign of Jonah is the Ninevites repenting and calling on the mercy of a God whom they do not know, while the prophet who does know God bemoans that mercy. The sign of Jonah is in the queen of Sheba coming from the ends of the earth to hear the wisdom of Solomon, when the king's very sons refuse to follow the wisdom. In the rest of the Gospel, the sign of Jonah is in the harlots and the publicans going into the kingdom ahead of the religious leaders of their time.

The sign of Jonah is in one who was rejected as a blasphemer by the religious leaders of his time, condemned to death as a criminal by the political leaders, rising up from the dead, sitting at the right hand of God, and being given a name that is above every other name, so that "at the name of Jesus every knee should bend, in heaven and on earth and under the earth" (Phil. 2:10).

Today people are again asking for signs. Even within the church we are asking for signs. Just as people asked for signs that Jesus was really the one sent by God, so do we today want signs that the church is truly the church of God. So we look at our statistics: Is the church growing? Is our membership declining? Is giving increasing? Where are some successful churches? And we deceive ourselves into believing that the sign of God's presence is in our bright statistical spots. Or we admire our own theological acuteness, or our plans for evangelism, or our organizational ability, or some thing or another at which we consider ourselves particularly adept—even commentaries on Scripture!

But it may well be that no sign will be given to us but the sign of Jonah. It may well be that the sign of a church in which the Spirit of

God is at work is precisely that the most unlikely folk are brought in, like the Ninevites at the time of Jonah, or like the queen of Sheba in the days of Solomon, or like the publicans and sinners in the time of Jesus. The sign of Jonah may well be that barriers of race and class that close and divide so many other communities are torn down in this community of the Spirit.

The sign of Jonah is not a comfortable thing. The book of Jonah tells us that when Jonah saw Nineveh repenting he wished he would die. Jonah was a good, religious man. He was part of the people of God, and he knew who belonged to that people and who did not. So are we, and so do we. We are religious people, church people. We know where the church begins and where it ends. We know the creeds, and we can name any doctrinal error the moment it appears. We know how to be prophets within the confines of Israel. But God's mission and God's purposes extend well beyond the confines of Israel or of the church. A church that does not heed this calling, but flees to the comforts of its own inner security, is like Jonah fleeing to Tarshish. Just as Jonah imperiled those who sailed with him, such a church should not be surprised if society at large tosses it overboard!

But the Gospel tells us that "something greater than Solomon is here," and that "something greater than Jonah is here." The one who will be considered a stranger (like the queen of the South) and considered an enemy of God (like the Ninevites in the time of Jonah) is greater than Solomon and greater than Jonah. And in this passage

---

Reformed pastor Jean de Léry, who had gone to Brazil as part of a failed Genevan enterprise, reported a conversation in which an aged Indian asked him why Europeans were so eagerly exploiting the Brazilian jungle. When told that these Europeans were trying to provide for their children, the old man said: "Is the land that nourished you not sufficient to feed them too? We have fathers, mothers and children whom we love. But we are certain that after our death the land that nourished us will also feed them. We therefore rest without further cares."

Being left with no response, Léry commented, in words that are reminiscent of Jesus' words about the sign of Jonah: "this tribe . . . will rise up in judgment against the plunderers who bear the name of Christians."

John Hemming, *Red Gold: The Conquest of the Brazilian Indians* (Cambridge: Harvard University Press, 1978), 16.

he invites all—the native Solomon and the alien queen of the South, the Israelite Jonah and the Gentile Ninevites—to acknowledge the mighty acts of God both in Israel and beyond, both in the church and beyond.

### 11:33–12:12  *Light and Truth*

### 11:33–36  *The Light of the Body*

Here Luke combines sayings that appear separately in Matthew (Matt. 5:15; 6:22–23). In Matthew the first of these sayings is a call to witness, to be a light for others, and the second draws the contrast between a healthy eye, full of light, and an unhealthy eye, full of darkness. By combining the two, Luke makes them fit in this section in which Jesus is in controversy with religious leaders. Granted, a light shines and guides the way of all those around it, or "those who enter," that is, who come within its reach. But if the eye is unhealthy, if it is full of darkness, it will not see the light. The implication is that those who reject Jesus and his teachings—those against whom Jonah is a sign—cannot see the light because they are full of darkness.

### 11:37–54  *At Dinner with a Pharisee*

Once again we find Jesus at a meal; indeed, in this entire section Luke seems to alternate between crowd scenes and meal scenes. In this case, the transition between the crowd and the meal is made explicit: "while he was speaking, a Pharisee invited him to dine with him." One may surmise that this was a fairly sympathetic Pharisee who was at least intrigued by Jesus' teachings. Yet hardly has the meal begun when conflict breaks out. The occasion is the Pharisee's expectation that Jesus would wash before dinner, which was commonly done, not for purposes of hygiene, but rather as an act of ritual cleansing. So from the very outset Jesus turns out to be a terrible guest. Against all laws of hospitality, he breaks into three "woes" against the Pharisees; and when the lawyers or teachers of the law declare that he is offending them, he replies with another series of three woes against them. Robert J. Karris shows the enormity of this breach of etiquette by translating the actions of Jesus into today's terms: "If you want to get in Luke's wavelength, think of those times when a guest in your house has changed TV channels on you or put the thermostat up ten degrees without your knowledge."[1] As we saw in the story of Mary and Martha, Jesus is not a very good guest. He has a tendency to take over. In this passage, Luke underscores that point by stating that "the *Lord* said to him. . . ." Luke would have difficulties with that sign commonly seen in Christian dining rooms, to the effect that "Jesus is the unseen guest at our table." No! Jesus will not be a guest. When the Pharisee invites him to dine, he is unwittingly inviting him to take over his dinner. Jesus cannot be one more name in our list of guests. When we invite him into our lives, we are inviting him to come not as a guest but as host and Lord.

The three woes against the Pharisees are preceded by Jesus' response to the Pharisee's concern over washing before eating. This response connects what Jesus now says with his comments on light in the preceding passage. Just as a body may be full of light or of darkness, so now what is important is what is inside, not what is outside. Jesus recommends that the Pharisees give to the poor from what is inside (that is, give from the heart) and this will truly cleanse them. The first woe insists on the theme of justice as an integral part of religion. The Pharisees are accused of being overly religious in their observances, tithing even the most minute herbs—which the law did not require—and yet neglecting justice and the love of God— which the law did require. The second woe echoes the theme of the great reversal that pervades the Gospel of Luke: the Pharisees are condemned for their self-importance. Finally, the third woe returns to the matter of what is inside and what is outside. Those who come to the Pharisees are unwittingly defiled by the latter's inner corruption, much as an unmarked sepulcher defiles those who walk over it.

Now the lawyers or teachers of the law intervene. Apparently they too are guests at the Pharisee's dinner, and they find what Jesus is saying offensive to them. Rather than apologizing, Jesus pronounces three woes against them. This disturbing guest insults not only his host but also his fellow guests! The first woe against the lawyers declares that they know the law full well when it comes to demand-

---

1. *Eating Your Way through Luke's Gospel* (Collegeville, MN: Liturgical Press, 2006), 43.

ing others to obey it, but ignore it when it comes to helping those others obey the law. The second charges that they are quite ready to honor the prophets of the past who died for their faithfulness, but refuse to honor the present prophets, thus making themselves guilty of the long tradition of violence that began with the death of Abel. The third accuses them of being "the dog in the manger" that will neither eat nor allow others to it, for when it comes to true knowledge, they keep others from entering, and they themselves do not enter.

Taken together, these six woes are a harsh indictment on religion as practiced by many both then and now. Religious people are often quite ready to tithe the mint and not practice justice, and to put on others burdens that we do not help them carry. Thus, like the Pharisees of old, we are meticulous in our every religious practice, but do little to make sure that justice is done, that the poor have food, or that the homeless have shelter. Or, like the lawyers of old, who set up burdens but then did not help others carry them, we declare abortion to be against the will of God, but do little to support unwed mothers or parentless children. In ancient times, the Pharisees paraded self-importantly in synagogues and marketplaces, and the lawyers honored the prophets of old while chiding those sent to them. Today we use our religion as a badge of respect, and we honor people such as Martin Luther King Jr. while we still do little to welcome the alien. In times past, the Pharisees defiled those who came to them unaware of their inner corruption. In recent times, we repeatedly read of religious leaders whose followers are led astray by the leader's sin. Finally, in times past there were students of the law who used their

> Another approach to this passage is to reflect on the positive directions that are implicit in the condemnations. What would the passage look like if it were changed from woes to beatitudes? As a blessing to the Pharisees, it would read: "Blessed are you Pharisees! For you practice justice and love while you pay a tithe on even your smallest source of income." . . . Similarly, as blessings on devout lawyers, it might read: "Blessed are you, lawyers! For you ease the burden of others and help them carry their loads."
> —R. Alan Culpepper
>
> "Luke," 250.

studies not to attain true wisdom but to take control of the law, thus preventing others from entering into its wisdom. Similarly, today we often turn theology into an esoteric discipline that, rather than leading people to the knowledge of God, makes such knowledge appear ever more recondite and unattainable. It is not only at the Pharisee's table that Jesus demands his role as host; it is also at our table!

The reference to the "Wisdom of God" merits some attention. Toward the end of the Old Testament period, the Wisdom of God had been hypostatized. This may be seen in Proverbs 8, where Wisdom declares her own existence with God from the beginning of creation: "The LORD created me at the beginning of his work, the first of his acts long ago. Ages ago I was set up, at the first, before the beginning of the earth." Some within the early church took up this tradition, speaking of God's Wisdom as the one who was incarnate in Jesus. This is particularly clear in the prologue of the Fourth Gospel, where most of what it says about the "Word" is parallel to what was also said about Wisdom. Eventually, it became common to speak of the incarnation of God's Wisdom (*sophia*) in Jesus. Thus the famous church of Saint Sophia in Constantinople was dedicated not to a female saint named Sophia, but to Jesus as the eternal Wisdom ruling over all things. In more recent times, much has been made of the fact that *sophia* is a feminine noun, thus affirming femininity of God. While much may be said in favor of such femininity, and it is necessary to correct the prevailing masculine image of God, the argument that *sophia* is a feminine noun does not carry much weight, for in Greek (as in many modern languages, but not in English) the grammatical gender of a word does not necessarily imply a gender in that to which it refers. (For instance, in Greek not only "wisdom," but also "truth," "faith," "justice," and "folly" are feminine, while "word," "heaven," and "bread" are masculine.)

### 12:1–3 *The Yeast of the Pharisees*

Now we move back to the crowd. At the end of the previous section, in verses 53–54, Luke has provided a transition, declaring that as Jesus went outside, the scribes and Pharisees began plotting against him. However, even amid a crowd of thousands, Jesus' words in verses 1–12 are addressed to his disciples, and the entirety of chapter 12 goes back and forth between words to the disciples (vv. 1–12, 22–53) and to the crowd (vv. 13–21, 54–59). Thus the picture Luke draws is of Jesus looking upon the crowd, the role of Pharisees in their lives, and Jesus commenting with his disciples on what he sees.

In this particular passage, Jesus uses the image of yeast. Here yeast represents the influence of the Pharisees. In 13:21 the same image will be used to indicate how the kingdom of God works in hidden ways. When the yeast is hidden in the dough, it seems quite insignificant and harmless. But as it works, it eventually affects all the dough. Likewise, Jesus implies, the teachings of the Pharisees, which seem quite harmless, are in fact dangerous. But their hypocrisy too, like the yeast whose effect is seen in the rising of the dough, will be uncovered.

Significantly, Jesus then applies the same point to his own disciples: "Therefore, whatever *you* have said in the dark. . . . And what *you* have whispered behind closed doors. . . ." It is not only the Pharisees that risk being hypocrites; the disciples also risk the same. They too may become like a hidden evil yeast. But if they do so, their hypocrisy too will be revealed.

### 12:4–12 *Who Is to Be Feared*

Since fear of those who may do us harm is one of the main sources of hypocrisy, Jesus—still speaking to the disciples—now turns to the subject of such fear. The entire passage deals with fearing those who can cause the disciples harm, particularly physical harm. Although from ancient times there were those who understood verse 5 as referring to Satan, who must be feared above all earthly rulers, most likely it refers to God, for the fear of God is the central theme of the entire passage. God is to be feared because, even more than killing the body, God can also cast one into hell (literally, Gehenna, a name drawn from a garbage dump near Jerusalem that seemed to be constantly burning).

Yet, paradoxically, the fear of God leads to trust and confidence. This God whom we are called to fear remembers the practically worthless sparrow, and every hair on our head. In 12:24–28 we shall find a similar argument: the God who cares for ravens and for lilies will take good care of us. There this will lead to trust in God on economic matters; here it leads to trust in God when opposition arises. Those who will oppose the followers of Jesus are not nearly as powerful as the God who has counted even the hairs on your head! This sort of fear of God should lead the disciples to valiant confession, knowing that the one whom they now acknowledge will acknowledge them in the end.

At the end of this passage we come to one of the most controverted passages in the history of biblical interpretation. What is meant by blaspheming against the Holy Spirit? Is it, as some claimed in the fourth century, denying the divinity of the Holy Spirit? Is it, as some claim in the twenty-first century, resisting or showing skepticism toward the extraordinary gifts of the Spirit? Is it apostasy— falling away after one has professed faith? Is the contrast between "speaking a word against" the Son of Man and "blaspheming" against the Holy Spirit?

As we look at the passage, we are struck by the announcement, on the lips of Jesus, that those who speak against him will be forgiven. We have just finished reading a series of passages in which people speak against Jesus, and even conspire to entrap him with their questions. Now Jesus announces that such people will be forgiven, but not those who blaspheme against the Holy Spirit. Thus, while much of the debate has centered on the matter of the sin against the Spirit, we often miss the word of grace in what Jesus declares. All those people who are accosting him, who will accuse him, who will murder him, will be forgiven!

In contrast to such a sweeping word of grace comes a word of judgment against those who blaspheme against the Holy Spirit. One cannot know who Jesus really is except by the Spirit of God. Therefore, to accept Jesus is not just a matter of one's own will; it can only happen in response to the Holy Spirit's call. Having done so, to then deny Jesus—as is likely to happen if one fears those who can kill the body more than one fears God—is to demean and deny the power of the Spirit that has led to the confession of faith in the first place. Furthermore, the passage does not end there, for Jesus promises his disciples that when they are brought before the authorities they are not to worry about what to say. When brought before those authorities who can kill the body, the Spirit will tell the disciples what to say.

If at that point they do not say what the Spirit tells them, but out of fear of the authorities say what those authorities wish to hear, they will be blaspheming against the Spirit. (It should be noted that Luke has a very high understanding of the role of the Spirit in the church. For instance, in Acts 5 Peter declares that Ananias and Sapphira have not lied to the church, but to God.) As Jesus would say later in the same chapter (Luke 12:48), "from everyone to whom much has been given [in this case, faith through the work of the Spirit], much will be required."

Even so, the text is rather harsh. Is the sin against the Spirit absolutely, completely unforgivable? It is difficult to reconcile such a notion with the teachings of one who declared that his disciples should forgive their enemies seventy times seven!

### 12:13–34 *Anxiety over Possessions*

### 12:13–21 *The Rich Fool*

Once again, amid a large crowd, a particular person draws the attention of Jesus. In typical Lukan fashion this person, a man, parallels the woman in 11:27. This particular man is interested in having Jesus come to his defense against a brother who he thinks is not treating him fairly in a matter of inheritance. Amid a crowd that is amazed at the teachings and deeds of Jesus, which are no less than signs of the kingdom of God, this man is concerned about his own wealth, and about how to deal with a brother who may be withholding what belongs to him. For him, Jesus is an opportunity to validate his claim to an inheritance. But Jesus will not be manipulated. Rather than taking sides with the man—or even against him—he challenges the very basis of his request. Even though he calls the man "friend," the parable that follows clearly shows him to be a fool.

A crucial difference between the God of the Bible and many of the prevailing religions of the time is that, while the main purpose of those religions is to manipulate or appease the gods so that they will do what the worshipers desire, the God of Israel and of the church is always sovereign, far above human attempts at religious manipulation. The purpose of biblical religion is not to have God do what we desire, but rather to have us do what God desires. Thus even though it is true (as we shall see in a moment) that in being overly concerned with material wealth the man in the story errs, it is also true that underlying that error is an even greater one: trying to use the power and authority of Jesus to get what he wants.

In this the man in the story is not alone. Throughout Christian history, the greatest challenge before the church has not been persecution—those who, in Jesus' words, can kill the body. Nor has it been disbelief—those who simply reject the proclamation of the church. The greatest challenge, both in the past and today, is what one could well term "Christopaganism," that is, a form of Christianity whose purpose is to manipulate God. Christopaganism lay at the foundation of the horror of the Crusades, when Christian faith—even sincere Christian faith—was used as a justification for wanton bloodshed, and when prayer was seen as a way to ensure victory over the "infidel." A subtler form of Christopaganism was the entire penitential system of the medieval church, against which Luther and Calvin protested. The notion that through one's good works one can persuade God to open the gates of heaven is no less pagan than the notion that by sacrificing a child one can appease the gods.

In more recent times, a blatant form of Christopaganism has become popular, promising people that if they will only join a certain church, or perform certain acts, or pray in a certain way, God will grant them what they wish. The only reason why God does not heal you, or does not give you the car you want, or does not force your spouse to be reconciled with you, is that you do not have enough faith. The success of the "gospel of success" is undeniable. The largest Brazilian-based international corporation is a church whose motto is "suffer no more," and which claims that people suffer because they do not know how to get God to solve all their problems. It also claims that if you have faith God will take your side against your enemies in whatever conflict you may find yourself. Jesus responds with an absolute refusal to be manipulated: "Friend, who set me to be a judge or arbitrator over you?"

At another level the issue in the Gospel text is one of material wealth, and therefore Jesus tells a story that shows the folly of those who trust in their wealth. This story is parallel to the one about the dishonest steward in 16:1–13. The two are connected by the question that the protagonist in each of the two stories asks: "What should/will I do?" (12:17; 16:3). Both deal with the question of material wealth and security. The man in the first story thinks he is secure in his position, and is not. The man in the second story acts out of a sense of insecurity, and thus secures his future. Significantly, while the man in the first story seems to act as would be expected of one in his social and economic position, Jesus calls him a fool; in the second story the actions of a scoundrel are commended as wise.

> He said within himself, "What shall I do?" And is not the answer ready? Do good. Do all the good thou canst. Let thy plenty supply thy neighbour's wants; and thou wilt never want something to do. Canst thou find none that need the necessaries of life, that are pinched with cold or hunger; none that have not raiment to put on, or a place where to lay their head; none that are wasted with pining sickness; none that are languishing in prison?
>
> —**John Wesley**
>
> "Sermon 119: On Worldly Folly," in *Works of John Wesley*, 7:307.

Specifically in the first story, that the man is concerned only about himself and his possessions is made abundantly clear by the constant repetition of "I" and "my." It is as if there were nothing else in the world but this man and his possessions. His greatest concern is that he does not know what to do with an exceedingly abundant crop; and his only solution is to build bigger barns so he can hold more and be more secure—so that "my" soul may "relax, eat, drink, be merry." The problem is that nothing of what he has—not even his soul—is his. It will be claimed when he least expects it, and all his plans will come to naught.

Jesus calls the man a "fool." At the level of mere common sense, the man's folly is obvious. He thinks he can attain joy and security by the accumulation of wealth. He imagines that he can really have control of his life and its end. He thinks he can plan for "many years," but he does not even have one more day to live. He is a fool because he forgets that, as is often said today, "you can't take it with you."

But the man is a fool also in a deeper sense. He is a fool because he acts as if there were no God. The words in Psalm 14:1 immediately come to mind: "Fools say in their hearts, 'There is no God.'

They are corrupt, they do abominable deeds." The fools to whom the psalm refers are not modern-day atheists, people who with their words deny the existence of God. They are rather people who, while still part of Israel, act as if there were no God. They do not care what God desires or commands, and the result is that they do abominable deeds. The man in the parable is a fool not only because he thinks he can secure his own life, but also because he acts as if there were no God. Presumably he is part of the people of God, and he knows that in the Hebrew Scriptures God repeatedly commends those in need to the care of those who have resources. This man knows this, and yet ignores it. This is what makes him a fool like those in Psalm 14. As Jesus says, he is ready to store up treasures for himself, but is not rich toward God.

### 12:22–34 *Anxiety and Trust*

Introduced as it is by the words "therefore" and "to his disciples," this passage is a further elaboration, for the benefit of the disciples, of the point made in the parable of the rich fool. The verb "to worry" appears repeatedly, thus showing that the issue is one of anxiety, suggesting a different answer to the fool's question, "What should I do?" The fool responds by building bigger barns; the disciples are to respond by not worrying. Just as the fool's first mistake was ignoring common sense, so is the first basis for the disciples' not worrying mere common sense: life is more than food, and the body is more than clothing; no matter how much you worry you cannot make yourself taller (or live longer, depending on how one translates v. 25). At this point, it is important to note that Jesus does not say that one should ignore food for the sake of life, or clothing for the sake of the body. Such an interpretation is quite common among those of us who have food and clothing in abundance. But those others who seldom have enough food or adequate clothing know that life cannot exist without food, and that a body without adequate clothing will not long survive. This should serve as a warning, lest we interpret this passage in ways that demean the struggle of those who are in real want of food and clothing.

The reasons Jesus gives for not worrying are grounded not only in common sense, but also in good theology. His disciples should not worry about these things because God knows that they need them. God feeds the ravens, who have no barns, unlike the fool in the parable. God clothes the lilies, who do not spin—in other words, do not perform the preliminary tasks that will eventually result in clothing. God knows that we need such things, and we are more important than the grass of the field, which God does clothe.

Although this entire passage has often been interpreted in the sense that food and clothing are not important (an interpretation that comes quite easily to those who have an abundance of both), what the passage says is exactly the opposite. We are not to worry about food and clothing precisely because God knows they are important! Indeed, they are so important that God provides them even to birds and grass. This is why it is "the nations of the world" (i.e., the Gentiles, the pagan world) that strive after these things. Their struggle is a result of their not knowing the God who provides even for ravens and for lilies. Thus when Christians who have all we really need still worry anxiously about having enough, and thus seek to accumulate more and more, we are falling once again into a form of Christopaganism (see commentary on 12:13–21).

The alternative to worrying is not a happy-go-lucky, careless attitude. On the contrary, it is a serious struggle, striving for the kingdom. This does not mean, as some might surmise, simply being more religious and pious. The kingdom of God is a new order, the new order that has come nigh in Jesus. It is an order in which God's will is done, as Matthew's version of the Lord's Prayer makes abundantly clear: "Your kingdom come, your will be done. . . ." Since it is God's will that even the ravens be fed, and the lilies clothed, to strive for the kingdom is among other things to make certain that all are fed and all are clothed. We are not to

> Asceticism and discipline are mutually incompatible. . . . Asceticism renounces possessions. Simplicity sets possessions in proper perspective. . . . Simplicity is the only thing that sufficiently reorients our lives so that possessions can be genuinely enjoyed without destroying us.
> —Richard J. Foster
>
> *Celebration of Discipline: The Path to Spiritual Growth* (San Francisco: Harper & Row, 1978), 82–83.

worry about securing such things, for they are important to God; but precisely because they are important to God we must oppose everything that precludes all from having them. This is why in the very passage about not worrying over food or clothing Jesus invites his followers to give alms (12:33), that is, to provide for those who are hungry or naked.

The ending of this section connects it with the parable of the Rich Fool, for the two are parallel: it is a matter of where one's treasure is. If on earth, as in the case of the rich man who decided to build bigger barns, it will have no lasting value. If in heaven, it will have lasting value, for in heaven neither do thieves steal one's treasure, nor do moths eat at it. So the matter is posed in terms similar to an investment consultant who tells us that now is a time not to invest in stock whose value will be declining, but in bonds whose value will rise. Verses 33–34 give clear guidelines as to how this is to be done: "sell your possessions"—your earthly treasure—and "give alms"—thus building up a treasure in heaven. In early patristic literature, one constantly finds the assertion that "when you give to the poor you lend to God," a theme drawn from Proverbs 19:17. In this passage one finds echoes of that theme.

It is this passage (and others like it) that stands behind John Wesley's famous advice to "make all you can, save all you can, give all you can." However, what Wesley meant by "saving" was quite different from our present understanding of that word. For us, "saving" is putting aside, stashing away—much like the rich fool of the parable. For Wesley, it meant to refrain from spending, so that one could have more to give. Thus quite often, in quoting Wesley, we are actually contradicting his spirit, which was much like Luke 12:33, and turn his words into an excuse for acting like the man in 12:18–19.

### 12:35–59 Be Prepared!

#### 12:35–48 Awaiting the Master

The theme of stewardship now comes to the foreground. In the previous section Jesus was teaching about one of the most common issues of stewardship, the management of possessions. Now he comes to another central issue of stewardship, the "in between" times. Significantly, the theme of stewardship will appear repeatedly as Jesus prepares for his departure, his "exodus" in 9:31. This is because stewardship, properly understood, is the life of believers in the time "in between." This motif will reappear, for instance, in the parables of the Dishonest Steward (16:1–13), of the Ten Pounds (19:11–27), and of the Wicked Tenants (20:9–19). In all of these, we are told that we are living in expectation of a future, and must therefore live and manage our resources according to that future, rather than to the present situation. In other words, as we read at the conclusion of the previous section, we are to build treasures in heaven rather than on earth, for the future rather than for the present.

Stewardship must not be divorced from eschatology. Too often the typical stewardship sermon says simply that all we have God has given us to manage. This leaves out two fundamental issues. The first is that we must not simply affirm that all we have has been given to us by God. We live in an unjust world, and to attribute the present order to God is to attribute injustice to God. It may well be that we have some things unjustly, and not as a gift of God. This matter will come up again in the parable of the Unfaithful Steward. The second issue that should not be left out of our discussions on stewardship is the crucial dimension of hope and expectation. We are to manage things, not just out of a general sense of morality or even of justice, and certainly not just to support the church and its institutions— which we certainly must do. We are to manage things in view of the future we expect. In the previous section, this was expressed in terms of building up treasures in heaven rather than on earth, and in terms of striving for the kingdom.

In this passage, that eschatological sense of expectancy or in-betweenness comes forth in the image of lamps that must remain lit. When we are expecting company we turn on the lights. If the company does not arrive, and we decide that they are not coming and we should go to bed, we turn the lights off. What for us is a fairly passive activity—all we do is flick a switch and the lights remain on—for people in the first century required frequent attention. One had to replenish the oil in the lamp. One had to adjust the wick. Today, we may go to bed leaving the lights on. Then, if one forgot about the lamp it would burn out. Thus keeping the lamp lit, as this passage instructs, is a matter that requires constant attention and watchfulness. This is the central theme of the passage.

The section may be divided in three, according to the central image employed. In verses 36–38 the disciples are said to be like slaves who await their master. In verses 39–40 they are placed in the position of the owner of a household, who must keep watch against a thief who will come when least expected. In verses 41–48 they are in the mid-range position of a manager or steward. Most often, such a manager was himself a slave who represented the master, and sought to have all the members of the household—that is, the other slaves—act in accordance with the master's wishes. It was crucial for such a manager to know what his master wanted, and to do it in the master's absence. In this last section, speaking to his disciples, Jesus intimates that, since they know what the master wishes, and since they have been given responsibility over the rest of the household, when the master returns they will be judged on the basis of their faithfulness to the absent master's wishes. Those who knew those wishes will be judged more severely than those who did not. Thus, while we might think that, because we are Christians, we have the advantage of knowing what God's intentions for the world are, the truth is also that any such advantage in knowledge also leads to a greater weight of responsibility. The servant who has no contact with the master, and does not know what the master wishes, is not as guilty as the one who does know what the master wishes and still disobeys. Furthermore, if that servant is a manager or steward, one placed over other servants, the responsibility will be even greater.

---

The world is crying out for keepers and tenders of its wonderful, frail beauty, and God desires to send us out as stewards into this astonishing, unique creation. Until we have been grasped by that Word and deed of our God; until we have begun to *be* who we are, no amount of exhortation or works will alter greatly the image of the church or the course of the world.

—Douglas John Hall

*The Steward: A Biblical Symbol Come of Age*, rev. ed. (Grand Rapids: Eerdmans, 1990), 244.

# FURTHER REFLECTIONS
## *The Absence of God*

The theme of the absence of God is central to the teachings of Jesus. In some of the parables, it is we who are absent from God. The lost sheep has to be found. The lost coin has to be found. The prodigal has to return. But in other parables it would seem that the issue is not our absence from God, but rather God's absence from us. We call these stories "parables of stewardship." And this is an excellent name for them, for stewardship is precisely what a steward practices when the master is away. While the master is there, a steward's role is limited. It is when the master is away that the steward must take responsibility. In one of his better-known parables (Matt. 25:14–30), Jesus tells of a man who, "going on a journey," called three of his servants, gave to each a large amount of money (five talents to one, two to another, and one to a third), and "then he went away." In other words, the parable is about how to manage while the master is not present. Similarly, the parallel parable in Luke—the parable of the Ten Pounds (19:11–27)—begins: "A nobleman went to a distant country"—he absented himself. In another parable in Matthew 25, the same chapter where we find the parable of the Talents, Jesus speaks of ten bridesmaids going out to seek the bridegroom. But the bridegroom is delayed—he is not present at the time when they expected him to be. Even beyond these, there are many other parables of absence in the teachings of Jesus. A master returns and discovers how a servant has been keeping his household. A thief comes at night, when people least expect him....

In Luke 20:9–18 Jesus tells another parable of absence: "A man planted a vineyard, and leased it to tenants, and went to another country for a long time." There is a parallelism between this parable and the story of creation. God

> The great temptation of the ministry is to celebrate only the presence of the Lord while forgetting his absence. ... As we become aware of his absence we discover his presence, and as we realize that he left us we also come to know that he did not leave us alone.
>
> —**Henri J. M. Nouwen**
>
> *The Living Reminder: Service and Prayer in Memory of Jesus Christ* (New York: Seabury, 1977), 46–47.

made the earth and all that is in it, and planted a garden, and gave it to the human couple to till. And it was all very good. And then God rested!

God's rest is an expression of the love that leads to creation. In the past, I have often spoken about how the doctrine of creation means that all things subsist thanks to God's providence, and that this is so much the case that if God's sustaining hand were to be removed for an instant, all of creation would disappear. This may be a good way to express an important truth. But as I look at these parables of absence, and join them with the biblical notion of God's rest, I see another dimension of God's creative love that needs to be stressed. God's love is such that God decides to create other beings besides Godself.

Just as earthly parents deciding to have a child are also deciding to create something beyond themselves, not entirely in their control, so God's decision to create the world and to create us is a decision to create something beyond Godself, and not entirely under God's control—even though we know that ultimately God's purposes shall prevail.

We often speak of the presence of God, and rightly so. But this other theme or metaphor of absence is also common in the Bible.

---

When a child is allowed to hold on to his mother's dress, can we say then he is walking along with her, just as his mother walks? Nay, we may not say so. First must the child learn to walk alone and on his own, before he can go the way his mother goes, and go as she is going. And when the child is learning to walk alone, what must the mother do? She must make herself invisible. That her tenderness toward him is the same and remains unaltered, that indeed it probably grows greater, just at the time when the child is learning to walk alone, we know very well; the child, on the other hand, may not always understand it. But what is meant by the child having to learn to walk alone and to walk on his own is, in a spiritual sense, the task set anyone who is to be somebody's follower—he must learn to walk alone and to walk on his own. Strange, is it not? . . . That heaven's care for us is unchanged, and is indeed, were it possible, still more solicitous in this hour of danger, we know very well, but perhaps we cannot always understand it, when we are learning.

—Søren Kierkegaard

*Gospel of Sufferings*, trans. A. S. Aldworth and W. S. Ferrie (London: James Clarke, 1955), 15–16.

Even apart from sin, God gives the human creature space, freedom to exercise its responsibility. In the story in the garden, after creating humankind, and giving them dominion over the rest of creation, God lets them exercise that dominion, even though it also implies the possibility of sin. And this absence, just as much as the divine presence, is a sign of love.

This image of parenthood may be taken one step further. Parental love is not manifested only in the act of procreation, and not only in the many actions of feeding, nurturing, and guiding, but also in a parent's acts of absence. Out of love a parent finds it necessary to step back and let a child try its wings, even at the risk of pain and failure. A parent who is always present, guarding a child from every risk and every hurt, is not a very good parent. A child whose parents are always hovering around, guarding the child's every step, will never learn to walk. And a child who is never given the responsibility of making decisions, even at the risk of error, will never grow up. Out of love, a parent must step back. Likewise, God's parental love is manifested, not only in creation and in sustenance, but also in God's apparent absence—in God's letting us run our lives and much of the world by ourselves, even at the risk of ruining both.

We are learning. We are learning to live as God's children in a world where the hand of our Eternal Parent is not always visible, in a world where God has placed us to be stewards of the absent Master, to grow as we could not were God always holding our hand and guiding our every step.

But then the divine absence has an added dimension: sin has come into the picture. This is indeed God's world. But it is God's rebellious world. This world, made by God, is also godless. It is a

> The mother may sometimes suffer the child to fall and to be distressed in various ways, for its own benefit. . . . And if we do not feel ourselves eased, let us at once be sure that he is behaving as a wise Mother. For if he sees that it is profitable to us to mourn and to weep, with compassion and pity he suffers us until the right time has come, out of his love.
>
> —Dame Julian of Norwich
>
> *Showings*, trans. Edmund Colledge and James Walsh, Classics of Western Spirituality (New York: Paulist Press, 1978), 300–301.

world of injustice and oppression, of war and prejudice, of hate and falsehood. In this world there is no guarantee of divine approval. The risk is still there. The talents must still be invested in a market that is always uncertain. Faithful Christians do not all agree on every course of action. We each and all must take the risk of acting according to what we believe to be God's will, like a faithful steward who makes a decision hoping that this is what the master would wish him to do.

### 12:49–53 *What to Expect*

This passage is the first of three sections that are apparently disjointed (vv. 49–53, 54–56, and 57–59). What holds them together is the theme of eschatological expectation, and how it must impact the life of believers in the present. Eschatological hope is not just a matter for the future. If we really expect the future we claim to await, this should have an impact on the way we live in the present.

The previous section ends with the announcement that "even more will be demanded" from those slaves who know what the master wants. Now we are told that things will not be easy. Jesus himself will suffer a "baptism" of suffering. And his disciples will suffer also, for opposition will be such that there will be bitter division even within households. Those servants who know what their master wishes will act differently than the rest. This will cause stress and division. It is as if in a parade some begin marching to a different tune. The rest—those who march to the common tune—will accuse them of upsetting the parade, and will seek to suppress or oust them.

### 12:54–59 *No Excuses*

The eschatological emphasis of the entire section now leads to warnings. The servants know that the master is coming. We know that the future belongs to the reign of God. But, given the potential cost, it is not surprising that we are strongly tempted not to see the signs of the new time that is emerging. To forecast the weather, one looks at the clouds and the wind. The same should be possible by looking at the signs of "the present time." There is a new order coming! But people refuse to see it, and seek to continue life as if nothing were happening. Hypocritically, although we know what the master wants, we find all sorts of reasons to continue living as if the present order were permanent. We all stand accused and are on our way to trial. We can continue insisting on our innocence, and face the judge and the ensuing penalty, or settle matters with our accuser before the time of trial.

### 13:1–9 *The Parable of the Barren Fig Tree*

This passage is often divided at the end of verse 5, as if the question about those who suffer undeservedly were separate from the parable that follows. But they belong together, and in a way the parable is Jesus' response to the question posed in the preceding five verses.[2]

This is a text most of us avoid, because it raises a number of thorny questions, particularly the age-old question of why human tragedies occur. When tragedy strikes, the first question we ask is, Why? Why did my child have to die? What evil had he done? Was it perhaps for some evil I did? Why does famine strike in Africa? Is it perhaps because of some particular sinfulness of the Africans or their leaders? Why does a particular hurricane hit New Orleans and not Georgia? Why did those people die in a plane crash and not others? These are all questions that it is quite natural to ask and quite impossible to answer (see pp. 69–72, "Further Reflections: Demonic Powers and the Mystery of Evil"). This is one of the reasons why we tend to stay away from this passage in the Gospel of Luke.

The other reason is that the passage does not answer those questions. As pastors, we often have to deal with this sort of question, and wish we had a ready-made answer, one that would immediately console the bereaved, enlighten the perplexed, and reassure the doubting. But Jesus does not give us, as we would like, a ready-made answer that we could give to the mother whose teenage son has just died in an automobile accident, like a doctor prescribes a pill to a patient. Rather, all that he does is to tell us that a certain answer is wrong, and then he moves on to tell us that such tragedies,

---

2. Some of this material, with slight variations, was published earlier in Justo L. González and Pablo A. Jiménez, *Púlpito: An Introduction to Hispanic Preaching* (Nashville: Abingdon, 2005), 95–100.

unexplainable and mysterious though they may be, do call survivors to greater obedience.

Jesus is on his way to Jerusalem, and has been speaking about what it means to be a faithful people. In that context, someone comes and tells him of a gruesome crime that Pilate has perpetrated: he has mingled the blood of a number of Galileans with their sacrifices. In other words, he has killed them just as they were offering their sacrifices to God. The details of what had taken place are not altogether clear. But several things are clear.

The first is that this terrible crime took place in the temple in Jerusalem, for this was the place where the Galileans would have come to offer sacrifices to God.

The second is that, precisely because it had taken place in the temple, it was a most horrible crime. It was not only murder but also sacrilege. One may well surmise that many Jews were reminded of the event, several decades earlier, when Pompey rode his horse into the Holy of Holies. Or that other time, centuries earlier, when the temple was destroyed and the people led into captivity. We are certainly reminded of the murder of Becket before the high altar in the cathedral of Canterbury, or more recently, of the murder of Archbishop Oscar Romero under similar circumstances in El Salvador.

Third, what becomes clear when we read the entirety of the Gospel is that some Jewish leaders in Jerusalem bore a great deal of animosity toward all Galileans. Indeed, many Jews viewed the Galileans as second-class Jews, as standing somewhere between true Jews and heathenish Gentiles.

For all these reasons, those who are telling Jesus of Pilate's crime are raising several questions in one. They are raising first of all the age-old question of the reason for such seemingly meaningless suffering. Second, they are raising the question of whether good Jews should not be incensed at Pilate and all the Romans. As in so many other places in the Gospel narrative, they are trying to place Jesus in the difficult position of having to appear either unpatriotic or subversive. If he condemns Pilate's act, he will be accused of inciting rebellion against the Romans. If he plays down its importance, his listeners will be outraged at his religious and human insensitivity. Finally, they are raising the question of the relations between Galileans and other Jews. In telling him of the horrible thing that has happened to these Galileans they are raising the commonly held belief among Jews that Galileans were less faithful than other Jews. Perhaps this is the reason why Jesus responds: Do you think that these particular Galileans were worse sinners than other Galileans? And then he sharpens the question by bringing it closer to home and referring to an incident in Jerusalem: Those eighteen upon whom the tower of Siloam fell and killed them, do you think that they were worse offenders than all the others who dwelt in Jerusalem?

This entire text is particularly poignant for those of us who, when speaking to someone about hunger in various parts of the world, have heard the response that these people are suffering from famine because of their sin. Or, when speaking of the suffering in our inner cities and our minority enclaves, we have also been told that such misery is the result of those people's sin. Certainly, famine and misery are the result of human sin, although very likely not the sin of those who are suffering and dying. Jesus brings the matter closer to home by asking: "Or those eighteen who were killed when the tower of Siloam fell on them—do you think that they were worse offenders than all the others living in Jerusalem?" In today's terms, this is like asking, Do you believe that those who perished in the Twin Towers were worse offenders than all others living in New York? When we put the matter in such terms, it is clear that whatever we say about the suffering of those far away must be consistent with what we are ready to say about the tragedies that strike closer to home, and even about our own suffering.

Jesus carries the matter one step further, and shows that we are posing the question in the wrong way. The surprising thing is not that so many die but that we still live. If it were a matter of sin, we would all be dead. Twice Jesus says: "Unless you repent, you will all likewise perish." And then he illustrates his meaning with a parable.

The parable is the story of a man who found that a fig tree in his vineyard was not producing fruit. His normal reaction would be to have it cut down, and he gives instructions to that effect. But a conversation ensues with the outcome that the owner of the vineyard agrees that for one more year the tree will be allowed to stand. It will even receive special care. But if at the end of that time it has not produced fruit, it shall be cut down.

What does the parable mean, in this context? It clearly means that those of us who survive, those Galileans who were not killed by Herod, or those Jews on whom the tower did not fall, or those of us who have not died from famine, or those who were not in the Twin Towers on September 11, are living only by the grace of God, and that our continued life is for the purpose that we bear fruit.

It also means that even our apparent blessing and abundance are not necessarily something of which we should boast. The tree that has produced no fruit receives special attention and added fertilizer, not because it is so good, but rather because it is so poor.

In order to understand the poignancy of the parable, one has to remember what a vineyard looks like at the last possible time when one would normally come looking for figs on a fig tree. The vineyard would have already yielded its grapes, and would have been severely pruned. It would all have been cut down, and one would see nothing but dry and gnarled stumps. In the midst of this scene of apparent desolation stands a verdant fig tree. It has never been pruned. Now it will receive even better treatment. The vinedresser will dig around it, and give it an exceptional dose of fertilizer. To a casual observer, the tree would appear to be specially blessed, and the vines cursed and forgotten, and one would think that the fig tree must be particularly valuable if it is treated with such care. This is what one would expect on the premises of the so-called gospel of prosperity: good things are a reward for faith and fruitfulness. But the truth is exactly the opposite. The fig tree is receiving special care because it has yet to give the fruit it was meant to bear.

This is not one of the more popular parables of Jesus. There are probably many reasons for this. But quite possibly one of the main reasons is that we would like to think that we have comfortable houses, when so many are homeless, or a substantial income, when so many are poor, or all kinds of food to eat, when so many are hungry, or a relatively healthy body, when so many are ill, because we have somehow been particularly faithful. This is why the "gospel of prosperity" is so attractive among those who are prosperous: they can now claim that God has blessed them in a special way because they are faithful believers.

This text, however, leads us to think otherwise. Could it be that the reason why some of us have been given all these advantages is that otherwise we would have great difficulty bearing fruit? Could it be that all these things of which we so pride ourselves are really just so much manure, piled on us because otherwise we would be such lousy fruit trees? Further, as in the case of the fig tree, could it be that our apparent advantages and privileges are also a warning about impending doom lest we bear fruit?

What is a question for us as individuals and as families is also a question for us as denominations and as individual congregations. We tend to admire the big church with the tall steeples, the large staff, and the professional choir. We tend to think that the fact that a church has many resources at its command is a sign that it has been faithful. But this parable raises the possibility it may be otherwise. Could it be that our own abundance has been given to us in an effort to lead us to bear fruit, to share those resources, to share of ourselves, and that the reason we survive is not our great budget, our nice music, our fine sermons, our beautiful buildings, or our sophisticated theology, but this miraculous grace of the Owner of the vineyard who has decided to give us one more chance?

### 13:10–17 *Jesus Heals a Crippled Woman*

This well-known passage is a further sign of the growing controversy between Jesus and the religious leaders of his nation. Yet, as is so often the case, precisely because we know it so well, we miss the drama that is unfolding. For in this text we have not just a miracle of healing, but the convergence of ancient and seemingly invincible powers, all coming to meet that Sabbath day in that synagogue.

It was the Sabbath, and a woman who had been ill for a long time, bent over, unable to stand up straight, comes into the synagogue. The text tells us that it was an evil spirit that crippled her. We do not know what the modern medical diagnosis might be. The point is that the woman cannot stand up straight, and that is demonic (see pp.

69–72, "Further Reflections: Demonic Powers and the Mystery of Evil"). With that woman there comes into the synagogue what we religious folk often try to forget: the reality of the power of evil, the reality of human suffering.

It was the Sabbath, a day devoted to rest since the most ancient times of Hebrew tradition and by none other than the very Creator God. But a day of rest that humans, by dint of ever more meticulous legislation, had belabored into a day of greater difficulties.

It was the Sabbath, in the synagogue—precisely where the laws referring to the Sabbath were studied, analyzed, and exaggerated. It was the Sabbath, and there in the synagogue was also Jesus, Lord of creation and Lord of the Sabbath. What will he do? On the one hand, in that woman's suffering Satan himself confronts him. On the other, in the entire atmosphere around him, in the very law of Israel, in the leader of the synagogue, the weight of tradition seems to say that there is nothing to be done. Jesus faces the bent-over woman, oppressed by the weight of Satan himself. To her oppression of eighteen years the religious leaders would add another of umpteen centuries: It is the Sabbath! It is a day for religious matters! Jesus saw the woman, and he called her, and he spoke to her, and he laid his hands on her, and immediately she stood up straight and began praising God.

But the leader of the synagogue was a religious man who knew the Law: "There are six days on which work ought to be done; come on those days and be cured, and not on the sabbath day." But Jesus took him to task, as well as others like him: "You hypocrites! Does not each of you on the sabbath untie his ox or his donkey from the manger, and lead it away to give it water? And ought not this woman . . . be set free from this bondage on the sabbath day?"

The confrontation points to the always lurking possibility that very good religious principles may be turned into allies of the powers of evil. The leader of the synagogue was defending religious principles derived from the very law of God. Yet in that very defense he was siding with the powers of evil that held the woman bent. Similar events abound in Christian history. What most of the inquisitors were defending was true; yet their very defense was evil. Servetus was burned in Geneva because he denied what was true; yet his burning was a demonic act. All of this is a warning to us orthodox

Christians, lest we too defend traditional doctrine and morality and in so doing allow ourselves to become agents of overbearing pride, of prejudice, and of oppression.

### 13:18–21 *The Mustard Seed and the Yeast*

At the end of the previous section, as a result of Jesus' healing the crippled woman and of his discussion with the leader of the synagogue, the entire crowd rejoices and praises Jesus for the great marvels he performs. But Jesus, instead of speaking about the great and marvelous, speaks about the small: about a mustard seed that someone planted, and a bit of leaven that a woman put into a mass of flour. Once again, in typical Lukan fashion, a story about a man is paralleled by a story about a woman.

The kingdom of God, Jesus tells the crowd, is like a mustard seed hidden in the ground, or like a bit of yeast hidden in the bowl of flour. God is not like the powerful of the earth, who must do everything with might and noise. God is like a woman who quietly puts a bit of yeast in the dough or like a man who plants a tiny mustard seed.

These are not just commonsense observations. Everyone knows that mighty oaks come out of small acorns. This is also a christological assertion. The one who is speaking has just shown his mighty power in the episode in the synagogue; but he was born a poor and small mustard seed in a humble manger, as a child he had to go into exile in Egypt, and he is preparing to face the most formidable powers of evil. In that confrontation, he will seem weak and insignificant like a mustard seed or a bit of yeast. Yet in that

> When Jesus says the *whole* is leavened, he's not kidding. The lump stands for the whole world. It's not some elite ball of brioche dough made out of fancy flour by special handling. And it's not some hyper-good-for-you chunk of spiritual bread full of soy flour, wheat germ, and pure thoughts. It's just plain, unbaked bread dough, and Jesus postulates enough of it to make it even handle like the plain old world it represents: that is, *not easily*. Indigestible in its present form, incapable of going anywhere, except in a handbasket.
> —Robert Farrar Capon
>
> *Kingdom, Grace, and Judgment: Paradox, Outrage, and Vindication in the Parables of Jesus* (Grand Rapids: Eerdmans, 1989), 100.

very smallness he will be making the way to his final triumph. Jesus himself is the yeast and the mustard seed of the kingdom of God. This point is made starker in the case of the mustard seed, which according to the parable becomes a tree. This has frequently puzzled interpreters, who know that a mustard plant is much smaller, and therefore many have tried to explain the problem away by claiming that Jesus is not referring to mustard but to something else. Yet that may be precisely the point. Jesus' hearers would know that it was absurd for a mustard seed to grow to such a size. Thus in what some see as a botanical error there may well be an intentional irony, showing that Jesus is not speaking merely of the commonplace—big oaks from small acorns grow— but of the apparently impossible truth that in this Jesus who stands before his listeners, and who will be despised and rejected, the kingdom of God is coming.

> What an unspeakable comfort it is to know that in the midst of man's mischief, in the midst of his scheming and bad speculations, his shaping and misshaping, his activism and his failures, there is still another stream of events flowing silently on, that God is letting his seeds grow and achieving his ends.
> —Helmut Thielicke
>
> *The Waiting Father: Sermons on the Parables of Jesus*, trans. John W. Doberstein (New York: Harper & Brothers, 1959), 86–87.

And, since every christological assertion also has ecclesiological implications, the disciples are called to be the insignificant mustard seed and the unnoticed yeast that announces the coming kingdom. Like Jesus, the church is not called to proclaim its power, its influence, its political clout, or its prestige. The vindication of the church and of believers is best left to the absent master when he returns.

### 13:22–30 *The Narrow Door*

The passage is well known. What we often miss is the connection between the words of Jesus and the life of the early church—and ours. For Christian readers when Luke wrote the Gospel, the claim of those left outside, that they had eaten and drunk with Jesus, would be particularly poignant. As a church, their main act of worship was

Communion, a weekly meal they shared with Jesus. Thus the words of Jesus, that some would claim to have eaten and drunk with him and still be left out, would remind them that simply being part of the worshiping community did not guarantee that the door would be opened to them.

The joint reference to a meal and to a door brings to mind the oft-quoted verse in Revelation 3:20: "Listen! I am standing at the door, knocking; if you hear my voice and open the door, I will come in to you and eat with you, and you with me." Although commonly understood as a call from Jesus to open our individual hearts, in its original context this text is addressed to a church that, although believing itself to be particularly rich and blessed, had shut the door on the Lord who was supposed to be the host at its table. While the church celebrates the Lord's Supper, he stands at the door and knocks!

To us also, the connection between the passage about doors and our Communion services is made apparent by the common practice of employing the last verse (Luke 13:29) in our celebrations of the Lord's Supper. When we do so, the attitude is often one of rejoicing in the manner in which the Lord's Table foreshadows the final banquet, where "they shall come from east and west, from north and south." However, reading this last verse in the context both of the words that precede it and of the closing statement of the next verse that "some are first who will be last," this passage is also a warning. It is a warning that we must take care lest, having attended church and celebrated Communion regularly, we find ourselves locked outside and pleading to be let in on the basis that we ate and drank with the Lord.

### 13:31–35 *The Lament over Jerusalem*

There has been much discussion among interpreters of this passage about the actual intent of the Pharisees who warn Jesus, for some find it difficult to imagine Luke depicting any Pharisees as well intentioned. But the passage says nothing about the reason why these Pharisees warn Jesus about Herod's designs.

Whatever the case might be, Jesus responds by telling them to go back to Herod—whom he calls a "fox"—and tell him that Jesus will complete his work. Jesus' message is rather cryptic, for he will take much more than three days on his way to Jerusalem. For this reason, some take it as a reference to the three days in the tomb. There is no doubt that he is connecting his response to his passion, as indicated by the reference at the end of verse 35.

The lament over Jerusalem connects the fate of Jesus with that of those who have gone before him. Some take his claim that he has "often" desired to care for the children of Jerusalem as an indication that he is speaking of his own participation in the ongoing work of God—as the Wisdom of God to which reference has already been made in a similar context in 11:49.

The image of himself caring for the children of Jerusalem as a mother hen takes care of her brood gives particular significance to his calling Herod a fox. A hen guards her chicks against foxes. Jesus wants to protect the children of Jerusalem not only from what we would consider spiritual or religious ills, but also from the exploitation of those who lord it over them.

There is no doubt that in this passage Jesus bemoans the disobedience of Jerusalem. But Christians should draw the conclusion that Jesus bemoans also the disobedience of his church and its members. Us too Jesus wishes to protect like a mother hen—and to protect against all evil, spiritual as well as political.

### 14:1–24 *Jesus, a Disturbing Guest*

The entirety of chapter 14 parallels 13:10–35.[3] Both sections open with an act of healing on the Sabbath, both then move to lessons on humility, and both end with warnings to those who believe they are secure in their relationship with God.

Jesus has barely arrived at the home of his host when he upsets the assembly by once again healing on the Sabbath. (The Greek can be translated, as in the NIV, in the sense that Jesus was already at dinner or, as in the NRSV, in the sense that he was on his way to dinner.) This passage is very similar to 13:10–17 (on which see

---

3. See Culpepper, "Luke," 283.

above). It presents the male counterpart to the woman healed in the synagogue. Since the conflict that such acts of healing on the Sabbath entail was already shown in the story of the crippled woman, now the story of the man with dropsy is briefer, and does not repeat those points of conflict, with which the reader of the Gospel would be familiar by now. Thus the story seems to serve two purposes: first, to present an episode about a man to parallel the one about a woman; second, to set the stage for the conflicting dinner scene that follows.

Not content with this act that his host and the other guests might find objectionable, Jesus then seems to take hold of the dinner and the conversation, as if he, and not the Pharisee, were the host. As was made clear in his visit at the home of Mary (10:38–42), Jesus will not be a passive guest. On the contrary, he will take charge, and in a sense become the host. He now challenges both his host and his fellow guests by means of three parabolic utterances (vv. 7–11, 12–14, 15–24), all having to do with dinners, hosts, and guests. The first of these is addressed primarily to his fellow guests, whom he has seen vying for the places of honor. At a superficial level, Jesus seems to be simply criticizing them and suggesting the wiser course of acting humbly and taking the places of lesser honor, so that the host will give them a better place, and they will have real reason to be proud. But at a deeper level one can see the eschatological reference of his words. Jesus speaks of a "wedding banquet"—a subtle reference to the final day of celebration, repeatedly depicted in the Bible as a wedding feast. Then he concludes his remarks by applying them to the larger, eschatological dimension

> Can we imagine the women witnessing these actions and hearing this story? By custom they were often not even provided the lowest seats but were relegated to the serving or cooking area or even outside. From such a perspective they could laugh at the arrogance of those choosing the first places and the delightful reversal by those in the last places who are invited to come up higher. This is exactly what Jesus is saying to them. They have been last. They have been abased and humbled. Jesus will exalt them.
>
> —Loretta Dornisch
>
> *A Woman Reads the Gospel of Luke* (Collegeville, MN: Liturgical Press, 1996), 170.

of the final judgment and the new order of the kingdom, which reverses the present human order: "For all who exalt themselves will be humbled, and those who humble themselves will be exalted."

Having criticized his fellow guests, Jesus now turns to the host, and dares find fault with his guest list. One can surmise that, just as his earlier words were a direct response to what he saw his fellow guests doing, so are his words about whom to invite a direct response to the host's choice of invitees. What Jesus now says and proposes is contrary to all rules of etiquette. Then, as today, it was quite common for people to invite to a dinner those who were of equal social standing with them—family, friends, colleagues. Since having a distinguished guest at dinner results in honor and prestige for the host, one seeks to invite such people—in Luke's text, "rich neighbors." When one holds such a dinner, the guests are expected to return the invitation. To us, this would seem normal. But Jesus sees things differently: when a former guest invites you, you have already been repaid. While we might consider this an advantage, or at least the normal order of things, Jesus proposes inviting those who cannot repay. After listing four main categories of people who are usually invited to such dinners— friends, brothers, relatives, rich neighbors—Jesus suggests four other categories—the poor, the crippled, the lame, and the blind. Surprising as this may seem to us, it would have been even more surprising for the host whom Jesus is addressing, for it was precisely such people whom a good Pharisee would consider not only unworthy but also religiously unclean. Thus Jesus is rejecting both social and religious convention. In today's vocabulary, one could say that Jesus is telling his host to invite not the worthy, nor even the "worthy poor," but the unworthy, irreligious, sinful poor.

As in the earlier advice to the other guests, in this case too the point of reference is eschatological. The reason not to invite those who are worthy is that they will probably repay you, and in that case all you have achieved is some social interchange. The reason to invite the poor, the crippled, the lame, and the blind is precisely that they cannot repay you, and you can expect payment only at the final day, "at the resurrection of the righteous." In Spanish-speaking lands it is customary, when someone does you a great and unmerited favor, and particularly when a beggar receives alms, to say, "Dios se lo pague" (may God repay you). The implication is that the favor received is unpayable, and therefore much more meritorious. Here again one hears echoes of Proverbs 19:17: "Whoever is kind to the poor lends to the LORD, and will be repaid in full."

Finally, Jesus addresses another commensal, who (perhaps hoping to defuse the situation) has spoken a religious truism, "Blessed is anyone who will eat bread in the kingdom of God!" He tells a parable about a great dinner that the original invitees refused to attend. They all had their excuses, some lamer than the others. This would be a grievous insult to the host—people turning down his invitation as if he were unworthy of them. But this particular host, sure of the value of his dinner, sends his servant out to invite precisely the supposedly unworthy. Furthermore, when these are not enough, he sends his servant out again, "into the roads and lanes," to "compel" people to come in. The image of compelling people to attend the banquet is both realistic and significant. In a society of profound social distinctions, the "unworthy" would not dream of attending a feast given by the rich and honorable. One can imagine the picture of a peon in a large hacienda being invited to sit at the table with the owner. He will be reluctant and will stay away. Or invite an immigrant maid serving a wealthy employer to sit at the table with the family. She will probably feel awkward and reluctant to accept the invitation. After all, the table is not supposed to be for her. It will take persuasion, and probably even some pressure, to get people to accept such an unexpected invitation. They will have to be "compelled." Likewise, in the parable, Jesus is referring to people who do not expect to be invited. They feel that they do not deserve the invitation, and need to be compelled to enter.

The point of the parable is the sharp contrast between the "worthy" invitees who found something more important or more interesting to do than attending the feast, and the "unworthy" ones, who would be so surprised at such an invitation that they would have to be compelled to enter. Within the context of its clearly eschatological reference, the parable is overpowering: the good religious folk who found something more interesting to do than planning to attend the feast will be left out, and the questionable and despised ones who did not even expect to be invited will be pushed into the banquet hall.

The eschatological references of the three speeches of Jesus at this dinner—to the guests, to the host, and finally, through a particular guest, to the entire assembly—should not detract from their applicability to everyday life. At a certain level, Jesus is declaring that it is not the religious and respected folk who will be the guests of honor at the final banquet. But he is also establishing the connection between the eschaton and the present. To be exalted in the end, one has to take the most humble places now. To be repaid in the end, one has to give now without expecting to be repaid. To be invited to the banquet one has to accept the invitation that is now given. Those who give excuses will be left out of the banquet hall. Those who serve only those who can repay them have already received their reward. Those who seek honor as if they deserved it will be humbled. The present has eschatological significance.

In interpreting this passage, we should not forget that for its first readers (as for Christians through the ages) the central act of worship was a meal. At Communion, even though we prepare the table and invite people to participate, Jesus takes over. He is the host, and we are his guests. All too often, however, Christians have claimed control of the Table as if it were ours, and not his. We decide whose belief is sufficiently orthodox to share Communion with us, who is sufficiently good and pure, who belongs to the right church. Rather than following Jesus' instructions, we seek the places of most honor, sometimes signaling this with actions and vestments that make clear who is in charge. Rather than inviting those who seem most unworthy and cannot repay us, we invite the worthy, those who support the church, people like us at whose tables we might well sit later in the week. Rather than going out and compelling people to enter, we shut the doors in various ways. Yet Jesus takes over, just as he did at the home of the Pharisee, and turns our unworthy meal into a sign, a promise, and a foretaste of the final heavenly banquet.

### 14:25–35 *The Cost of Discipleship*

Luke does not tell us how the dinner ended. He simply places Jesus back among "the crowds." It is to them rather than to the Pharisees and the lawyers that, in a final embodiment of what he was saying at the home of the Pharisee, he spells out the meaning of true discipleship. Following the parallelism between chapters 13 and 14, he warns those who would follow him of the cost of discipleship. In chapter 13 he lamented over Jerusalem, over the failure of the people of God to acknowledge and follow the will of God. Now he turns to the crowds around him. It is not only Jerusalem and all it represents that should take heed of the danger of disobedience; it is also this entire crowd that travels with him. If Jerusalem must be disabused of the notion that it will be easy to be the people of God, now this crowd of followers is also disabused of the notion that it will be easy to be a disciple of Jesus.

Discipleship requires radical obedience. Love of family must not stand in the way. In verse 26 to "hate" the family does not mean to have evil sentiments for them, but rather to forsake them for the sake of the kingdom. A disciple of Jesus will not use supposed family responsibilities to avoid obedience. And this is then paralleled by the saying about carrying the cross. Taken in context, this is not just a call to sacrifice, as we often think. The cross is an instrument of legal punishment and torture. So to take up the cross is parallel to "hating" the family. A disciple of Jesus must be ready to carry the burden not only of tensions in the family, but even of civil disobedience to the point of legal punishment. This was often the experience of Luke's first readers. By the time he wrote, it was clear that things would not be easy within the Roman Empire. This is still the experience of countless Christians throughout the world.

Pointing to this idea, Jesus uses two brief parables about counting the cost. One does not begin to build a tower without considering what it will take to finish it. And a

> The cross is laid on every Christian. It begins with the call to abandon the attachments of this world. It is that dying of the old man which is the result of the encounter with Christ. As we embark upon discipleship we surrender ourselves to Christ in union with His death—we give over our lives to death. Since this happens at the beginning of the Christian life, the cross can never be merely a tragic ending to an otherwise happy religious life. When Christ calls a man, He bids him come and die.
>
> —Dietrich Bonhoeffer
>
> *Cost of Discipleship*, 73.

king does not go to war without considering how strong the opposition is and how he will attain victory. Likewise, one should not
become a follower of Jesus without considering the cost, the opposition, and the final outcome. (What does this say about our common
practice of inviting people to raise their hand, or to come to the altar,
to "accept Jesus," with little or no warning about the actual cost of
such a decision?)

Verse 34, whose parallels in Matthew and Mark appear in different contexts, makes clear that a lukewarm disciple is useless,
like insipid salt. Even more, it is harmful, for if it were placed in the
manure pile it would result in damage to the crops. This saying also
serves to close the chapter with a word that reminds us once again of
the banquet that opened the chapter.

### 15:1–32 *The Lost, the Found, and the Never Lost*

### 15:1–7 *The Lost Sheep*

We now come to three parables that are often used in evangelism to
address those who are "lost": the lost sheep, the lost coin, and the
lost prodigal son. Yet in proposing
them Jesus is not primarily addressing the "lost," but rather the never
lost. Verses 1–3 make this clear.
"Tax collectors and sinners" were
coming to listen to Jesus. (Note
the connection between this attitude of listening and the last words
of the previous chapter: "Let anyone with ears to hear listen!") The
response of the pure religious folk
who are admired for their piety and
their theology ("the Pharisees and
the scribes") is to grumble because
Jesus welcomes these sinners and
eats with them. Note the stark contrast in verses 1–2 between "the tax

> The poor man's sins are
>     glaring;
> In the face of ghostly warning
> He is caught in the fact
> Of an overt act:
> Buying greens on Sunday
>     Morning.
>
> The rich man's sins are hidden
> In the pomp of wealth and
>     station;
> And escape the sight
> Of the children of light,
> Who are wise in their
>     generation.
>                   —Lord Byron
>
> In Helen Gardner, ed., *The New Oxford
> Book of English Verse, 1250–1950* (New
> York: Oxford University, 1972), 562.

collectors and sinners" and "the Pharisees and the scribes." Note also that the reference to eating connects this section with chapter 14, most of which was devoted to the matter of eating, whom to invite to dinners, and how to behave at such dinners. According to verse 3, it is to "them"—the Pharisees and the scribes, the never lost—that Jesus addresses the three parables in chapter 15. All three are popular in Christian tradition and art, and are often found in church windows.

The first parable is about a shepherd who loses one of his hundred sheep, and about his efforts to find that one lost sheep. Traditionally, we read it as an illustration of God's extraordinary love for the lost, and that is a good and proper reading. What we miss, however, is that the parable speaks also about the other ninety-nine sheep that were never lost. Note that the shepherd leaves them "in the wilderness" (literally, "in the desert") and goes after the lost one. This would be a harsh word for those among the audience who were complaining that Jesus was eating with sinners. According to the parable, the shepherd is willing to abandon the faithful ninety-nine sheep in the desert while seeking for the lost one. The Pharisees and scribes who complained that Jesus was eating with sinners would get the point: they are the ninety-nine sheep that were never lost, but that precisely for that reason would be left in the wilderness while the loving shepherd went after the lost one. To make the point even sharper, Jesus closes the parable with the declaration that "there will be more joy in heaven over one sinner who repents than over ninety-nine righteous persons who need no repentance." In other words, there is more joy in heaven for one of

> Yet was it wise to leave the ninety-nine and wander away searching for the one? ... Does the lost individual matter or are "the people" alone important? Indeed, it is the shepherd's willingness to go after the one that gives the ninety-nine their real security. If the one is sacrificed in the name of the larger group, then each individual in the group is insecure, knowing that he or she is of little value. If lost, he or she will be left to die. When the shepherd pays a high price to find the one, he thereby offers the profoundest security to the many.
>
> —Kenneth E. Bailey
>
> *The Cross & the Prodigal: Luke 15 through the Eyes of Middle Eastern Peasants* (Downers Grove, IL: InterVarsity Press, 2005), 31.

these sinners with whom I am eating who repents than there is for the lot of you, who claim never to have been lost!

Quite often in our Christian interpretations of this parable we miss (or we suppress) that all-important point: Jesus is speaking to the supposedly never lost about God's preferential attention to the lost! Most of our church windows depicting this parable have the loving shepherd in the foreground, often carrying the lost sheep. The other ninety-nine seldom appear, or if they do they are just part of the landscape. It would be helpful to imagine a different composition of the same picture, with the ninety-nine abandoned in the wilderness, and the shepherd walking away in search of the lost one.

Part of the beauty of the parables is that they attain new and different meanings according to the role in which we place ourselves within them. In this particular parable, we tend to place ourselves in the role of the lost sheep. As the hymn says, we once were lost, and now are found. There is great reason to rejoice in this, and we do well to remember that we all have gone astray, like lost sheep. But suppose we put ourselves in the place of the ninety-nine that were not lost. How would we feel about being left in the desert while the shepherd goes after the straying one? In that case, what would we hear Jesus telling us? Are we being warned about our own supposedly superior piety and behavior, about our reluctance to see others whom we consider unworthy be given at least as much importance as we are—and perhaps even more? Or, remembering that we are not only sheep, but also shepherds, what does the parable mean if we read it as shepherds who are to be imitators and followers of the Good Shepherd? In this case, what would the parable mean for our church programs, for our budgets, for our committees and commissions?

> Ordinarily in Christian proclamation, the woman is just the filling in the "sandwich" between the all-too-familiar story of the lost sheep and the long, interesting parable of the lost ("prodigal") son. Between the man and his sheep and the man and his son, the woman and her coin are metaphorically "swept under the rug."
>
> —Linda Maloney
>
> "'Swept under the Rug': Feminist Homiletical Reflections on the Parable of the Lost Coin (Lk. 15:8–9)," in *The Lost Coin: Parables of Women, Work and Wisdom*, ed. Mary Ann Beavis, Biblical Seminar 36 (London: Sheffield Academic Press, 2002), 34.

How much of all this, now devoted to the ninety-nine (us), should be redirected to the ones who are lost?

### 15:8–10  *The Lost Coin*

Once again Luke parallels a story about a man with one about a woman. While in the parable of the Sheep one's immediate reaction would be to imagine God as the shepherd who seeks for the lost sheep, in the parable of the Lost Coin one should equally see God as the woman seeking the lost coin. This second parable makes little or no reference to the nine coins that were not lost. There is also no reference to the ones who do not need repentance. Now the focus is on the lost, on the joy at its being found, and particularly on the actions of the woman seeking the lost coin. Thus, while the parable about the sheep would immediately lead people to think in terms of their role as sheep (either lost or not), this other parable focuses on God and God's attitude toward the lost. While it is possible to speak of sheep in terms of attitudes, and thus to blame the lost for having strayed, the same is not possible in the case of a lost coin. Thus the parable of the Lost Coin is more "theological" in the strict sense of the word, for it forces the reader to think about the nature and actions of this God who, like a woman, seeks a lost coin. She insists on her search, lighting a lamp, sweeping, searching carefully. Reading this parable in connection with the previous one, the focus shifts from the lost, the found, and the never lost, to the searching God—the shepherd searching after the one lost sheep, or the woman searching after the one lost coin. The reason why the "holier than thou" attitude of the scribes and Pharisees (and of so many of us today) is unacceptable is not just that it is in bad taste, or that religious people ought to be more forgiving, or that such attitudes scare people away. All those may be true; but the real reason for seeking and loving the lost is that ours is a seeking and loving God.

> Much as the ancient housekeeper of the New Testament, while possessing nine coins, searched for the tenth which she had lost, so we too, while acknowledging the dominance of male language in scripture, have lit a lamp, swept the house, and sought diligently for that which was lost.
>
> —Phyllis Trible
>
> *God and the Rhetoric of Sexuality*, Overtures to Biblical Theology (Philadelphia: Fortress, 1978), 200.

### 15:11–32 *The Lost Son*

Now we come to one of the best-loved parables of Jesus. It is loved both for the manner in which it expresses the love of God as that of a father waiting for a lost son, and for its subtle psychological and religious nuances. As in the previous two parables, Jesus is addressing the religious and pious folk—the scribes and the Pharisees. Since most of the space in the narrative is occupied by the story of the younger son, the traditional title of the parable is the Prodigal Son. But the father and the older son are also important to the story.

Interpreters have correctly pointed out that the younger son is practically telling his father, "I can't wait for you to die." His father's very existence is an obstacle to his goals. In this regard, if we consider the parable to refer to God as father and to us as God's children, this young man's attitude is similar to those fools who according to Psalm 14:1 claim that there is no God so that they can do as they please. This younger son wished for his father not to exist, so he could do as he pleased with his father's goods.

In this context, the parable has a dimension of stewardship, and accurately describes those of us who wish to manage our goods, our time, and our entire lives as if they were really and solely ours—as though they did not belong to the God whose existence we deny, if not in so many words, certainly in our management of life and its bounties. As in Psalm 14, there is today much practical atheism—practical either in the sense that, while claiming to believe, we act as if there were no God, or in the sense that people, perhaps even unconsciously, decide to be atheists because that will give them greater freedom in all their affairs.

This younger son going "to a distant country" sets an interesting contrast with the many parables of stewardship, where it is the master, or God, who goes to a distant land (see pp. 165–68, "Further Reflections: The Absence of God"). However, he is not as wise a manager as he thought he would be—nor are we.

The first surprise of the parable is the father's response to his repentant son. He is "filled with compassion," and receives him with great honor. This is the point that is most often stressed when this parable is used in the context of evangelism. Indeed, for many this is the end of the story.

But then the older son, who has hardly been mentioned before, now refuses to join his father's feast. He refuses to enter, not because he is a bad son, but because he considers himself too good a son! He is angry because he has been "working like a slave" for his father. He has been ever obedient. Yet his father celebrates the prodigal's return with a largesse that the elder son has never experienced.

In the context of this set of three parables, one may well imagine that the scribes and the Pharisees who had been criticizing Jesus for eating with sinners would understand that Jesus was depicting them as the elder son. They have always remained faithful and obedient to God. They even work for God as slaves. One would expect that God would show some gratitude! But the God whom Jesus proclaims is quite different. This is a God who, like a shepherd who loses a sheep, or a woman who loses a coin, is thrilled when the lost are found!

Here again, how we interpret the parable and apply it to ourselves depends on what we assume to be our role in the cast of characters. Most commonly, we see ourselves as the prodigal who has been welcomed by the ever-loving father. Obviously, such an interpretation of the parable must never be left entirely behind, for once we forget that we are forgiven prodigals we risk assuming the attitude of the elder son. Yet at the same time we remember that God has forgiven us merely out of lovingkindness, we must also confess and accept the possibility of our being in the position of the elder son. We are members of the church. Many of us are leaders in the church. We study the Bible; we preach, inviting others to return as the prodigal returned; we write books; we serve in programs for the well-being of those around us; we constantly seek to obey God's will. It is others who must return, others who must acknowledge their sin and accept God's loving forgiveness. When we hear this parable, no matter how conscious we are that we are forgiven prodigals, we hear it from a position similar to that of the elder son—or of the scribes and Pharisees. Like them, we risk turning our obedience and faithfulness into something derived not from love but from obligation, into a sort of slavery in which there is no delight. Even worse, when that happens we present to the world not the loving father of the prodigal, but the relentless and stingy taskmaster that the elder son thought his father to be. We may constantly invite others to come to the arms of the loving Father; but the very tone of our lives and of our invitation to "sinners" may present to the world not the loving father whom the prodigal discovered, but the harsh, begrudging father that the elder son thought he had.

It is important to note that all three parables in Luke 15 end on a note of joy. There is joy in heaven; the angels rejoice; there is a banquet in celebration of the return of the prodigal. If the ninety-nine sheep resent being left in the wilderness while the shepherd looks for the one that has strayed, they will be unable to rejoice when it is found. If the elder son resents the ease with which his father forgives his errant brother, he shuts himself out of the father's banquet and, even more, out of the experience of his father's gracious love. If the scribes and Pharisees see Jesus' practice of eating with tax collectors and sinners as a lack of religious purity, they will miss the joy of love. If Christians pretend to preach the gospel while seeing ourselves as faithful children of God and looking at others as prodigal sons, we too will miss the joy of the gospel. And a gospel without joy is no gospel; it is not good news!

### 16:1–13 *A Commendable Scoundrel*

This is a parable we should all read and consider before attempting to interpret any of the other parables of Jesus. It certainly undoes the common notion that the parables are nice stories about commendable people whom we ought to imitate. There is no doubt that many of the parables speak of such people: a sower, a loving father, a loving shepherd, a woman baking bread, a woman keeping house and looking for a lost coin. Then there are others that speak of people who are not so admirable, for instance, a fool who seeks to ensure his future by building bigger barns, or a man who, having been forgiven a huge sum owed to the king, is not willing to forgive a paltry debt that another owes him. But this parable speaks of a man who is undoubtedly a scoundrel; and yet it praises him and his wisdom! It is not uncommon to see on our church windows portrayals of a father receiving a son who had strayed, or of a sower spreading seed, or of a Samaritan helping the man by the roadside. But I have never seen a window depicting a man with a sly look, saying to another,

"Falsify the bill, make it less than it really is." Yet it is precisely this sort of man that the parable turns into an example!

This leads us first of all to the conclusion that we cannot take the parables of Jesus as mere moral teachings and examples. We clearly understand that if any of us are responsible for the administration of another's property, we are not to cheat the owner. We understand that we are not to steal from our employer. Yet this is precisely what the man in this parable does. Just as we cannot take this parable as justification for an employee's dishonesty, we should not be able to take the parable of the Talents as justification for wise investments in the stock market. That we take one and not the other as an example to imitate is a clear indication of where we stand as interpreters of Scripture.

The parable itself is fairly straightforward. A steward has not actually been fired yet, but is certainly on notice. In this regard, he is in a situation similar to all human beings, who for the present have a life, goods, talents, relations, and time to manage, but are also on notice of our firing. We do not know when we will be dismissed from our temporary management of all these things, but dismissed we will be. The present order is not permanent, and our authority over life, goods, and all the rest is only temporary. We may well imagine that, until given notice, the manager felt quite secure in his position. So do we, until we are reminded that our management too is provisional—that what we have is not really ours, and will be taken away from us.

The manager asks himself, "What will I do?" This is the same question that the rich fool asks himself in 12:17. Significantly, in both cases it is a matter of possessions and material resources. The rich fool has more than he can use, and decides to build bigger barns. He is a fool, not because he decides to build barns, but because he thinks that he can assure his continued well-being by doing so. The manager in chapter 16 asks the same question, not because he has too much, but because he suddenly

> The parable of the unjust steward is full of eschatological significance. The whole context of that story is the consciousness of the End—which implies accountability.
> —Douglas John Hall
>
> *The Steward: A Biblical Symbol Come of Age* (Grand Rapids: Eerdmans, 1990), 48.

realizes that what he has will be taken away from him. Thus there is a contrast between the two men. The fool thinks that he really owns what he has, and that he even owns his life. The manager knows that he does not really own what he has. The fool takes for granted that the present order will continue indefinitely. The manager realizes that there is a new order about to be established.

The manager could well follow the path of the fool. He could have said, "Since my stewardship is coming to an end, I will enjoy it while I have it." This is the attitude of many today, as it has been throughout history. People say: "Life is short. You can't take it with you." In both statements, they are right. We are all like the manager of the parable. But then they add, "Therefore, enjoy it while you have it." When such is our attitude, we are no wiser than the rich fool in chapter 12.

Then, the manager could have taken exactly the opposite tack. He could have said, "Since these things belong to the passing order, I will no longer pay any attention to them. I will not be here to enjoy them forever; therefore I might as well ignore them and think about something else." This is the attitude of those who claim that, since material things are passing, one should ignore them and concentrate on the spiritual, which is permanent. In Christian tradition, this has been the attitude of gnostics who have seen the world and material reality as an impediment on the way to eternity. In a way, it is also the attitude of many Christians who insist that what is important is the future spiritual life, and that what we do with the present—and particularly its opportunities for service—is not important.

But the manager in the parable does not follow either of these two paths. What he does is use the authority he still has in the present order to feather his bed for the future order. When his firing becomes effective, he will be rewarded in the new order for the use he made of what he had in the old order.

This is a parable of stewardship. Whatever we now have is no more than a temporary management. We have all been given notice. And the parable invites us to be like this wise steward, who was ready even to cheat the present order for the sake of the new order he knew was coming. Jesus concludes the parable with a moral that reminds us once again of Proverbs 19:17: "Whoever is kind to the poor lends to the Lord, and will be repaid in full."

Although perhaps shocking, the parable is for the most part straightforward. There are, however, two points of difficult interpretation that should at least be mentioned. The first is in verse 8, and the second in verses 9 and 11. In verse 8 it is not clear whether the "master" who praised the manager is the man in the parable or Jesus himself. In saying "his master," the NRSV has decided for the first of these options; but the Greek text is ambiguous on this point. At any rate, no matter whether the one who praises the manager is his master or Jesus, there is no doubt that in telling the story, and then in the explanation that follows, Jesus is using this dishonest steward as an example of the shrewdness he is proposing. Then, in verses 9 and 11, Jesus seems to connect dishonesty—or more literally, injustice— with wealth. Does he mean, as later some of the great theologians of the church claimed, that all wealth is the product of injustice? Or does he mean simply that this manager's wealth is dishonest because he is using it for his own purposes, and falsifying records? It is impossible to provide a definitive answer on the basis of the text itself.

### 16:14–31 *Listen to the Law and the Prophets*

The rest of chapter 16 is best read together, for otherwise verses 14–18 seem to be little more than a digression or a series of disconnected and cryptic comments. But those verses provide an introduction and a larger context for the well-known parable of the Rich Man and Lazarus (16:19–31).

This section begins by connecting what follows with the preceding. This connection is in the response of the Pharisees. They "heard all this"—meaning what Jesus has just said—and they ridiculed Jesus. (There seems to be an inconsistency between 16:1 and 16:14, for in v. 1 we are told that Jesus was speaking "to the disciples," and now v. 14 begins by declaring that the Pharisees heard what he was saying. Probably the "all this" refers not only to the parable of the Dishonest Manager, but also to the three parables in chap. 15. This would make it easier to see the connection between the preceding and what follows.)

According to Luke, there is a connection between the Pharisees' love of money and their ridiculing Jesus. This is a significant insight. Theological positions and religious opinions are not entirely disconnected from economic interests and agendas. The Pharisees consider themselves better than the "sinners and tax collectors" in part because they think they belong to a "better" social class. And the reason why they ridicule Jesus' declaration that no one can serve both God and wealth is that they themselves love wealth. Note the connection between verse 14, which affirms that the Pharisees were "lovers of money," and verse 15, where Jesus tells the Pharisees that "God knows your hearts." The Pharisees seek to justify themselves "in the sight of others" by claiming that what Jesus teaches is ridiculous. Jesus tells them that God sees things differently than do humans.

Jesus' general response to the ridicule of the Pharisees, both directly beginning in verse 15, and by means of a parable beginning in verse 19, is to insist that what he is teaching is in full agreement with the Law and the Prophets. This theme of obedience to the Scriptures of Israel connects the parable of the Rich Man and Lazarus with its introduction in verses 14–18, which otherwise seems a series of disconnected commentaries having little to do either with the preceding discussion or with the parable that follows. Thus it would be wrong to interpret verse 16 in the sense that after John the Law and the Prophets are no longer valid. It is true that now "the kingdom of God is proclaimed"; but it is also true that the Law is still there. Not one of the little hooks by which various letters in the Hebrew alphabet are distinguished will pass away. It is precisely this continued authority of the Law and the Prophets that Jesus will illustrate in the parable of the Rich Man and Lazarus. The apparently disconnected commentary on divorce in verse 18 is a further example of the authority of the Law. Now, however, "the kingdom of God is proclaimed" in accordance with the Law and the Prophets. The phrase that the NRSV translates as "everyone tries to enter it by force" can also be translated (as the NRSV itself suggests in a footnote) as "everyone is strongly urged to enter it." This latter option may be preferable, for it connects what Jesus is now saying with the earlier parable in 14:15–24, where the servants are instructed to "compel people to come in." In the context of chapter 16, this would seem to mean that the Law and the Prophets compel people to accept the preaching of the kingdom and enter into it.

In verse 19, without further introduction, Jesus begins the story of the rich man and Lazarus. Traditionally, the rich man has been called "Dives" or "Divas." The Vulgate says, "homo quidam erat dives" (which simply means that a certain man was rich), and out of this the supposed name of the man has evolved. But the parable does not give the man's name. This is significant as one more of Luke's many examples of the great reversal. Normally, it is important people who have a name. They have recognition. They are somebody. But in the parable the rich and apparently important man has no name, and the poor and insignificant man does. From the very beginning of the parable, Jesus is illustrating what he has just said, that "what is prized by human beings is an abomination in the sight of God." The very name "Lazarus" means "God helps"; and the parable will show that this is indeed the case.

Since this is the only parable of Jesus in which a character is given a name, and since this name is the same as the brother of Mary and Martha whom Jesus raised from the dead (John 11:1–45), popular piety has linked the two. Thus images of "St. Lazarus" usually depict not the brother of a woman who at least had a home and could offer hospitality to Jesus, but a beggar dressed in rags and surrounded by dogs. At a certain level, such confusion is wrong. But at another level it illustrates part of the point Jesus is making: the despised man, whom people might consider accursed, is blessed, and even deserves the title of "Saint."

The parable begins by depicting the rich man and his life, and then contrasting it with Lazarus and his condition. The rich man is dressed "in purple and fine linen." Roman law codified who had the right to wear purple, at that time a very expensive dye. Thus the original hearers and readers of this parable would understand that the rich man was sufficiently respected to merit this particular honor, and also indirectly that he had achieved this with the approval of Roman authorities. He is an important, respected person—which immediately reminds us of what Jesus has just said in verse 14, that "what is prized by human beings is an abomination in the sight of

God." He is so rich that he has sumptuous feasts, not only on special occasions, but every day.

Then there is Lazarus. Between him and the rich man there is a gate. The gate is another sign of the man's wealth and importance—he lives in what today would be a luxury gated community. He has the means to keep out undesirables such as Lazarus, who is not allowed into the inner circle beyond the gate. Lazarus is not only starving, but also apparently unclean and accursed by God, being licked by unclean dogs. From the point of view of human prestige, wealth, and even religiosity, the rich man is far above Lazarus.

Then they both die, and things are completely reversed, even in the way Jesus refers to their death. Lazarus died and was "carried away by the angels to be with Abraham," while the rich man simply "died and was buried." However, the great contrast is in the final outcome of each one's life: the rich man ends up in Hades, while Lazarus is carried to Abraham's bosom. Even after such a reversal of fortunes, the rich man considers himself more important than Lazarus, whom he wants sent, first to him, and then to his brothers.

(At this point, Abraham says that "a great chasm has been fixed, so that those who might want to pass from here to you cannot do so, and no one can cross from there to us." These words have often been used as proof that one's fate is finally decided in the present life, and that after death there is no hope of redemption. While that may indeed be the case, these words appear in the course of a parable on a totally different subject, and so are not a strong foundation for such a claim.)

The most common interpretation of this parable deals with the responsibilities of the rich vis-à-vis the poor. Thus throughout the Middle Ages this parable became standard fare in sermons about the need to give alms. Sometimes it was said that all that the rich man would have had to do to be saved was to feed Lazarus, or to give him alms so he could buy food. Quite often the image of St. Lazarus covered in rags and surrounded by dogs was placed above or next to the poor box, where alms were collected for the poor. As to the poor, the parable was used as a means for them to be consoled, knowing that they would be rewarded in heaven.

Such an interpretation, while perhaps helpful, misses the point of the great reversal that is so central to the Gospel of Luke. The parable is not only about a rich man who ignored the poor, but also about the rich man ending up in poverty, and the poor man in abundance. The man who had daily feasts now does not even have water to cool his tongue. The one whose sores had been licked by unclean dogs, and who therefore was not even worthy to be counted among the faithful children of Abraham, is now in the bosom of Abraham. Once again we hear echoes of Mary's song: "He has brought down the powerful from their thrones, and lifted up the lowly; he has filled the hungry with good things, and sent the rich away empty" (1:52–53).

However, there is more to the parable than the great reversal. In verses 29–31 the parable is connected with the theme that Jesus was discussing just before it: the authority and guidance of the Law and the Prophets (vv. 16–17). This is what binds the parable with its introduction. Jesus is telling his hearers, who are "lovers of money," that they do not need special signs or wonders to know what they are to do. They have the Law and the Prophets, which are firmer and more durable than both heaven or earth (v. 17). He is also telling them that their love of money prevents them from truly listening to the Law and the Prophets. At the end of the parable, when the rich man wants Lazarus to be sent to warn his brothers, Abraham tells him that they already have "Moses and the prophets," and that this should be enough for them. When the man insists that they would repent and do right "if someone goes to them from the dead," Abraham replies that this is not so. If they are not willing to obey Moses and the prophets, they will still remain disobedient "even if someone rises from the dead." In other words, there is no miracle capable

> So there will be no one appearing from the dead, no voice from heaven will sound, nor will there be any miracle in the clouds. *None* of this will come to you—you who are one of the rich man's five brothers. We have only the Word, the Word made flesh and crucified, that namelessly quiet Word which came to us in one who was as poor and despised as his brother Lazarus. For he really wanted to be his brother.
>
> —Helmut Thielicke
>
> *Waiting Father,* 50.

of leading to faith and obedience when one has vested interests and values that one places above obedience to God, such as "the love of money" of the Pharisees whom Jesus is addressing. The rich man's brothers would not obey, even though they had Moses and the prophets. One coming back from the dead would still not convince them. Love of money does that, perverting one's vision so that even the greatest of miracles can be explained away.

Luke's early readers would immediately realize (as we do) that the one saying this was one who would indeed return from the dead. Many treatises have been written trying to prove Jesus' resurrection. The premise behind such books is that if we can prove that Jesus did rise again people would have no option but to believe. But that is not the case. The man's brothers would not believe. The main obstacle to faith is not lack of proof; it is an excess of other interests and investments—of time, money, dreams, and so on.

Furthermore, all would seem to indicate that the rich man and his brothers thought they had things squared away with God. He wore purple. One may well imagine that his daily feasts were attended by religious, political, and economic leaders. To any observer, it would have seemed that the rich man was blessed by God, and Lazarus shunned or even damned. Certainly, abundance of goods, power, and prestige must be a blessing resulting from one's righteousness and religious observance. And one who lives among unclean dogs is proof of the other side of the coin: he must be accursed because he is not as religious as the people at the feasts.

But the truth is exactly the opposite: the rich man is accursed, and Lazarus is blessed. So much for the "gospel of prosperity" that many find so attractive today! It may be as weak a reed as the rich man's trust in his riches.

## 17:1–19:27

### Preparing for Discipleship

The journey to Jerusalem continues. In this last phase of the journey, Luke centers his attention on the teachings of Jesus to his disciples, particularly on his teachings about the kingdom of God. The controversies with the religious leadership will continue, even though for a time they do not occupy the center of the story. Eventually, these controversies will lead to the cross. But for the time being, in the last stages of Jesus' journey to Jerusalem, he is preparing his disciples for the continuous, lifelong trek after him, carrying their crosses and knowing that the kingdom of God is at hand.

## 17:1–10 *The Nature of Faith*

Interpreters have often been puzzled by the odd collection of four apparently unconnected themes in these verses: being a stumbling block to others, forgiving, having the faith of a mustard seed, and being faithful servants. Where there are parallels to these themes or sayings in the other Gospels, they do not appear jointly, as they do in Luke. Leaving aside matters of sources, literary composition, and the rest, one may well assume that Luke has joined these four sayings for a reason, and that they should therefore be considered jointly. All four sayings are addressed to "his disciples," in contrast to the previous section, which was addressed to the Pharisees who mocked Jesus and his teachings.

The first saying (vv. 1–2) places the rest in their proper setting. It is a warning to the disciples. They have just heard Jesus rebuke the Pharisees. But the disciples are not like the rich man, who loved his possessions and his privilege above the Law and the Prophets. They have left all behind to follow Jesus. They have every reason to be smug! In that context, Jesus' words sound an ominous note of warning, and the entire passage should be read as part of that note.

The warning is that, even though people will continue to stumble, any who become a stumbling block for others bear a responsibility even greater than the ones who stumble. Forgiveness will come to the foreground in the next saying. But this does not mean that God will simply overlook the sin of those who lead others into sin, who cause them to stumble. Their fate will be worse than being thrown into the sea with a millstone tied to their neck. At this point, it may help to remember that to the mind of the time the sea was a symbol of chaos and of evil. Being thrown into the sea is then more than just drowning; it is also being cast into the region where evil reigns.

The transition into the next, apparently unconnected saying (vv. 3–4) is, "Be on your guard!" On the basis of the preceding, it is a warning that the disciples are in danger of becoming stumbling blocks to "these little ones." And, surprisingly, this has to do with forgiveness! One would expect that the disciples could make others stumble by their poor moral behavior, by their lack of faith, by their own apostasy. But the possible stumbling block on which Jesus focuses is unwillingness to forgive.

While these words on forgiveness find their parallel in Matthew 18:21–22, the emphasis here is slightly different. Matthew speaks of "seventy times seven"; Luke, of "seven times a day." What Luke is stressing in this entire section is the continued life of discipleship. Forgiveness must then be not only unlimited, but also daily and repeated. It is a continued practice, rather than just a magnanimous action.

As one looks at the history of Christianity, and more so at its present situation, it is clear that reluctance to forgive has been and continues to be one of the most common, if not the most common, stumbling block on the way of others to faith. Too often we Christians are so self-assured in our righteousness, in our orthodox beliefs, and in our certainty on what it is that God wills that we convince ourselves that we have reason not to forgive those whose beliefs, lifestyle, or understanding of the will of God differ from ours. We know that this is uncharitable; yet we justify it by our adherence to the true faith, or to the straight and narrow. In so doing, we may well be precisely the sort of stumbling block that Jesus is talking about in this passage. And we would do well to heed the words about the millstone!

From the obligation to forgive we move in verses 5–6 to the oft-quoted saying about "faith like a mustard seed." Here the transition from one subject to the next is provided by the disciples' request, "Increase our faith!" Read in the context of the foregoing, this points to the wise recognition that what Jesus is demanding of them is impossible. Forgiving even our worst offenders seven times a day? That would take much faith indeed! Hence the disciples' request.

Jesus' response about "faith like a mustard seed" is capable of several different, and even contradictory, interpretations. First, what the Greek says is not "the size of a mustard seed," but simply "like a mustard seed." If the point of the saying is the size of the seed—and by implication, of faith—then Jesus is saying that their problem is the smallness of their faith. This is the most common interpretation, and is based on other passages where the point about a mustard seed is indeed its size, particularly Matthew 13:32 and Mark 4:31, where Jesus refers to the small mustard seed as a sign of the kingdom. But if one understands "like a mustard seed" as meaning faith of the same sort as the mustard seed has, then the meaning of the saying is different. The "faith" of the mustard seed is the certainty of its goal. It "knows" it is to become a mustard plant. And it does. In that case, the faith that is required of the disciples is one that makes them trust in the final outcome of their discipleship and in the coming of the kingdom, and to trust in such a way that they will be able to forgive those who do not agree with them or who offend them.

Then there is the matter of the mulberry tree. The grammar of the saying itself is confusing. In Greek one expresses a hypothetical saying ("if") in two different ways, depending on whether the statement is according to fact or contrary to fact. In this particular saying, however, the first part of the saying, about having faith, is stated as according to fact (the disciples do have faith like a mustard seed), while the second part, about the mulberry tree, is stated as contrary to fact (the disciples cannot order a tree to move about).

The most common interpretation is that Jesus is promising the disciples that faith will allow them to do the seemingly impossible. It is on this basis that Christian healers often tell people that if they believe, they can be healed—which is tantamount to saying that if they remain ill it is their own fault for not having enough faith. But there is another possible interpretation. What would be the point of ordering a tree to uproot itself and to be planted in the sea? A mulberry tree belongs on land, not in the sea. The very notion is ludicrous and, if accomplished, would amount to no more than a spectacular feat of magic. Thus one interpretation (unusual, but plausible) is that if the disciples had more faith they would not know what to do with it and would misuse it. The proper use of the power of faith is always coupled with obedience, such as that of the mustard seed, which is called to be a mustard plant and will indeed become such a plant.

> God is lord and man is his
> servant. Strictly speaking
> man's relationship to God as
> that of a servant to a master
> certainly excludes the thought
> of a reward, or at least limits it.
> For the servant is his master's
> own property, his slave whose
> body and mind belong to him,
> and who has no special claim
> on a reward.
> —Günther Bornkamm
>
> *Jesus of Nazareth*, 138.

Then, given the context in which the saying appears in Luke, there is still another possible interpretation. Jesus has just commanded to do the impossible: to forgive others seven times, and then to do it all over again the next day. The disciples ask for more faith in order to be able to obey this injunction. Jesus recognizes that what he is asking of his disciples is difficult and requires much faith, even more faith than would be necessary to command a mulberry tree to uproot itself and be planted in the middle of the sea. This last interpretation would then lead into the fourth and last of the sayings in this section, which has to do with the impossibility and yet the need to obey the Master in all things.

The final saying or theme in this string (vv. 7–10) takes the form of a short parable. It begins with what at that time would be a ridiculous proposition, which immediately reminds us of the mulberry in the middle of the sea. The parable begins by focusing on a slave's master. Apparently, this is a fairly small household, in which a single slave is expected first to work in the fields—"plowing or tending sheep"—and then to prepare the master's meal and serve him. In that setting, the slave returning from the fields would not expect the master to feed him. On the contrary, he knows that he must now prepare food for the master and serve him. This is no more than would be expected of the slave, and the master would not even thank him for doing it.

At this point the focus of the parable shifts. The parable began by referring to the master—"who among you would say to your slave"—and now it shifts to the slave: "So you also, when you have done. . . ." The point then is that all that a slave can do for a master is no more than is his due, and that the same is true of the disciples. Going back to the beginning of this series of sayings, this would mean that, even when the disciples have forgiven someone seven times daily, and done this day after day, they have done no more than is expected of them.

Taken together, these four sayings are both an indictment and a word of grace, both law and gospel. They set impossible standards. They show how faulty all human discipleship is. Yet they also free the slave—and the disciples—from the burden of believing that one can do all that is expected, and therefore should somehow earn God's love by means of absolute obedience. One could easily apply to them Luther's saying to the effect that the law is like lightning striking a tree: it kills the tree, and yet it makes its branches point skyward.

> We are accustomed to require an ethic to be practicable. If this is what we want, then we should turn to Aristotle! The ethic of the Gospel is not practicable because it is serious. . . . To take . . . the Will of God seriously, leads to the admission that it is impossible to do it. But the impossibility is no excuse.
>
> —Emil Brunner
>
> *The Mediator: A Study of the Central Doctrine of the Christian Faith*, trans. Olive Wyon (Philadelphia: Westminster, 1967), 419.

In centuries past Jesus' words about "unworthy servants" have played an important role in the debate between Protestants and Catholics regarding the "counsels of perfection," the "works of supererogation," and the "treasury of merits." Theologians during the Middle Ages developed a distinction between what they saw as commandments and what they called "counsels of perfection." The commandments are to be obeyed by all. The counsels are to be followed by those who seek to move beyond mere obedience and on to perfection. Thus the counsel of voluntary poverty is based on Matthew 19:21, where Jesus tells the rich young man who has always obeyed all the commandments, "If you wish to be perfect, go, sell your possessions, and give the money to the poor" (words that do not appear in the parallel passage in Luke 18:18–25). And the counsel of celibacy is based on Paul's words in 1 Corinthians 7:38: "he who marries . . . does well; and he who refrains from marriage will do better." Since following such counsels of perfection is more than is required by the commandments, those who follow them are performing "works of supererogation," and the merit accrued by such works goes into the treasury of merits that the church manages, mostly through the sacrament of penance and the penitential system.

As the debate over works and their merits became heated in the course of the Protestant Reformation, those who rejected the very notion of merit before God and insisted that salvation is by grace alone as a free gift of God had recourse to this parable in Luke: those disciples who have done all that is commanded to them are still no more than unworthy servants. Thus what from one perspective appear to be harsh words, pointing to every disciple's failure if measured by the law, are actually words of grace, pointing to the love of the Master even for these unworthy slaves.

### 17:11–19 *The Healing of Ten Lepers*

Luke tells us that this event happened in "the region between Samaria and Galilee." While the geographical reference is unclear, and has led many interpreters to conclude that what we have here is a sign that Luke was weak in his knowledge of the geography of Palestine, one may simply understand this as meaning that he was in the general area between the two regions, much as people in the United States refer to "the borderlands," meaning a fairly wide strip at the border with Mexico. In any case, the reference is Luke's way of reminding us that Jesus is still on his long journey from Galilee to Jerusalem. It also provides the background for the story itself, in which a Samaritan plays an important role.

The story is fairly straightforward, and its details need not detain us here. The theme of gratitude for God's wondrous and unmerited gifts connects it with the previous parable, about the master owing nothing to the slave. In this case, the Samaritan who returns is grateful for what Jesus has done, while the others seem to take it in stride, almost as if it were their rightful due.

There is, however, another dimension to the story, a dimension that resonates with Luke's theme of the great reversal. The worst part of being a leper was often not the disease itself, but the ostracism it entailed. The law of Israel made this very clear: "Command the Israelites to put out of the camp everyone who is leprous" (Num. 5:2). Furthermore, the lepers themselves were made responsible for the enforcement of such ostracism, announcing their condition to any who might approach them: "The person who has the leprous disease shall wear torn clothes and let the hair of his head be disheveled; and he shall cover his upper lip and cry out, 'Unclean, unclean.' He shall remain unclean as long as he has the disease; he is unclean" (Lev. 13:45–46). To be a leper was not only to suffer a physical illness, but also to be cast out from family and society.

On the other hand, a leper was not without hope. Since various diseases were included under the general heading of leprosy, allowance had to be made for those whose symptoms disappeared. For them, the law provided a detailed procedure, which included an examination by a priest, and then a complex ritual of cleansing (Lev. 14:2–32).

Given such circumstances, the story in Luke has added dimensions. First, one notes that Jesus does not immediately heal the ten lepers. He merely tells them to go and show themselves to the priests, as if they were already healed. Significantly, all ten have enough faith to heed his word even while they are not yet healed. It is along the way to see the priests that they are healed. Upon noticing that they are indeed healed, one returns to thank Jesus, and the other nine continue along their way to healing and to restoration to their communities. We tend to ignore these nine, or to classify them as unbelieving ones; but the text says (or at least implies) that they believed Jesus, and even that they obeyed him by continuing on their way to see the priests.

But the oddball among these ten, upon discovering that he has been healed, postpones his visit to the priests and returns to thank Jesus. In so doing, he is disobeying Jesus (or at least postponing his obedience), who had told him to go before the priests. But even more, by his very act of gratitude he is postponing his restoration to his family and community. In a way, his actions are an application of what Jesus said earlier, about not loving "father and mother, wife and children, brothers and sisters," above him and the new community of the kingdom. (See the commentary on 14:25–33.)

What is most surprising is not just that this one leper returned to Jesus, but also that the one who returned was a Samaritan—as Jesus says, a "foreigner." Presumably the other nine (or at least most of them) were Jews. All ten were outcasts because of their leprosy. This one is doubly outcast, for he is a Samaritan. The one who has healed him, Jesus, is a member of the Jewish community, which despises Samaritans. One could even say that there is a hint that the reason why he was doubly grateful for his healing was that he had a double experience of exclusion, and that he therefore could be doubly surprised by Jesus' act of healing—not only a leper but a Samaritan leper! Thus the great reversal takes a new twist: those who are most marginal and excluded are also able to be most grateful to this Lord who includes them. Those whose experience of community and rejection is most painful may well come to the gospel with an added sense of joy.

When one joins this story with the previous saying about forgiving "seven times daily," their meaning for today's church should be clear: Forgive even those whom you consider absolutely unforgivable—forgive them particularly—for they may well have a fuller understanding of the saving power of the gospel than you do!

### 17:20–37 The Unexpected Kingdom

A number of factors make this one of the most difficult passages to interpret in the entire Gospel of Luke. First, there is no obvious connection between it and the rest of the Gospel narrative. Beginning here and on through 18:30, Luke gives little or no indication as to when or where the events he narrates took place. The setting in 17:20 could not be more vague: "Once." This is followed by "Then" (17:22 and 18:1), and by other similarly vague settings: "He also told this parable" (18:9); "People were bringing even infants to him" (18:15); "A certain ruler asked him" (18:18). It is only in 18:31, after another vague "Then," that we are reminded that Jesus is on his way to Jerusalem, and the journey narrative resumes.

Then there is the matter of the two possible translations of the word *entos* in verse 21. This could mean either "within" or "among." Translated as "within" (as the NIV does) it would seem to mean that the kingdom of God is within each believer, thus turning it into a matter of inner feelings and attitudes, or of a personal relationship with God. While this interpretation is quite common, it presents the difficulty that it is not to his disciples but to the Pharisees that Jesus directs these words. If, on the other hand, we translate "among," there could still be two different meanings. Jesus' saying could mean that the kingdom is in relationships among people. Or this could be a christological statement, meaning that, because Jesus is there among them, the kingdom is present in him and therefore among them.

Then there is a question as to what is the point at issue. In the first part of the narrative (vv. 20–21), the Pharisees ask when (v. 20), and Jesus answers in terms of where (v. 21). Then, beginning in verse 22, Jesus addresses his disciples mostly in terms of when. Yet the disciples' final question in verse 37 is, "Where, Lord?"

The general thrust of the passage is clear and includes a central warning. There have been periods when people continued living their ordinary lives—eating and drinking, marrying and being given in marriage, buying and selling, planting and building (vv. 27–28)—totally oblivious to catastrophic events that were about to take place: the flood and the destruction of Sodom. Significantly, those "days" or times are not named after such people, but after those who saw a different future, a different turn of events—Noah and Lot. Now Jesus is announcing similar circumstances, "the days of the Son of Man" (v. 26). The implication is that, even while people continue living their ordinary lives as if nothing significant were happening, the disciples should see a different future and act as those who know of such a future, as did Noah and Lot.

This is a warning that has been particularly valuable throughout history at times when Christians have been generally accepted and even respected by society and its structures of power and prestige. It is too easy for Christians in such conditions to forget that, like Noah before the flood and Lot before the destruction of Sodom, they know a different future that the world does not know. In such cases, Christians are tempted to continue living as usual, as if nothing had happened or would happen in Jesus Christ—as Jesus would say, "eating and drinking, buying and selling, planting and building." Such activities are good and necessary; but they must all be undertaken and managed under the overarching Christian hope for "the days of the Son of Man."

Within that general content, there is another warning. Jesus is once again telling his disciples that life will not be easy. He himself "must endure much suffering and be rejected by this generation." The days are also coming when the disciples "will long to see one of the days of the Son of Man," but will not see it. Exactly what is meant by "one of the days" is not clear. Is Jesus talking about moments of victory and hope that would be as glimpses of the final "day that the Son of Man is revealed"? Is this phrase parallel to the "days of Noah" and the "days of Lot," so that what the disciples will long to see is proof that, even though the world goes on as before, these are the days of the Son of Man? Whatever the exact meaning of the phrase, there is no doubt that Jesus is warning his disciples about difficult times to come—times that will be particularly difficult because, like Noah before the flood or Lot before the destruction of Sodom, life will seem to go on as usual, and they will be marching to a different tune than those around them.

Then the passage contains a third warning. Distressed in those coming days, the disciples will be tempted to believe those who will say to them, "Look there!" or "Look here!" While such calls are particularly attractive to harried disciples, Jesus warns them to pay no heed. Significantly, in this context Jesus gives an illustration that at first sight would seem to contradict what he has just said about not being able to recognize the kingdom by mere analytical observation. Now he tells his disciples that they have no need to listen to such presumed prophets, for the day of the Son of Man will be unmistakable, and will be seen by all, "as the lightning flashes and lights up the sky from one side to the other" (v. 24).

This warning is particularly valuable for Christians who for whatever reason are marginalized or rejected. In such circumstances, it is altogether too easy to flee into wild eschatological expectations, believing "prophets" who (look again at vv. 20–21) claim to know when or where the kingdom is coming. While such claims may seem far-fetched to Christians who are able to continue buying and selling, building and planting, as if nothing had happened, they are quite attractive to those who have nothing with which to buy even the basic necessities of life, and who only plant what others will eat and build houses that others will enjoy. (One may well imagine that

Noah, mocked by all his neighbors, would see in the least drop of rain a sign that the flood was finally there.)

Beginning at verse 31, the text brings home the examples of Noah and Lot. In those other days, only those who had prepared for the hidden but certain future survived. Likewise, on "the day that the Son of Man is revealed" people's fates will be sealed, and at that time it will be too late to choose the future one rejected earlier. To choose such a future may indeed be to make life less secure in the present order; but, in words that echo his earlier teachings, Jesus reminds his disciples that "those who try to make their life secure will lose it, but those who lose their life will keep it" (v. 33).

The general warning about the need to decide for the future order—to decide between securing one's life and losing it—comes to the foreground again in verses 34–35. (One is surprised at the words "that night" after a passage in which constant references are made to "days." It may be a dramatic way to end the conversation. Or it may be a reference to the coming of the Son of Man unexpectedly, like a thief at night [12:39–40].) Here we have two pairs: two in bed, and two grinding grain. Grammatically, masculine pronouns are used for the two in bed. This would be the normal usage in Greek grammar even if one were a man and another a woman. But we are explicitly told that the two grinding grain are women, and therefore we may have here one more of the many cases in which Luke pairs up sayings or stories about men with others about women. In any case, the point is clear: people who seem to live identical lives at present in fact belong to different futures—and on "that night" it will be too late to change matters.

Finally, there is the cryptic saying at the very end of the passage, "Where the corpse is, there the vultures will gather" (v. 37). Its obscurity is further complicated because the word translated as "vultures" could also mean "eagles." In that case, some have suggested that what Jesus is saying is that, just as the eagle swoops unexpectedly on its prey, so will the day of the Son of Man come unexpectedly. It is also possible that the meaning of the aphorism is that the evil one will swoop unexpectedly upon his prey. Finally, there may be an added twist. The eagle was the symbol of the Roman Empire, and particularly of its conquering legions. We know that in

first-century Palestine Jews saw the eagle as a symbol of an occupation they hated. Is Jesus subtly suggesting (as Revelation would
openly declare later) that the empire serves the powers of evil, and
swoops like eagles on the children of God? It is impossible to tell.

### 18:1–8 *A Parable on Prayer*

Again, Luke says little as to the setting of this parable. He simply says,
"Then. . . ." However, that very introduction would seem to indicate
that there is a connection between the parable Jesus is about to tell
and the preceding section about the coming of the kingdom and
about living at a time when they will long to see the day of the Son
of Man. This impression is then confirmed by the last words in this
section, "when the Son of Man comes, will he find faith on earth?" In
other words, the parable itself is couched within the context of living
in the difficult time of waiting for the day of the Son of Man. During
such a period of suffering and awaiting vindication, the only way to
remain faithful is to focus continually and persistently on the promise of the coming order. This is why immediately after the section on
the difficult days that the disciples must live through while they wait
for the day when the Son of Man is revealed, Luke has Jesus telling "a
parable about their need to pray always and not to lose heart."

The parable itself is fairly straightforward. As in many other parables, Jesus contrasts two characters. One is a powerful and ruth-
less judge; the other, a widow who has suffered injustice. A Jewish
listener would immediately relate this to the constant injunctions in
the Hebrew Scriptures to do justice to the widow and to protect her,
as well as the orphan, the poor, and the alien. The reason for such
injunctions was that widows normally had no one to speak for them
or to protect them. In the social order of the times, in most cases a
woman needed a man to speak for her and to claim her rights. Since
a widow usually does not have such a man, it is the responsibility
of the entire people of God to care for her, and to make certain that
justice is done. But in the story the judge, who does not fear God,
has no reason to do what God commands, and refuses to intervene
in favor of the widow. Eventually, however, the widow's insistence
forces him to act. (What the NRSV translates as "wear me out"

could also be translated as "hit me under the eye," or "give me a black eye," with the same possibility as in English, or taking this literally as a physical attack, or as besmirching the man's reputation.) Thus not out of a sense of compassion or of justice, but simply out of annoyance, the judge vindicates the widow.

Jesus then comments that, if this unjust judge will listen to the persistent pleas of the widow, much more will God listen "to his chosen ones who cry to him day and night." The judge refused to do justice for a while. In contrast, God will not "delay long," but "will quickly grant justice" to them. This contrast between the judge's delayed reaction and God's prompt response must be stressed. Otherwise, the parable may be understood (and has often been understood) in the sense that God is like that unjust judge, and will eventually answer prayer, not out of justice or compassion, but out of sheer fatigue at the insistence of petitioners. Such an interpretation would seem to place God on the side of the believer's adversary, just as the judge in the parable, by not acting, took the side of the widow's opponent. Nothing could be further from the intention of the parable. What Jesus is saying is that God, who is loving and not unfeeling as the judge is, will respond promptly, and will not delay and demand insistent petitions, as does the judge.

Why then the need "to pray always and not to lose heart"? Because the disciples are living, as was said in the previous section, in the difficult days when they long for the day of the Son of Man and their open vindication. They are like Noah being mocked by his neighbors. The only way to remain firm in such a situation is to pray constantly, and thus to receive vindication from the Lord. The open manifestation of such vindication may not be until "the day when the Son of Man is revealed." But those who pray receive prompt assurance of their vindication.

Given some of the more common interpretations of this parable, it is also important to say something about what it is that the disciples are to pray for. The parable is not about praying for things we want. It is not about being "blessed" with a fortune as the result of insistent prayer. It certainly is not about being successful in the present days. It is rather about being vindicated even at a time when such vindication seems illusory, like Noah and Lot knowing that they were right even while their neighbors might disagree, and eventually being openly vindicated.

### 18:9–14 *A Parable on Humility*

The next section in the Gospel of Luke is the parable of the Pharisee and the Tax Collector. Once again the parable is introduced rather vaguely, with no indication of its connection to the larger narrative of the Gospel: "He also told this parable. . . ." Thematically, this parable is a bridge between the previous one and what follows. The previous parable dealt with prayer, and so does this one. What follows will be the words of Jesus about children entering the kingdom, and the story of the rich ruler, where—as in the present parable—pride and self-importance are shown as an obstacle in the way to the kingdom.

> Satan lies in ambush ready to catch you by surprise at the very time of thanksgiving. . . . He makes you drunk on pride on the lovely and sweet sound of your voice, the beauty of your chants that are sweeter than honey and the honeycomb. The result is that you do not realize that these belong to God, and not to yourself.
>
> —Martyrius
>
> In Arthur A. Just, ed., *Luke*, Ancient Christian Commentary on Scripture: New Testament 3 (Downers Grove, IL: InterVarsity Press, 2003), 279.

As we read this parable, we must take care lest we allow the reference to the Pharisee to turn it into a parable about hypocrisy. While on occasion the Gospels do speak of the hypocrisy of the Pharisees, in fact the Pharisees were among the most religious—sincerely religious—people in Israel. Their desire to be obedient to the law led them to study it assiduously, and to discuss how it ought to be interpreted and obeyed in all circumstances of life. Thus the parable is not about hypocrisy and sincerity but rather about the great reversal that is so clear throughout the Gospel of Luke. And this time the great reversal is religious! Note the parallelism between this parable and what Jesus had said earlier about guests at a banquet. Those who sit in the places of honor will be abased, and those who take the lowlier places will be honored. Both the Pharisee and the tax collector stand, one "by himself" and the other "far off." One stands by himself so as not to be contaminated by others less pure than he. The other stands far off because he does not consider himself worthy. Yet, the one who stands far off is in fact nearer to God.

All that the Pharisee says he does he should be doing; and all he says he is not, he should not be. Tithing and fasting are good religious practices, commended by Scripture; and being a thief, a rogue, an adulterer, or a tax collector (a collaborator with the occupying Romans) were not commendable activities. Jesus is not saying that people should not do what the Pharisee does (fasting and tithing) nor that they should become collaborators with the powerful and the ungodly, as tax collectors were. He is saying that, when the Pharisee uses his piety and religious practices to consider himself better than the tax collector, he will not be justified; and that even a tax collector who acknowledges his sin and his shortcomings will be justified. The reversal is that the one who brings piety, purity, and obedience, and who trusts in all these, is farther away from God than the one who simply brings misery, weakness, and dependence.

As in other parables, what we see in this one depends on where we place ourselves in the story. Our normal reaction is to identify with the tax collector, for we are not proud or hypocritical, as we presume the Pharisee was. But, as religious people, we are repeatedly tempted to take the stance not of the tax collector but of the Pharisee. We do not do evil things that others do; we serve God and help our neighbors; we attend church and give offerings. . . .

And, like many other parables, this one has the power to catch us unawares, and even to do so repeatedly. There is a story about a Sunday school teacher who, after a great lesson on the parable of the Pharisee and the Publican, led his class in prayer: "Lord, we thank you that we have your word and your church, and that therefore we are not like the Pharisee. . . ." The contradiction between what the parable says and what this teacher did is obvious. But we fail to see that in the very act of pointing to that contradiction, and perhaps even chuckling at this teacher's incomprehension, we are secretly saying, "Lord, I thank you that I am not like this teacher, who did not even understand your parable. . ."!

> How far does this reign of
> God reach? At this point
> our senses, our imagination,
> our reason and our mind
> all fail. It is as great as the
> length of eternity, which
> cannot fail nor have an end.
> It is as great as the width
> of love, which cannot be
> restrained. It is as high as
> sublimity itself, which cannot
> be comprehended.
> —St. Bonaventure
>
> *On the Kingdom of God* 15, my trans.

## 18:15–30 *The Way into the Kingdom*

The parable about the Pharisee and the Publican is followed by two episodes in which people's attitudes and actions provide occasion for Jesus to teach on what is required to enter the kingdom. At this point, Luke picks up on Mark's narrative, and the two Gospels are parallel once again.

### 18:15–17 *The Children*

Luke retells the story, which was already found in Mark, changing very little. The words of Jesus about little children are commonly interpreted as commending their innocence, their sweetness, and other such qualities. This is particularly true in our modern culture, where we tend to romanticize children, and forget that they too have the capacity to be obnoxious, spiteful, and so on. In the ancient world, people's attitudes toward children were very different. They often considered children worthless and even disposable. In the Greco-Roman world, it was perfectly legal to abandon a child one did not wish to raise. Children were commonly seen as a source of family income in the future, and of security in old age—or as a way to pass on the family name and traditions. Children were excluded from most activities, and there were few institutions defending them. Thus the main point of the story is probably not that one has to become as innocent or as sweet as little children, but that the kingdom of God belongs to people such as these infants, who seem to be of no importance.

The particular infants in this story were being brought to Jesus so "that he might touch them." The passive role of such infants must be noted. They are brought by others to Jesus, and the disciples try to prevent it. By changing Mark's "children" to "infants," Luke is underscoring their vulnerability. And it is precisely to such that the kingdom of God belongs!

This passage (and its parallels in the other Gospels) has often been used as an argument for infant baptism, and is frequently found in baptismal liturgies. To argue that Jesus' words refer in any direct way to baptism would probably go too far. But the passage may indeed be seen as a response to the argument against the baptism of infants, that they should not be baptized because they can have no faith. In this story, what makes the kingdom of God theirs is their very inability to decide things for themselves. The kingdom does not belong to them (or to us) because—like the Pharisee in the parable—they (or we) tithe and fast. The kingdom does not belong to those who are able to understand what it means. The kingdom belongs to them, and to us, out of God's sheer, unmerited favor. There may be many valuable arguments against infant baptism (for instance, that it has been practiced in such a way as to make the civil society practically coextensive with the church, and physical birth practically a guarantee of Christian rebirth). But the argument that infants cannot be baptized, because there is something they cannot do and we can, comes perilously close to the Pharisee's pride in his own piety and obedience (18:11).

In any case, the passage has meaning quite apart from the debated matter of infant baptism, and its implications are not limited to children. This is quite clear in verse 17, where the word "whoever" implies that *all* must receive the kingdom of God as infants. So the passage is about any who would receive the kingdom.

How we interpret this passage has much to do with where we place ourselves within the story. Obviously, we would like to place ourselves in the role of the little children, and that is a legitimate goal. But when we claim that our role is that of the little children we are coming perilously close to the Pharisee in the parable. Perhaps we would do better to consider the possibility that we might be like those disciples who tried to stop those who were bringing the little children. This has often been, and still is, the great temptation of the church and of the faithful. Just as we are tempted to boast of our piety, like the Pharisee, so are we tempted to set rules, regulations, and standards that effectively keep people away from the church and from its Lord. Churches in every city are surrounded by people who are almost as vulnerable as infants—unemployed people, people who have never known anything but violence, homeless people, people without proper immigration papers. We do not openly say we do not want them. We simply set up systems, standards, practices, and expectations that exclude them. By our clothing we hinder those who cannot dress as we do. By our liturgies we hinder those who did not grow up in the church. Yet, like it or not, it is to such that the kingdom of God belongs!

### 18:18–30 *The Rich Ruler*

Following the same outline as Mark, Luke now tells us another story about a very different person. This is the story about a man who is traditionally known as "the rich young ruler," although Luke does not say that he is young. In Mark (Mark 10:17–22) he is a rich man, and in Matthew (Matt. 19:16–22) he is a rich young man. It is Luke who presents him as a rich "ruler." In so doing, he is establishing a marked contrast with the children of the previous story. They are the epitome of powerlessness and vulnerability; this man is rich and powerful.

Before moving to the central message of the story, we do well to consider the possible theological significance of some of its apparently minor points. The first is the dialogue between Jesus and the ruler. The latter calls Jesus "Good Teacher," and Jesus replies with a question and an assertion: "Why do you call me good? No one is good but God alone." What does Jesus mean by such words? Is it an act of humility, in which Jesus acts like the tax collector in the parable? Is he saying that he is not good? Or is the meaning of his words exactly the opposite, that only God is good, and that the ruler has somehow given Jesus an attribute that belongs to God, but which Jesus does not deny? Does it reflect an early Christology that held that only after the resurrection is Jesus worthy of worship, in which case his words represent both a rebuke and a promise? Throughout history, all these interpretations have found their proponents and advocates.

Then, one should note that the call to be "perfect," which appears in Matthew's version of the story (Matt. 19:21), is absent from

Luke's version. As noted above (see commentary on 17:7–10), Matthew's version of the story has provided the basis for the distinction between the commandments and the counsel of perfection—the former being obligatory for all, and the latter only for those who choose the way of perfection. Luke, however, is not referring to a higher form of obedience, or to a more perfect life. This would contradict much of what he has said up to this point, that there is nothing one can do to merit the kingdom, which in fact belongs to those who cannot do much—such as the infants in the pericope immediately preceding. Thus in Luke's Gospel the "one thing still lacking" is precisely to come to the point where things are actually lacking. For the ruler to sell all he has and give it to the poor implies joining the ranks of the poor. What is "lacking" is for him to become like one of the powerless "little children" of the preceding story. The reference to having "treasure in heaven" by giving alms to the poor may well be an allusion to Proverbs 19:17: "Whoever is kind to the poor lends to the LORD, and will be repaid in full," a text that is constantly lurking at the background of many of the sayings of Jesus about wealth and poverty.

Luke does not say that the man left, as do Matthew and Mark. In the Lukan account, the ruler is still present as Jesus comments on the event. He is sad, but apparently he has not given up. Yet it is clear from his very sadness that he will miss the joy of the kingdom. Quite possibly, Luke is writing this account at a time when the presence in the Christian community of some who are in better economic condition than others poses problems and raises questions, much as was the case in Corinth when Paul wrote 1 Corinthians. Having the ruler listening to Jesus' words would prefigure what would be the reality of Luke's church, where the poor and the not so poor would listen to the Gospel together.

It should also be noted that here, as in the parable of the Good Samaritan, Jesus opens his response by recalling the commandments of God. Jesus does not say that these are invalid, nor that they should not be obeyed. By the middle of the second century, there were Christians (notably Marcion) who claimed that there was a radical difference between the god who gave the Jewish law and the Father whom Jesus proclaimed. They claimed—quite erroneously—that this was what Paul taught. Since Luke had been Paul's companion, these people accepted only an abridged version of Luke's Gospel, abridged mostly by deleting all references to the Hebrew Scriptures or to the God of Israel. While such positions are rare today, many still believe that there is a radical opposition between the Old and the New Testaments, and that Jesus somehow came to correct the errors of Judaism. Nothing is further from the truth. Throughout Luke, as well as throughout the New Testament, the faith of Israel is affirmed, and so are the commandments given by God to the children of Israel.

While affirming the permanent value of the law, however, one should take care lest this passage become simply a harsher legal demand. At the same time when the Marcionites were proposing to do away with the law, others (notably Tertullian) were speaking of the gospel as a "new law of Christ," higher and more demanding than the law of Israel. (Eventually some went further, speaking of an even more exacting "law of the Spirit.") This too is a misinterpretation of the text. Jesus is not saying that, besides obeying the earlier commandments, his followers must sell all they have and give it to the poor. (Later, in the story of Zacchaeus [19:8–9], we find a rich man who simply gives half of what he has—and Jesus declares that salvation has come to him. And in Acts 5:4 we are told that Ananias and Sapphira had no obligation to sell their property.) He is calling the powerful man who trusts in his riches to give up that in which he trusts, and to join the powerless in their plight. The Pharisee in the previous parable trusted in his own piety; the ruler trusts in his own money and power. Both must be undone if salvation is to come to them.

> And it is not more sinful to be rich than to be poor. But it is dangerous beyond expression. Therefore, I remind all of you that are of this number, that have the conveniences of life, and something over, that ye walk upon slippery ground. . . . I know how plausibly the prophets of smooth things can talk in favour of hospitality; of making our friends welcome; of keeping a handsome table, to do honour to religion; of promoting trade, and the like. But God is not mocked: He will not be put off by such pretenses as these.
>
> —John Wesley

"Sermon 112: The Rich Man and Lazarus," in *Works of John Wesley*, 7:250.

When the ruler is saddened because he is rich, Jesus replies with a word of lamentation, to the effect that for the rich to enter the kingdom is as hard as for a camel to go through the eye of a needle. Interpreters have often sought to soften these words, for instance, by suggesting that Jesus was referring to a gate in the city walls called "the eye of the needle," and that camels could only enter it by being rid of their burdens or by kneeling in humility. But Jesus' words are radical. He means what he says: just as it is impossible for a camel (the largest animal known in Palestine) to go through the eye of a needle (as narrow an opening as one could imagine), so it is impossible for the rich to enter the kingdom.

Once again, however, this is not a law, so that those who obey it will make their own way into the kingdom. It is rather one more affirmation of the need to accept the kingdom as a gift of God's grace—or as the infants of the previous passage are nurtured. No matter what the rich do, they cannot attain the kingdom. But what is humanly impossible is possible for God. Thus the entire story is an affirmation of both law and grace. The rich must set aside their wealth and their trust in it. But even so, salvation is ultimately not the result of human action—not even of the radical action of giving everything to the poor—but of divine grace.

The note of grace is sounded again, as the final note of the pericope, when Peter reminds Jesus that he and the other disciples have left their homes in order to follow him. Jesus promises them a reward greater than anything they may have had to give up—and "very much more." The promise that this will be true "in this age, and in the age to come," may be surprising. Jesus is not proclaiming a "gospel of prosperity," urging people to give so that they may become wealthier. He is telling Peter and the others what would clearly be the experience of the church by Luke's time. Even though many had to give up their families and their homes, they would find a wider family and a greater home in the community of the church. This would be true "in this age"; but it will be true even more "in the age to come." Thus the passage, which includes the story about a man who was saddened because his possessions would not allow him to follow Jesus, concludes with the joyful note of the promise of the coming kingdom, and of its presence now in the community of faith.

## 18:31–34 *A Reminder*

Jesus predicts his passion once again, this time more fully than before. Two points stand out in this summary of the passion. The first is that, while elsewhere (for instance, in 9:22) Jesus speaks primarily of the role of Jewish leaders in his passion, here he stresses the actions of Roman authorities. He predicts that he will be "handed over" presumably by Jewish authorities "to the Gentiles." The role of Jewish authorities is mostly one of "handing over"; it is the Gentiles—the Romans—who will kill Jesus. The second is that the disciples do not understand what Jesus is saying. This is a repeated theme in the Gospel, whenever Jesus refers to his upcoming passion. Reading these stories after the passion and resurrection, believers would understand them. Reading them also after Jewish resentment against Roman law led to Jewish rebellion and the Roman destruction of the temple and of much of Jerusalem, these words would also find echo among Jewish Christians. Readers would be reminded of the political context of the passion, which had taken place in a province where Roman rulers feared Jewish hopes for liberation. This prepares the reader for the next section, about the healing of a blind man.

## 18:35–43 *A Blind Man*

The story about the blind man has often been connected with the parable of the Good Samaritan. The latter is set on the road to Jericho, and so is the former. In the parable, religious people pass along the road and do not stop; in the story, Jesus does stop and responds to the needs of the man at the roadside. There are also connections between this story and the passage about the little children, for in both people try to hinder others from coming to Jesus.

However, there are also political nuances that move the story toward the events in Jerusalem. This may be seen in the title "Son of David," which the blind man gives Jesus. The connection between Jesus and David appears early in the Gospel of Luke (1:27, 32; 2:4, 11, 32); but no one mentions it again until this incident shortly before the entrance into Jerusalem. Luke 20:41 attests to the widespread expectation that the Messiah would be "David's son." We can thus understand why, when the blind man shouts, "Jesus, Son of David," people—"those in front," a phrase whose meaning is not quite clear, but which probably refers to part of the band of disciples—try to silence him. To call someone "Son of David" was to raise messianic hopes about the liberation of Israel from the yoke of Rome. It was a dangerous thing to say; and it would certainly endanger Jesus and his disciples, for Rome could hardly tolerate such talk. But the blind man will not be silenced, and shouts even more loudly. While people try to silence the man who cries out for liberation, Jesus stops and listens to him, and then he frees him from his blindness. The man's liberation may not be the political event some expected; but neither is it a vague promise of future joy in heaven, coupled with a call to acceptance of his condition. It is an immediate liberation from the material condition that holds him in subjection.

By healing him, Jesus himself is taking a material risk. The man called him "Son of David"; and now Jesus shows that he indeed has power by healing the man. To those present, this would be proof that the blind man was justified in calling him "Son of David." In that context, it is possible to understand the affirmation at the end, that they "praised God," not just in the sense that they praised the God who had healed the man, but also in the sense that they praised the God who had finally sent the Son of David. The stage is now set for the entrance into Jerusalem and the events that will follow.

### 19:1–10 *A Tax Collector*

The journey continues, and in Jericho Jesus meets Zacchaeus. This story appears only in the Gospel of Luke, and picks up on two themes that have appeared repeatedly throughout the Gospel: the acceptance of the worst of sinners, and the use of wealth and resources. From the beginning of his ministry, Jesus had clashed with those who presumed on their piety and their obedience to the law as guaranteeing their salvation, and insisted on a great reversal that would result in great joy at the conversion of sinners and the finding of what was lost. Now that last person who repents and rejoices at Jesus' call is a rich tax collector. Tax collectors in general were despised as collaborators with the Roman regime, as exploiters of the powerless, and as often contaminated by ritual uncleanness. Major tax collectors had others performing the same duties under them. That Zacchaeus was rich implies that he was not just one of many tax collectors, but an important one. A sinner among sinners! It is not surprising that the "right" people would grumble at Jesus' call to him. Yet it is he whom Jesus calls, in whose house he wishes to dwell, and upon whom Jesus pronounces salvation. He is one more example of the lost that have been found (see 15:1–32).

On the use of wealth, this story may be read as a commentary on both the parable of the rich fool and the story of the rich ruler. Zacchaeus stands in contrast with the fool that thought his possessions were truly his, and with the ruler who was saddened because he wished to hold on to what he had. This story also corrects the possible interpretation of the story of the ruler as making it a law to sell all and give it to the poor. He decides to give to the poor half of his possessions—not all, as the ruler was told. He adds that, if any of his wealth is ill-gotten, he will repay it fourfold. Jesus accepts this as a true act of repentance, and announces, "Today salvation has come to this house." When it comes to the use of possessions, it is not just a matter of setting aside a certain proportion to give to the poor—be it 100 percent as in the case of the ruler, 50 percent as in the case of Zacchaeus, or 10 percent as in the practice of tithing—and then claiming the rest for oneself. It is not just a matter of obeying a commandment—be it the tithe or giving all to the poor. It certainly is not just a matter of some token almsgiving. It is a matter of free, liberal, loving giving. And it is also a matter of being willing to recognize the possibility that one's wealth may be unjustly acquired. In short, it is a matter of love and justice entwined.

### 19:11–27 *Waiting for the Kingdom*

The journey to Jerusalem is coming to an end. It is a long journey that has occupied nine chapters of the Gospel's narrative. At this point of high expectation, Jesus tells a parable, and Luke explains that this was because, on approaching Jerusalem, Jesus' followers "supposed that the kingdom of God was to appear immediately." Since this parable is similar to the parable of the Talents (Matt. 25:14–30), its significance at this point of the narrative is frequently overlooked. The relationship between these two parables is the subject of much debate that need not detain us here. At any rate, the parable of the Ten Pounds (or minas) is different from the parable of the Talents on several significant points.

First, it is not about "a man" who goes on a journey, but about a king who is claiming his kingdom. When we today hear about such a king, it may sound like one of those tales that begin, "Once upon a time, there was a king. . . ." But this was not the case for Jesus' hearers. It was common for vassal kings to depend on greater powers for their authority. Shortly before the birth of Jesus, Herod had become king of Judea thanks to Rome's support. When Herod died, his son Archelaus went to Rome in a failed attempt to have this title confirmed. At about the time of the birth of Jesus, Herod Antipas had unsuccessfully sought from Rome the title of king. The entire Herodian family was known for its abuses, and in some cases for defying Jewish customs and laws. Given that background, the parable is alluding to the political realities of the time, and the cruel and vindictive king of the parable is not an outlandish figure of fiction.

Second, the two parables differ radically on the amount each servant receives, and on the distribution itself. The first of the three servants in Matthew's parable receives five talents, approximately the equivalent of 30,000 days' wages for a common laborer. The other two receive lesser amounts, but even a single talent would amount to 6,000 days' wages. In contrast, in Luke's parable all ten servants receive the same amount; and the pound (or mina) they receive is approximately a hundred days' wages. In total, this king gives his servants the equivalent of a thousand days' wages, while the man in Matthew gives them forty-eight times that much. As a result, in the parable of the Pounds the rewards seem out of balance with the achievement of each servant: one who gives the king roughly the equivalent of a year's wages receives authority over ten cities!

Third, in the parable of the Talents there is no opposition to the absent master, while in the parable of the Pounds "the citizens of his country hated him and sent a delegation after him" to oppose the man's confirmation as king—which would immediately remind the early hearers of this parable of the Jewish delegation that had been sent to Rome, to oppose Archelaus's bid for kingship.

Where the parable of the Pounds stands in the Gospel of Luke makes it much more than a parable about stewardship (which it also is). This is primarily a parable about the need to decide in favor of or against a king whose authority has not been confirmed. It is a parable about the ultimate risk of discipleship, which is based on the conviction that this one whom the disciples serve is indeed king—a point that will become very much an issue in the rest of the Gospel. It is a parable about being faithful to an absent king whose power is opposed by many in his own land, and who can give his servants no more than a paltry pound or mina.

Ultimately, stewardship itself is a political issue. Would-be disciples have to choose between the present order and the order of the king whose kingdom has not yet been revealed. That king does not give his disciples large sums of money, nor power, nor influence. But what they have, they must use in expectation of the coming kingdom.

> There are really only two ways to take a thing seriously. Either you renounce it or you risk everything for it. Either you fling away your pound or you use it and trade with it. There is no third choice. The kind of Christian who is merely conservative and those who want only the Christian "point of view"—those people want this third choice, which doesn't exist. Throw your Christianity on the trash heap, or else let God be the *Lord* of your life.
>
> —Helmut Thielicke
>
> *Waiting Father*, 145.

# 19:28–24:53

# *Jerusalem*

Luke has constructed the main body of his narrative (9:51–19:27) around the theme of the journey to Jerusalem. In spite of its apparent digressions, that earlier section of the Gospel may be seen as the disciples' training and preparation for the events that will take place in Jerusalem, culminating in the parable of the Ten Pounds (19:11–27), warning the disciples not to expect the immediate establishment of the kingdom.

## 19:28–46

### *Entrance to the City*

The instructions that Jesus gives his disciples, and the apparent ease with which the disciples carry them out, have often been explained away as merely showing that Jesus had already made the necessary arrangements. This probably misses the point of the story, which is precisely to indicate that the events about to take place in Jerusalem are not the result of chance, but are part of a larger and mysterious plan. Throughout the narrative of the passion, while Jesus is made the victim of conspiracies and political interests, he is still the victor, for in some mysterious way all that is happening is in God's hands. He is the strange king who conquers by means of suffering and apparent defeat, and whose power, greater than any other on earth, seems to be trampled under the power of religious and political authorities.

The disciples still do not understand. In spite of all his warnings to the contrary, they still expect Jesus to come into his kingdom immediately, and they celebrate his arrival at Jerusalem as if this were the beginning of his enthronement. At this point of apparently impending victory, it is not just the inner circle of his followers but "the whole multitude of the disciples" that acclaim the new king now marching toward Jerusalem.

The entry itself exemplifies the profound paradox of the suffering Messiah, or the crucified King. Triumphal entries were common enough to be recognized by the early readers of the Gospels, and rare enough to retain their sense of the extraordinary. Since time immemorial, conquerors claiming a city would enter it in a procession. In Rome generals returning from exceptional victories were celebrated with a *triumphus*, a solemn procession where the victor exhibited the spoils of war, surrounded by the leaders of his armies, as well as by conquered kings and rulers and by numerous captives destined to slavery. The victor, wearing a crown of laurel, would ride on a chariot pulled by white horses (white being the color of victory) and would finally go to the temple of Jupiter to offer sacrifice. All along the way, soldiers and the citizenry in general would shout acclamation and sing hymns in honor of the conqueror. In Jerusalem itself, three centuries earlier, Alexander the Great had entered in solemn triumph, and had then offered sacrifices in the temple.

> Ride on! Ride on in majesty!
> In lowly pomp ride on to die;
> O Christ, Thy triumphs now
>   begin
> O'er captive death and
>   conquered sin.
> —Henry H. Milman (1827)

Jesus' entry into Jerusalem both parallels such solemn entries and contrasts with them. This strange king does not ride a chariot, but a donkey. Yet even within that sign of humility there is a paradox, for in riding a humble ass Jesus is claiming for himself the ancient prophecy of Zechariah 9:9: "Lo, your king comes to you; triumphant and victorious is he, humble and riding on a donkey, on a colt, the foal of a donkey." People acclaim him as earlier their ancestors acclaimed Alexander, or as the Romans acclaimed Caesar and Pompey. He does not wear a crown of laurel, but soon will wear one of thorns. Alexander rejoiced over his conquests; Jesus will weep over Jerusalem. Alexander—a Gentile—entered the temple and, with the acquiescence of its authorities, sacrificed in it; Jesus will enter the temple and denounce what is being done in it.

Even though Jesus will not seek to depose the Roman and Jewish authorities, the scene is politically charged. Judea is part of the Roman Empire. No one can claim to rule over it without the support of Roman authorities (see the commentary on 19:11–27). Yet Jesus' disciples loudly proclaim him king. It is no wonder that the Pharisees wish to silence them. Politically, the Pharisees tried to walk a fine line between open rebellion and total capitulation before Roman authorities. While not supporting the Zealots, they valued the measure of religious and political freedom Israel had, and sought to prevent anything that could arouse the ire of Rome. (See an example of this in John 11:45–53.) Now this man enters Jerusalem surrounded by a crowd acclaiming him as king. For the good of the nation, and not just for religious reasons, he must be silenced. And once again, Jesus' response is paradoxical. He does not wish to claim the kingdom as his disciples understand that action; yet he accepts their acclamation, which foreshadows what will later be discovered—that he is indeed king, and king over all kings of the earth.

Only Luke among the canonical Gospels includes the scene of Jesus weeping over Jerusalem. It is an important counterpart to the triumphal march, and a correction to an overly simplistic interpretation of it. (And probably should be included in our Palm Sunday readings, so as to avoid many a triumphalistic celebration of that day.) In spite of appearances, Jesus knows that he will not be well received in Jerusalem. The main point of the story is that Jerusalem does not know "the things that make for peace," or has the wrong idea of what peace is and what brings it about. The Pharisees who have urged Jesus to stop the acclamations he is receiving are a prime example of not knowing the things that make for peace. They are so afraid of what Rome might do that they cannot see what God is doing. Rome offers its famous Pax Romana, and in their defense of this false peace the Pharisees—and with them all the religious leadership of Jerusalem—are ready to ignore the things that make for real peace. But the "peace" they thus achieve will not last long.

Jerusalem will be besieged and destroyed, and what little measure of peace it has will be wiped out.

It is easy to connect this with the siege and conquest of Jerusalem by Titus in the year 70; but it is more difficult to see what it says about all our present attempts at peace. We trust the peace of armaments, the peace of vigilance, and even the peace of isolation from those whom we fear; but we find it difficult to trust and practice the peace of love. The Jesus who wept over Jerusalem still weeps over our cities and our nations.

The triumphal entry leads directly to the temple. This is exactly parallel to what Josephus says about Alexander's triumphal entry into Jerusalem, except that Alexander went to the temple and offered sacrifice under the guidance of the high priest, while Jesus goes to the temple in order to cleanse it. The high priest in Josephus's account betrayed the faith of Israel by capitulating before Alexander. In the Gospel, Jesus goes to the temple not to offer sacrifice but to oppose what is being done in it—not to be cleansed by a sacrifice, but to cleanse the temple in what amounts to a sign that the price of such cleansing will be his own sacrifice. One could say that he is the true high priest who undoes what the high priest and others are doing: polluting once more the faith of Israel not only by serving the interests of Rome, but also by allowing the temple to be used for economic interests. But one can also say that he is the sacrificial victim. In cleansing the temple, Jesus is asserting his authority to restore the faith of Israel; but he is also setting in motion a series of events that will soon lead to his death.

## 19:47–21:38

### *Teachings in the Temple*

#### 19:47–20:8 *By What Authority?*

For an undetermined length of time (which Christian liturgical tradition shortens to about half a week) Jesus teaches in the temple. The account of his teachings is sandwiched between two reminders (19:47–48 and 22:2) that the Judean leaders sought a way to kill

Jesus, but did not dare do this too openly for fear of "the people." Significantly, the "leaders of the people" are held back by fear of the people. It will be later (23:13) that "the people" will turn against Jesus. (This is parallel to the early chapters in Acts, where the leaders do not dare take harsh measures against the followers of Jesus because they fear the reaction of "the people." There too, through a series of events and a conspiracy, "the people" finally come around to the side of the leadership [Acts 6:12].)

This confrontation between "the people" and "the [supposed] leaders of the people" may be dismissed by some as not being of theological significance. After all, it does not fall under any of the traditional headings of theology: God, creation, sin, and so on. But the truth is that the perspective from which one interprets reality is of great theological significance. Theology done by "the leaders of the people" is different from theology done by the people. Unfortunately, too much theology has been done by "the leaders of the people" with little attention to the experiences and the struggles of the people. This may be the reason why we may think that the contrast in Luke–Acts between "the people" and its supposed leaders is only part of the background—which is a natural thought for us, who are among the "leaders of the people." Fortunately, late in the twentieth century and early in the twenty-first a new generation of theologians arose—mostly among people previously marginalized in the theological enterprise, such as ethnic minorities, the colonized, and women—who questioned much of the theology done by "the leaders of the people."

> Mark and Luke teach us, first, that the class of men that constituted the Church was of the lowest order, while His opposition came from the priests and scribes and all the chief people. This is part of the foolishness of the cross, that God overlooked the excellencies of this world and chose foolishness, that is, the weak and despised.
> —John Calvin
>
> *Harmony of the Gospels, 3:9.*

The first confrontation (19:47–20:8) has to do with the question of authority. Those in authority—the chief priests and the scribes—question the authority of Jesus, who in turn responds with a question that silences them, at least for a while. The significance of this passage goes beyond the polemical issue at the time, and far beyond any polemics with Judaism. The question of authority was also asked of the apostles by the Sanhedrin (Acts 4:7). It is easy to read these accounts in the Gospel and in Acts and lay blame on those leaders who were unable to recognize Jesus' authority. But those of us who have positions of responsibility in the church constantly find ourselves having to decide on issues of authority. The Council of Nicea had to decide: should the teachings of Arius be allowed? Innocent III had to decide on St. Francis's authority. Leo IX had to decide on Luther's authority. Luther had to decide on the Anabaptists, on Zwingli, and on many others. The Church of England had to decide on John Wesley. How do we make such decisions? To what degree are our decisions determined, as in the case of the Gospel account, by political and personal considerations? Are our finite decisions ever final? We need to give more attention to the difficult situation in which positions of leadership place us, constantly having to decide on what is true, while knowing that we are fallible, and constantly having to decide on what is good, yet knowing that we are not good.

When we join this with what was said above about the contrast between "the people" and "the leaders of the people," we realize how difficult and perilous our task is. Theologians are supposed to know what is true, what is best doctrine; yet, if we presume on that knowledge, we risk missing the very core of the gospel, which is good news to the people—not necessarily their leaders—and yet is hidden from the wise and the intelligent (10:21).

### 20:9–19 The Wicked Tenants

This is another parable of absence, and of responsibility in view of the absence of the master—that is, a parable of stewardship (see pp. 165–68, "Further Reflections: The Absence of God"). In other parables of absence, the servants are generally left behind, hoping that they will do their master's will during his absence. In this case, the absence is not total. The absentee owner sends his representatives, and eventually his own son, only to have the former beaten and insulted, and the latter killed. At this point, as in the other parables of absence, the master returns to give their due to his servants, or in this case, to his tenants or sharecroppers.

Although fiction, this parable (like so many others) cuts deeper than truth itself. Jesus is using the story to show the utter stupidity and wickedness of the "tenants." And there is no doubt who these are, for "the scribes and chief priests realized that he had told this parable against them" (20:19). The result is that their hatred increases, and the only reason why they do not "lay hands on him" is that "they feared the people."

It is easy to read this parable as announcing that Israel's inheritance would be taken away and given to the church. Indeed, this was the most common interpretation during the patristic and medieval periods, when it was often used in anti-Jewish polemics. Such an interpretation, however, is contradicted by the Gospel text itself. The parable is not told against Israel, but against the scribes and chief priests, and "the people" take no offense at it. Jesus is not saying that the vineyard will be taken away from Israel, but that it will be taken away from the scribes and chief priests, and given to the common people. This is one more case of the great reversal that is central to the Gospel of Luke.

At any rate, the parable is God's Word to us, not because it tells us about Jews and Gentiles, but because it speaks to us and to our condition. The parable is addressed to any who have been entrusted with God's vineyard, the vineyard of creation. In this sense, it is parallel to other such parables (for instance, that of the Watchful Slaves in 12:35–48); but there is an added dimension here: the owner of the vineyard, although absent, sends representatives—including, as a last resort, his own son. Within its historical context, early readers of the Gospel of Luke would have understood that this was a reference to the many prophets sent to Israel (see 11:47–51), and then to Jesus himself. On this point, this parable reminds us of that of the Rich Man and Lazarus, where Jesus says that the man's rich brothers already have the Law and the Prophets, and will heed no further warning. But that parable is also about us. We too, like the rich man's brothers and like Israel, have been offered repeated opportunities to render to God what is God's. We have a fairly good idea how we are to manage our lives and how we are to manage all of creation; and yet we do not do it. Upon hearing this parable, we have no option but to cry, "Heaven forbid!"

The parable is further explained by the quotation from Psalm 118:22. This must have been a very important text for early Christians, for it is quoted not only in this passage and its parallels (Matt. 21:42; Mark 12:10), but also in Acts 4:11 and 1 Peter 2:7. It is a strong affirmation of the great reversal as it applies to Jesus himself. The religious leaders are supposed to be expert builders; yet they have rejected the keystone, or cornerstone, chosen by God. Religious people, particularly religious leaders (then as well as today) have difficulty accepting such a reversal, particularly since it also implies that our positions of leadership may well be taken from us in favor of others we might consider less holy, less orthodox, or less theologically astute. This too is part of the great reversal.

### 20:20–26  On Paying Taxes

The background for this episode is at the end of the previous section (20:19). The teachers of the law and the chief priests (those to whom Jesus referred in the parable of the Wicked Tenants) seek to destroy him, but fear the reaction of the people. They therefore plan a more devious approach: to force Jesus to take a political stance on a controversial matter. They will force him to choose between antagonizing Roman authorities—with the result that he will be handed "over to the jurisdiction and authority of the governor"—and alienating the people by seeming to favor Roman rule. To do this, they will send "spies" who, pretending to ask an honest question, will ensnare Jesus. The question is simply stated: "Is it lawful for us to pay taxes to the emperor, or not?" But Jesus' response to this seemingly simple question could have dire consequences. Rome would not tolerate any who refused to pay their taxes, and inciting others not to pay would be interpreted as an act of rebellion. On the other hand, Jewish national sentiment rightfully resented Roman oppression, exploitation, and taxation. Furthermore, the question has to do with more than money. It is couched in terms of obedience to the law: "Is it lawful. . . ?" From the point of view of Roman authorities, it is not only lawful, but obligatory. But Jewish law is more debatable. Zealots claim that to pay taxes to the emperor is to break the law of Yahweh. At the other extreme, Jewish tax collectors are agents of Roman exploitation. In between, many Sadducees are supported in their aristocratic positions by Rome, and are willing to collaborate with the empire, while most Pharisees follow a path of neither rebelling against Rome nor collaborating with it. Thus, "Is it lawful . . . ?" actually means, "which law are we to obey, Rome's or God's?" No matter what Jesus answers, he will be in trouble.

The request for a denarius seems innocent enough; but Jesus will use it to confound those who seek to entrap him. This is a Roman coin bearing the image of the emperor and an inscription that would most likely declare him "son of the divine Augustus." By the very act of carrying such a coin, these conspirators are already showing that they are not as pure as one might think. Why would they want to keep an object that is in itself blasphemous? Is this not breaking the law of Israel? So Jesus tells them to return it to the emperor whose it really is.

> This is not meant as a timeless general proposition, but is to be considered, like all of Jesus' teaching, in the light of the coming kingdom of God, which is already present in Jesus' words and deeds and has begun to realize itself. Through this interpretation of "Render unto God all things that are God's," the other part receives the meaning of a temporary, interim obligation, soon to end. For the reign of Caesar passes, but God's reign comes and does not pass away.
> —Günther Bornkamm
>
> *Jesus of Nazareth*, 123.

Thus, without attacking Rome or saying that one should not pay taxes, Jesus undermines the existing order even more radically than his enemies could have imagined. If you are so pure, let the emperor keep his idolatrous coins!

Then Jesus adds what in this context could well be called "the other side of the coin." It is not just a matter of giving the emperor the things that are his—his idolatrous and blasphemous coins—but also of giving God what is God's. Interpreters disagree on what this may mean. The "things that are God's" encompass all things. Thus interpreted, Jesus is urging that all things be given to God—which in turn implies an obedience such that one is ready to reject Caesar's ungodly coins. Others have pointed out that, since the word translated as "head" in 20:24 is literally "image," Jesus is distinguishing between money, which bears the image of the emperor, and people, who bear the image of God (Gen. 1:26). In this case, Jesus is telling his hearers to give up on Caesar's money and give their own selves to God.

What should be clear is that Jesus is not simply saying that some things belong by right to the state, and some to God. In spite of its common usage in that direction, this passage is *not* about separation of church and state—certainly not about the state having some rights and the church others. The passage is rather about radical obedience. By reminding them that they carry Roman coins, Jesus lays bare the duplicity of his interlocutors. By telling them to give to God what is God's, he is calling them to obedient faithfulness.

When we then place ourselves within this passage, we should not see here a call to give part of our allegiance to the state and part to the church. It is rather a call to give our entire allegiance to God, and to shun compromises that make it easier to live in the present order without really questioning or challenging it.

### 20:27–44 *The Resurrection and the Kingdom*

This is the first time Luke mentions the Sadducees, who will appear repeatedly in the early chapters of Acts. For the sake of his Gentile readers, he explains that the Sadducees do not believe in the resurrection. On the matter of the resurrection, Jesus agrees with the Pharisees, who do believe in it. So the Sadducees are questioning both him and the Pharisees.

Like the previous passage, this one also begins with a captious question. In this case, it has to do with the "law of levirate," the commandment that, if a married man died childless, his brother should take the widow as his wife, and thus produce children to continue the line of the deceased (a common practice throughout the ancient Near East). The conundrum that the Sadducees pose is, "In the resurrection, . . . whose wife will the woman be?"

Jesus cuts the Gordian knot by simply declaring that the coming age is different than the present, and the resurrected "neither marry nor are given in marriage." Later Christians took these words as a call to celibacy, for by being celibate one prefigures, announces, and even begins to enjoy the coming order of the kingdom. This interpretation has often been joined to an asceticism that tends to denigrate the body and its functions, particularly its sexuality.

A better interpretation is simply to say that Jesus is arguing that the conditions of the present age do not obtain after the resurrection. The question, "Whose wife will she be?" ignores the radical newness of the coming kingdom. There are many similar questions that have no answer (and that are similar to those that the Corinthians seem to have been asking, and to which Paul responds in 1 Cor. 15): How old will I look? Will I have a body like that of my youth, or one that looks more like I looked when I died? Jesus does not attempt to answer such questions, but simply calls his listeners to trust the God who has made all things, and who will make the kingdom come to pass.

An interesting note having to do with marriage is that Jesus says that in the new order people "neither marry nor are given in marriage." For a woman to be "given in marriage" implies subjection to others: the father who gives her, and the groom who takes her. In an order of peace, justice, and freedom, people are not "given" to others.

Having responded to the objections of the Pharisees, Jesus counterattacks with his own argument: Moses says that God is the God of his ancestors and, since God is not a God of the dead, but only of the living, this means that for God those ancestors are still alive.

Finally, Jesus insists on the radically new character of the kingdom he is proclaiming. Verses 41–44, which at first sight seem to be a digression in the narrative or a completely independent saying, are actually part of the response to the Sadducees and to any others who do not realize the radical newness of the kingdom. The argument about the Messiah as David's son is a way of showing that the kingdom that the Messiah will bring is much more than the restoration of David's kingdom. While the Messiah will be of the lineage of David, this does not make him lesser than David. In fact, David himself called him Lord.

## 20:45–21:4 *Scribes and Widows*

While dividing the text into chapters and verses is a useful way to refer to particular passages, it often obscures the connection between the end of one chapter and the beginning of the next. Such is the case here, for we usually read the words about the scribes as quite separate from the words about the widow who offered two copper coins, when in fact the two explain one another. They are connected by means both of contrast and of a common theme. The contrast is between the pompous and greedy scribes and the poor widow who gives all she has. The common theme is provided by the widow herself. Part of what Jesus condemns in the scribes is that "they devour widows' houses"; and then he points to a poor widow as an example for all, including the scribes. Thus taken together the end of chapter 20 and the beginning of chapter 21 are one more example of the great reversal that Jesus brings about. The scribes are the religious leaders, those who best know Scripture, those who sit in the synagogues in places of honor, those whom all respect. Yet they make their wealth and gain their prestige while taking all that poor widows have—"devouring" them. At the service, the contributions of the rich are noted. But Jesus takes particular notice of a widow (one of those whom the scribes devour) giving all she has. Her offering, though apparently small, is greater than the seemingly greater ones of the rich.

> In no religion is the "character of protest" so vital as in the messianic faith of Christianity. One cannot grasp freedom in faith without hearing simultaneously the categorical imperative: One must serve through bodily, social, and political obedience the liberation of the suffering creation out of real affliction.
> —Jürgen Moltmann
>
> "Toward a Political Hermenutics of the Gospel," in *New Theology No. 6*, ed. Martin E. Marty and Dean G. Peerman (Toronto: Macmillan, 1969), 78.

## 21:5–38 *Eschatological Announcements*

The rest of chapter 21 is devoted to a series of announcements and warnings about the time to come, or rather, to what is constructed as a single discourse about future events and the disciples' lives as they await such events. The setting is the temple, where Jesus has been teaching, and the occasion is the admiration of "some"—not necessarily the disciples. In response to such admiration, Jesus comments that the time will come when even the temple will be utterly destroyed, a destruction so thorough that "not one stone will be left upon another."

The words that follow (vv. 7–36) are susceptible to different interpretations. Many see them as a sort of program of future events (much like a TV guide that tells us what comes next) so that the disciples may know when the end is coming. This interpretation seems to be bolstered by verse 31: "So also, when you see these things taking place, you know that the kingdom of God is near." Its main drawback is that it contradicts Jesus' many warnings that it is impossible to know when the end will come (in Luke's own writings, see Luke 12:35–40 and Acts 1:7). Another possible interpretation is that Jesus expected the kingdom of God to come very soon, possibly on the heels of the destruction of Jerusalem. This understanding of the text finds support in verse 32: "this generation will not pass away until all things have taken place." Its main difficulty is that presumably Luke was writing well after the fall of Jerusalem, and he knew that the end had not come; even more, he was writing at a time of relative peace when persecution of Christians both by Jews and by Romans had abated. Jerusalem had been destroyed; the original generation had passed; and still the end had not come. It is difficult to imagine that he would have put in Jesus' mouth prophecies that history had proven wrong.

For these reasons, it seems best to interpret the text as bearing the same general thrust as many of the parables of stewardship: telling the disciples how to behave while awaiting the end. On this score, Jesus' main warning is not to believe any who claim to know when the end will come: "Beware that you are not led astray; for many will come in my name and say, 'I am he!' and, 'The time is near!' Do not go after them" (v. 8). As a corollary of that main warning, Jesus then tells them both about the destruction of Jerusalem (21:9–11)—which Luke knew at the time of his writing—and about how even before that fall his disciples would be persecuted (21:12–19)—of which Luke also knew, as Acts well shows. The siege and destruction of Jerusalem are described in terms, and even with words, that are parallel to the account of Jewish historian Flavius Josephus. Verses 12–19 are almost an outline of what Luke will later tell in Acts about the subsequent history of the Christian community, although obviously the phrase "not a hair of your head will perish" must be taken as either a hyperbole or even better as a sign that even death is not defeat, for at the time of this writing Luke already knew of the deaths of at least Stephen and James. Even before the fall of Jerusalem and its awesome events of death and destruction, the disciples of Jesus will be persecuted.

Then, beginning in verse 25, Jesus tells his disciples that even the destruction of Jerusalem is not as catastrophic an event as they should expect. That destruction is just a sign or a foretaste of even more ominous events. Now he speaks of "signs in the sun, the moon, and the stars," as well as "roaring of the sea and the waves"; and these affect the entire inhabited world, the *oikoumenē* (v. 26). It is at that time that "they will see 'the Son of Man coming in a cloud' with power and great glory."

Two points are significant about this coming of the Son of Man. The first is that he comes "in a cloud." This reminds us of Acts 1:9, 11, where the disciples see Jesus being lifted into heaven by "a cloud," and are then told: "This Jesus, who has been taken up from you into heaven, will come in the same way as you saw him go into heaven."

The other important point about the coming of the Son of Man is the contrast between the common reaction and what should be the disciples' attitude. "People will faint from fear and foreboding of what is coming," while the disciples are told to "stand up and raise your heads, because your redemption is drawing near."

This latter contrast is indicative of the main difficulty many Christians have with eschatology. Many of us are so well installed in the present order that we look at its passing not with hope, but rather with dread. We are not among those who are to "stand up and raise your heads, because your redemption is coming near," but rather among those who "faint from fear and foreboding of what is coming upon the world." We convince ourselves that the kingdom of Christian hope is a nice idea, but little more than a chimera. It is not rational. It is the expectation of a bygone age of superstition, still kept alive by ignorant people who should know better. But perhaps our thinking on this matter is tainted by our own secret hope, which is no longer the hope for the new order, but rather the hope that the present will never pass away. And so, just as Augustine used to pray, "Give me chastity, but not just yet," we pray, "Thy kingdom come," and then silently add, "but not just yet." It is precisely because of this that Jesus warns: "Be on guard so that your hearts are not weighed down with dissipation and drunkenness and the worries of this life, and that day does not catch you unexpectedly, like a trap" (vv. 34–35).

For these and other reasons, eschatology has very bad press among many "mainline" Christians. Eschatology is left to those who claim to know that we are now on the fourth or the fifth trumpet of the Apocalypse; or that the beast is X or Y; or that the "rapture" will take place this coming Wednesday. But the fact of the matter is that the gospel of Jesus Christ is unintelligible without eschatology—without the hope and the promise of a coming order of love, peace, and justice. Were we to take the very Gospel of Luke we have been reading, and tear out every page that speaks of the promise of the kingdom, or of the day of the return of the absent Master, very little would be left!

The short parable or simile of the Fig Tree (vv. 29–33) illustrates this point, leaving us without excuse. The tree tells us that summer is near; it is a sign of things to come. We may not be ready for the coming future; but it is coming as surely as the first leaves on a tree presage summer. We wish the present season would continue. We do not want things to pass away. But all things ("heaven and earth") will pass away. No matter how settled we may be in the present season, the new order is coming, because, as Jesus says, "my words will not pass away."

But we prefer a "gospel" without eschatology—a "good news" without hope—because for many of us such "good news" is not so good. We prefer a gospel without eschatology, because the good news of the great reversal that Luke has been proclaiming all along does not seem so good to us. If the promised great reversal is for the benefit of sinners rather than properly religious folk, for the exploited, for the poor, for those who have no other hope, where does that leave us? How can such a reversal be a promise of hope for us who are now, so to speak, on top of the heap? This is why, while for most Christians eschatology is a matter of hope, for many others it has become a matter of fear. When the latter is the case, change ceases being a promise and becomes a threat.

There is only one way, and it is to this that Jesus refers in verses 12–19. It is the way of living now as those who know that a different future awaits. It is a difficult way, for those who live out of a different order than the existing one will necessarily clash with the present order. The good news does not at first sound so good: "they will arrest you and persecute you. . . . You will be betrayed even by parents and brothers, by relatives and friends; and they will put some of you to death." This sounds so alien to us! Persecuted for being a Christian? Rejected by family and friends for our faith? That may have been true in the first century, but not in these enlightened times of ours! Yet the truth is that more Christians died for their faith in the twentieth century than in three centuries of persecution under the Roman Empire. And the truth is also that, while many of us experience a certain malaise about the apparent decline of Christianity (or at least of our "mainline" and respectable churches), throughout the world Christianity is growing by leaps and bounds among the poor and the disinherited, many of whom know that their faith will not make things easier for them—it will probably make things even more difficult.

What then about those of us who are not poor or disinherited, whose religion makes us socially respectable, whose mainline churches are the moral and social mainstay of our communities? If all that Luke says about the great reversal is true, there is only one way open to us: solidarity. The doctor of the law cannot suddenly become a Samaritan. He is who he is. The only alternative left to him is to act like the good Samaritan. The Pharisee cannot leave behind his faith, his piety, and his obedience to the law. The only alternative left to him is to join "sinners" in their pain and their trust in God. Zacchaeus cannot undo the evil he may have done while becoming rich on the basis of exploitation and collaboration with an oppressive regime. The only alternative left to him is to use the wealth and the power he has acquired to undo as much as he can of the evil he has produced. Those of us whom society considers respectable "mainline" Christians must understand that the gospel of Jesus Christ, and the promise and hope of the great reversal, make the very phrase "mainline Christian" a contradiction in terms—that the very name of "Christian" requires being at the sidelines, at the margins where people suffer and are exploited or ignored. This is the proper consequence of genuine Christian hope—and it is precisely for that reason that we would much rather leave eschatology aside.

# FURTHER REFLECTIONS
## *A Future to Live From*

In order to recover the full dimension of eschatological hope, we need to recover the full dimension of the future. For most of us, all present and future events are the result of past causes. Indeed, when we say that one event "causes" another, we take for granted that the cause comes first, and the consequence follows. But this is not the only way to think of causality. What we now know as "causes" are what the ancients would have called "efficient causes," because for them there were also "final causes." While an efficient cause precedes its result, as when a billiard ball hits another and causes it to move, a final cause is the goal that produces an event. One could say that, while efficient causes "push" things from the past, final causes "pull" them from the future. Things happen, not just because other things happened before, but also because they have a purpose. They happen "in order that...."

It is difficult for us to think in such terms, because modernity has been characterized by the great success of the physical sciences, and what such sciences study is precisely the efficient causes of things. If we wish to know why a billiard ball rolls into the pocket, we look at the other ball that hit it, then at the cue that hit the first ball, then at the arm that pushed the cue, and so on. This way of looking at things is important, for it allows us to foresee the consequences of our actions and of present events. I turn the starter key in my car knowing that it will produce a spark that will in turn produce a combustion that will make the engine run, and that when the engine runs I can move the car. Were there no efficient causes, or no generally predictable consequences of such causes, order would be inconceivable.

But then one can look at the same sequence of events from the opposite direction: I turn the key because I want internal combustion in the engine. I want internal combustion because I want the engine to run. I want the engine to run because I want to move the car. I want to move the car because I am going to visit my daughter. Thus it is not only the past that pushes the present, but also the future that pulls it. This is what is meant by "final causes."

> God's future is God's call to the present, and the present is the time of decision in the light of God's future.
>
> —Günther Bornkamm
>
> *Jesus of Nazareth*, 93.

These two dimensions are often present in medieval theological treatises, where God is said to be both the "first cause" (meaning the first efficient cause of all causes) and the "final cause" (meaning the ultimate goal toward which all things move).

Christian eschatology—indeed, the entire biblical view of history—must be viewed from the perspective of final causes, of the present being called toward a future, of God's final purposes being worked out. On the basis of that belief, when Christians look at the history of the world, or at our own lives, we must never forget that there is in all of history, as well as in each life, a "so that . . ." or an "in order that. . . ." Within this context, eschatology is a glimpse into that future so glorious that we cannot fully envision it or understand it, but for which we still hope and for which we live.

The future causes much of the present. I am now writing these words because they will be published; and they will be published because they will be read. Certainly, such hopes may never be fulfilled; but still it is out of them that these words are written, and without that hope they would not be written.

The other side of the same coin is that our faith in the future is either corroborated or belied by our present actions. If I say that I expect this book to be published, but do not write it, no one will believe that I really expect the book to be published. If I claim belief in a coming kingdom of peace, love, and justice, and meanwhile do not practice peace, love, and justice, all my protestations of faith will avail nothing.

Once we understand this, we see that eschatology is more than speculation about the "last things," or about whether the millennium comes before or after the Parousia. Eschatology is the very basis of our hope, and therefore of our Christian life. It is also the basis of our proclamation, and a corroboration of our belief in what we preach. Eschatological hope is the future out of which we live. And if we do not live out of this future, we find ourselves as in a position where, Paul would say, "our proclamation has been in vain and your faith has been in vain" (1 Cor. 15:14).

## 22:1–23:54
### *The Passion*

### 22:1–6 *The Plot*

Even as hope provides a vision of the future, the present cannot be avoided. Luke quickly brings us back to the present order, where people plot evil and work injustice. In this present order, religious sentiments, fear, and greed combine to serve the powers of evil. Ironically, all of this happens as the greatest religious festival in Israel is approaching. It is a feast that celebrates Israel's deliverance from the imperial yoke of Egypt; and yet the religious leaders of Israel now plot to turn Jesus over to the new imperial power, Rome. Luke tells us that they did this because "they were afraid of the people." Such fear may have been twofold. On the one hand, it is clear that they were afraid of the possible reaction of the people to the public arrest of Jesus. On the other, they may also have been afraid of the political consequences were the people to become too enthusiastic over Jesus. (In John 11:47–50 we are told that the chief priests and the Pharisees began plotting the death of Jesus because they were afraid that, were his fame and following to become too great, Rome would intervene to the detriment of Israel.) Many traditional interpretations of the plot to kill Jesus focus entirely on the religious issues involved, as if religion ever existed without a political, social, and psychological context. Here that context is one of imperial presence, popular hopes of delivery, and an elite trying to navigate between one and the other—and using its religious authority to that end. Although technically Judea was not a Roman colony in the sense in which that word was used then, it was a colony in the modern sense. The chief priests, the scribes, and the officers of the temple had to walk the fine line that local colonial elites always have to walk: they must please the imperial power without completely alienating the population.

Then, in verse 3, in comes Judas; or rather, Satan comes into Judas. With Judas and Satan, greed also enters into the picture. The elite are willing to pay a price in order to be able to arrest Jesus without causing a riot, and Judas is willing to provide them the means to do so in exchange for money. The stage is set for the betrayal and the arrest.

### 22:7–38 The Passover Meal

Passover was the great Jewish festival celebrating the liberation of the people from the yoke of Egypt. Its basic theme was remembrance leading to hope. This was introduced by the ritual question, "Why is this night different from all others?" The response began with the story of the first Passover, followed by a recital of other occasions in which God had delivered Israel, and usually concluded with a prayer for the liberation of the land of Israel from Roman rule—although one may well imagine that this last prayer was not always uttered in the Passover meals of those who supported Rome's power and benefited from it.

### 22:7–20 The Preparation and the Institution of the Lord's Supper

The story of the preparation for the Passover meal (22:7–13) raises the same sort of questions that were discussed in connection with the preparation of Jesus' entry into Jerusalem (19:28–40). Here again the main thrust of the story is that what is about to happen is not a matter of chance or the mere result of historical circumstance, but is part of a divine plan that is being fulfilled.

Luke's account of the Last Supper (22:14–20) differs in a number of respects from those of Matthew and Mark. Most notably, in Luke Jesus gives the cup to his disciples both before and after the bread, while in the other two Gospels the breaking of the bread occurs before the blessing and passing of the cup. This probably reflects various practices in the early church, for some ancient texts speak of the bread first, and then the cup, while others follow the opposite order. Even so, there is a structural uniformity in the use of practically the same verbs both in the Gospels and in ancient Christian literature: "he took . . . gave thanks [or blessed] . . . gave . . . saying. . . ." Thus, while there seem to have been variations in the manner in which the Eucharist was celebrated, there was also a degree of commonality.

The Lord's Supper, also known as Communion and Eucharist, has been at the very heart of the church's worship throughout most of Christian history. It has also been the source of some of the most bitter controversies among Christians and theological traditions. Thus one of the points of disagreement that arose during the Middle Ages between the Eastern and Western churches had to do with whether the Eucharist should be celebrated with leavened bread (as in the East) or with unleavened (as in the West). At other times, people have debated whether believers should come to the table to partake of Communion, or the elements should be brought to them. But by far the longest and most divisive controversies have centered on the manner in which Christ is present in Communion. In the ninth century, again in the eleventh, and particularly in the sixteenth (during the Reformation) and seventeenth, people condemned one another as miscreants and heretics because they did not agree on these matters. To this day, there are churches that will admit to Communion only those who agree with them as to the exact manner in which Christ is present in it.

The debates regarding the manner of Christ's presence in the Eucharist, and parallel disagreements on issues as to who is qualified to preside over it, how it should be administered, what sort of bread or wine to use, and so on, have obscured several dimensions of Communion that need to be highlighted, however briefly.

One of these dimensions is the connection between the elements employed in Communion and the meal itself. Traditionally (and still in many churches) the bread and wine are brought forward at the offertory. In a sense, they are our gift to the Lord. The bread and wine of Communion, unlike the water of baptism, are the result of human labor. In this they contrast with the water employed in baptism, which is used just as it is given in nature, with no human labor. Thus if the baptismal water points to the unmerited grace of God, the bread and wine in Communion point to the stewardship whereby God invited humans to share in God's work through our labor. God gives wheat and grapes; human labor turns them into bread and wine. In the offertory, the people of God offer their gifts to God. But then, in inviting believers to partake of God, we say, "the gifts of God for the people of God." We bring our gifts, but we are not the hosts. It is much as when we are invited to dinner and we bring our hosts a bottle of wine or a box of cookies. The table is still theirs. It is not our gifts that nourish us, but the meal that our hosts have prepared. We are responding to our hosts' hospitality with a much lesser sign of hospitality. Even if when sitting at their table we consume the wine or the cookies we brought, they are still the hosts, and we are the guests who in bringing a gift have offered a sign that we wish to partake of their hospitality not only by partaking of the meal, but also by being hospitable, as they are. In the Eucharist, the people bring their gifts to the table, but the meal is much more than what they brought. When the celebrant says, "the gifts of God for the people of God," we are being invited to share not only in what we offered, but also in what God is offering.

> From the Last Supper there stretches the unbroken chain of all those whom Jesus has sent out on his mission with his word. Link after link falls into place in this succession of the living bread and the earthly wine, this chain of human words and human signs.
>
> —Karl Rahner
>
> *Biblical Homilies*, trans. Desmond Forristal and Richard Strachan (Dublin: Herder and Herder, 1966), 52.

We also need to pay more attention to the possible meanings of the words, "Do this." They certainly mean that the followers of Jesus ought to gather periodically for a meal such as Jesus celebrated with his disciples. This is why through the ages Christians have responded to the wondrous gifts of God by gathering to break the bread and share the cup. This is also why through the ages, when cruelly oppressed or sorely tried, Christians have responded by gathering to break bread. But "Do this" may also be understood as referring to "my body, which is given for you." If this is the case, then "Do this in remembrance of me" also implies giving one's life and body for others. And this too Christians have done through the ages, often inspired by the eucharistic meal. It was of this that Ignatius of Antioch spoke on his way to martyrdom: "I am God's wheat, to be ground by the teeth of the beasts and thus be presented as pure bread of Christ. . . . Allow me to be an imitator of the passion of my God."[1]

Finally, we must look at the words "in remembrance of me" in their original context of a Passover celebration. As stated above, at the Passover meal the entire history of God's redemptive dealings with Israel was rehearsed, centering on God's great liberating act in bringing the people out of Egypt, remembering similar liberating interventions, and finally expressing the hope and the longing for a new liberation. At the Passover, not only the past but also the future is remembered. The Passover is a celebration of the certain hope that the God who brought the people out of Egypt will again lead the people into renewed life and freedom. Likewise, when we "do this" in remembrance of Jesus, we remember not only his cross and resurrection, but also the promise that we will again drink with him of the fruit of the vine in the kingdom of God. Significantly, the most ancient extant eucharistic prayer has this eschatological dimension: "As this loaf was scattered over the hills, and has been gathered into one, so may your church be gathered into your kingdom from the very ends of the earth."[2] The same is true of most of the ancient eucharistic prayers that have been preserved; they rehearse the loving acts of God from creation to crucifixion and resurrection, all leading to the hope of the kingdom.

### 22:21–34 Betrayal, Dispute, and Denial
The three short accounts that follow the institution of the Lord's Supper are all set in the context of the same Passover meal, and this makes them all the more poignant and tragic. The first is the

---

1. *To the Romans* 4.1; 6.3, my trans.
2. *Didache* 9.4, my trans.

announcement of the betrayal by Judas (22:21–23). Theologians have been so engrossed in the questions of freedom, predestination, and predeterminism that we have often obscured the bitter irony of the narrative itself. Jesus has just declared that his body will be given up for them, and there sits Judas, who has already arranged to give up the same body in exchange for money. Presumably Judas too has eaten of the bread and drunk of the cup. He too has heard that the body of Jesus is being given up *for* him. And he knows that it will be given up *by* him!

Then there are the other disciples. Most of them have doubts about their own fidelity, except, presumably, Peter and Judas: Judas because he knows he is the one, and Peter because he is too sure of himself. The rest of the narrative will show that they had good reason to doubt themselves. But one thing is clear in the entire narrative: Jesus himself will remain faithful. Here again, the history of Jesus and his disciples parallels the history of Yahweh and Israel. The people will be unfaithful and will have to be called to repentance again and again; but God is always faithful. At Communion we do not celebrate our own faithfulness (tempted as we may be to do so) but the faithfulness of the Lord. If all who doubt our own faithfulness were barred from Communion, none of us would be able to come to the table.

The debate about who would be the greatest (22:24–30) is parallel to 9:46–48. In both cases, the argument about who is the greatest is placed immediately after Jesus announces the suffering that awaits him—which makes the argument even more inappropriate and petty. Here in chapter 22, the connection between this argument and the previous question of who will betray Jesus is not entirely clear. Without a word of transition, the disciples move from their doubts about their own faithfulness to the debate about their own greatness. Presumably, they thought that if they proved their faithfulness in some greater degree this should also result in greater honor. But once again the great reversal confuses their expectations—and ours. In human kingdoms, the path to greatness is mere loyalty to the king. As religious people, we tend to think that our greatness is in our loyalty to the King. But Jesus tells his disciples that their true greatness is in service. Does this mean that loyalty to the Lord is not important? By no means. But it does mean that true loyalty to this strange Lord of ours, who is among us as one who serves, lies precisely in serving as he himself serves.

In the announcement of Peter's denial (22:31–34), Luke presents Jesus addressing Peter directly, telling him that the entire group will be tested, and that even Peter will have to turn back from his fall in order to strengthen the rest. (In the Greek text, Jesus addresses the disciples in the plural, "sift all of you [plural]," and then turns to Simon in the singular, "I have prayed for you [singular]." The NIV makes this transition clearer than the NRSV.) Peter trusts in his own strength and fidelity, claiming that he will never abandon Jesus. But in fact Peter will come back and be able to strengthen his brothers because Jesus has prayed for him. As in the entire biblical narrative, what is certain and unmovable is not Peter's faithfulness but the Lord's. Peter will be able to return and follow the Lord, and strengthen the rest, not because he is faithful but because the Lord who has interceded for him is faithful.

The narrative about the supper ends with new marching orders (22:35–38). This is a puzzling passage, which only becomes clearer as we consider it in relation to the theme of rejection that dominates the entire scene. In 10:4 Jesus had sent his disciples with the instruction to "carry no purse, no bag, no sandals." Now he tells them that they must carry a purse and a bag, and presumably sandals, although they are not mentioned among the things the disciples are to take with them. During their earlier mission, the disciples had no need to carry provisions, for many would receive them. Now, as their Lord is about to be rejected, they too will be rejected. The time of general acceptance is past. Now comes the time of resistance and rejection. The time of the easy mission is past. Now mission requires endurance, preparation, and provision.

The reference to taking a sword has been much debated among interpreters. Is Jesus instructing his disciples to arm themselves, and to be prepared to respond to violence with violence? If so, this would seem to go against all his teachings and against all that the rest of the New Testament tells us about the early church. Furthermore, when the disciples take these instructions quite literally, and seem to make a quick inventory resulting in two swords, Jesus tells them that this suffices. Thus most probably the reference to swords is not an injunction to take up arms, but rather a symbolic reference to the difficult times to follow. Later in the same chapter, when one of the disciples wounds the slave of the high priest with a sword, Jesus rebukes him (22:51).

But perhaps more to the point is the context in which Jesus instructs his disciples to make provision for their needs. It is a context of rejection, opposition, and even persecution. Unfortunately, in times when the situation of believers has been quite the opposite, enjoying popularity, power, and respect, Christians and the church have all too often taken these words of Jesus as an invitation to amass wealth and resources.

### 22:39–53  On the Mount of Olives

We now move from the Passover meal to the Mount of Olives, where Luke tells us of Jesus' anguished prayer as he confronts the cross. Luke does not place this in Gethsemane, as in Matthew and Mark, nor in a garden, as in John, but rather on the Mount of Olives, where Jesus will also be arrested. One should also note that verses 43–44 do not appear in a number of ancient manuscripts, and that many scholars argue that the very structure of the passage suggests that they were not part of the original text.

There are two main topics in the passage: the prayer of Jesus, and the sleep of the disciples. On the prayer of Jesus, one notes two elements that are often in tension in our own views and practice of prayer: on the one hand, Jesus expresses his wishes; on the other, he submits to the Father's wishes. Quite often today we hear that if one insists enough, God will grant one's request. Just before writing these lines, I saw a preacher telling his television audience that if they are unemployed, and they pray hard enough, God will have to grant them their request. After all, he said, this is what God has promised, and God is bound by such promises! He was blunt: "Demand, and God will do!" Perhaps in response to this, there are those who claim that in prayer we should not place our wishes and petitions before God, for the purpose of prayer is not to ask, but rather to conform one's wishes to God's. Both of these views contradict much of what we find in Scripture, and certainly in this passage. Throughout Scripture (and certainly in the Psalms) there are prayers not only asking for God's help and guidance, but even arguing with God and protesting against God's actions and decisions. There are also numerous examples of prayers whose response is not what the petitioner requested, and is even contrary to it.

Significantly, in his prayer on the Mount of Olives, Jesus addresses God as "Father." Looking at prayer as a relationship between child and parent helps us avoid the two extremes mentioned above. When approaching a parent, one does not demand that something be done. Respect for the parent's authority and wisdom precludes that. But on the other hand, one who really trusts a parent does not simply say, "Whatever you say is all right with me." Trust in the parent's unyielding love allows the child to express wishes and feelings of which the parent may not approve. But the very act of expressing them is a sign of both love and respect. It is out of this relationship that Jesus is able to say both "remove this cup from me" and "not my will but yours be done." The two probably interpolated verses, 43 and 44, present an interesting paradox that is best understood in this context. An angel comes from heaven to give Jesus strength, and the result is not, as we would expect, that his fears are allayed, but rather that "in his anguish he prayed more earnestly." The more heavenly strength one has, the more one is able both to express one's anguish unashamedly, and to accept God's loving will.

The other central topic in the passage is the disciples' sleep, even when Jesus has told them to pray. Luke places this topic both at the beginning and at the end of the story, with the result that Jesus' own prayer in the middle of the passage illumines his call for his disciples to pray that they "may not come into the time of trial" (vv. 40, 46). He has long been warning them that his cross will also lead to their own. Now he seems to be warning them that they too will have times of trial such as he is now facing. Such times of trial are not to be sought. On the contrary, the disciples are to pray that they may be spared such times. But when such times come they must be faced in prayer much as Jesus faced his own trial in anguished prayer. This provided valuable guidance for Christians in the early centuries of the Christian church, when martyrdom was highly admired, but when it was also necessary to reject the attitude of those who actively sought it—the "spontaneous."

Although we often separate the arrest of Jesus (22:47–53) from his anguished prayer and his call for the disciples to pray, Luke makes the connection explicit: "While he was still speaking. . . ." In this he follows Mark 14:43: "Immediately, while he was still speaking. . . ." But, although Luke usually expands on Mark's narrative, here he takes the opposite tack: his story of the arrest is the shortest in all four Gospels. Such brevity underscores the importance of what is to follow. It is as if Luke were in haste to move on to the trials of Jesus, his death, and his resurrection.

The passage is connected to the foregoing by the reappearance of Judas and by the topic of swords. The last we heard of Judas, he was with the rest of the disciples at the Last Supper. Now he appears with his fellow conspirators. The implication is that while Jesus prayed and the disciples slept, Judas plotted. With regard to swords, the narrative on the Passover meal concluded with the disciples declaring that they had two swords, and Jesus telling them that this is enough. Now people come to arrest him "with swords and clubs," and the disciples offer to defend him "with our swords"—apparently two of them! One takes direct action and attacks the servant of the high priest. But Jesus rebukes him and heals the servant. The entire episode clearly refutes all bellicose or militaristic interpretations of the earlier passage.

Finally, one should note that once again what we have here is an attempt on the part of the religious leadership of Israel—"the chief priests, the officers of the temple police, and the elders"—to arrest Jesus when the people of Israel are not present (see 19:47–48; 20:1, 19, 26; 22:2). This theme of popular support for Jesus and his followers, and fear of the people on the part of the ruling elite, will appear again in the first chapters of the book of Acts (see Acts 3:11–12; 4:1–2, 5–6, 17, 21; 5:12–13, 17, 21, 24, 25–26).

## 22:54–65 *Denial and Mockery*

### 22:54–62 *Peter's Denial*

The stage is now set for the trial and death of Jesus. But before moving on to those events, Luke tells us of the fulfillment of Jesus' announcement regarding Peter's denial. While the other evangelists tell the story piecemeal, interspersing the denials with various events in the trial of Jesus, Luke tells it all at once. It all happens in rapid sequence in the high priest's courtyard. The time has come for the "sifting" that Jesus announced in 22:31. It is also the beginning of Peter's turning back to strengthen the others, as Jesus also announced at that time. Quite possibly, in placing the entire story of Peter's denials in a single passage, Luke is preparing the way for the story in Acts, where Peter does indeed strengthen the rest of the community. After we are told that Peter "went out and wept bitterly," he disappears from the Lukan narrative until 24:12, 34, then to reappear as a leading figure in Acts.

Of all the evangelists, only Luke tells us that after the last denial "the Lord turned and looked at Peter." Much has been made of these words and what might have been the mood of that look, whether of recrimination, of sadness, or of forgiveness. Calvin says that Peter "had to meet Christ's eyes to come to himself."[3] Like Calvin, most interpreters stress the themes of sin, repentance, and forgiveness. There is no doubt that this is central to the passage. Even though he had been forewarned, Peter still succumbed to temptation. And even though he had fallen into apostasy, he could still repent, be forgiven, and become a leader in the early Christian community.

> To wash away the sin of denial, Peter needed the baptism of tears. From where could he get this, unless the Lord gave him this too? . . . So even repentance is a gift from God.
> —St. Augustine
>
> In Just, ed., *Luke*, 350.

There is an irony in this passage that we often miss, and that comes to the foreground when we read this story in connection with the

---

3. *A Harmony of the Gospels: Matthew, Mark and Luke*, eds. David W. Torrance and Thomas F. Torrance, trans. A. W. Morrison, Calvin's New Testament Commentaries, 12 vols. (Grand Rapids: Eerdmans, 1972), 1:173.

three verses that follow. Jesus has repeatedly proven to his followers that he is a true prophet. In his own arrest and impending death, and in Peter's denials, his predictions have come true. Yet he will now be mocked as a false prophet.

There have been many debates as to who it was that condemned Jesus: was it Roman or Jewish authorities? In that debate, there has been much research into Roman and Jewish law, trying to establish who had the power to impose the death penalty, what were the rules governing procedures in the Sanhedrin, and so on. These matters are worth considering, for the notion that it was the Jews who killed Jesus has led to much prejudice, hatred, and outright violence against Jews. But Luke presents the story first of all as an act of senseless violence. It is not clear exactly who the men were who were guarding Jesus. Were they members of the high priest's household? Were they part of the mob that went out to arrest Jesus? Were they just bystanders who happened to be at the courtyard? It is impossible to tell; and in that lies the terrible message of the story. Pent-up violence can explode at any time and anywhere. Young men brought up in respectable households have been known to take bats and go hunting for minorities to beat up. Very normal and caring sons, husbands, and fathers, placed amid the tensions of war, have been known to commit rape and mayhem. Children bully one another in school, and the bullies soon have a following of others who both admire and fear them. A young man who feels excluded and rejected by his peers arms himself to the teeth and massacres his classmates. We tell ourselves that all of these are abnormal and aberrant behaviors. And they are. But they are also behaviors and tendencies that, in one measure or another, lurk beneath the surface in each one of us. Like Peter, we are ready to say, "Not I, Lord." But in so doing we ignore the power of sin and violence.

The power of violence lies in its ability to reproduce itself. This happens in two different but parallel ways. On the one hand, violence often creates a violent reaction, as in the case of the disciple who cut off the ear of one who came to arrest Jesus. On the other, violence also reproduces by contagion. The men who mocked and beat Jesus may well have been respectable folk who would never do something like that on their own. But now, in the heat of the moment, each inspiring the rest, they become a mocking and cruel mob.

These two ways in which violence exerts and extends its power require two different but parallel responses. The only way to prevent violence from begetting more violence is by reacting to it in ways that disarm and destroy it. This is what is often called "nonviolence"; but one could also say that it is "doing violence to violence." Violence can only be destroyed by peace (see pp. 123–25, "Further Reflections: Violence and Nonviolence"). Practicing peace, one undoes the power of violence—one "does violence to violence." In the rest of the Gospel story, Luke will show how Jesus does violence to violence—how, as Ephesians 4:8 would say, "he made captivity itself a captive," or, as others would say, he killed death.

The other response, the way to undo the contagion of violence, is to create a community in which love and forgiveness take the place of hatred and violence. This is the church, and it is to this that Luke will devote his entire second volume.

### 22:66–23:25 *The Trials*

Luke's account of Jesus before the council or Sanhedrin (22:66–71) is briefer than Matthew's (Matt. 26:57–66) or Mark's (Mark 14:53–64), and can hardly be called a trial. Here there are no witnesses, and the accusation of having claimed that he could destroy and rebuild the temple (Matt. 26:61; Mark 14:58) is also lacking. Also, in contrast to the other two Synoptic evangelists, Luke spells out that those bringing Jesus before the council were "the assembly of the elders of the people, both chief priests and scribes"; note once again the typically Lukan theme of the contrast between the people in general and the powerful among the people.

In Luke's account, the council's questioning of Jesus revolves around two titles: Messiah and Son of God. To the question of whether he is the Messiah, Jesus simply replies that no matter what he says, the council will not believe him. His answer to the second question is equally evasive: it is the council that says that he calls himself the Son of God. On this flimsy basis, the council says, "We have heard it ourselves from his own lips." In between, Jesus makes use of a third title that he much prefers throughout the Gospel narrative: Son of Man. In so doing he announces the great reversal that is at the very heart of the gospel story: the one who is about to be crucified, the Son of Man, "will be seated at the right hand of the power of God."

Eventually, it will be shown that both titles, Messiah and Son of God, do belong to Jesus. But significantly at this point he prefers to refer to himself as the Son of Man, a title that he has repeatedly used throughout the Gospel narrative to refer both to his coming sufferings and to his final victory. Thus this brief appearance of Jesus before the Sanhedrin, rather than a trial, sets the stage and provides the clue for what will follow.

Jesus is then taken before Pilate twice (23:1–5, 13–25), with a visit to Herod in between (23:6–12). Luke has already alerted his readers to the cruelty and injustice of both Herod Antipas (9:9) and Pontius Pilate (13:1). The preceding story about the hearing before the council has already indicated that the charges will at best be flimsy; but now they become false and insidious. They are false, because Jesus had not forbidden nor even discouraged the payment of taxes to the emperor. On the contrary, he had undercut the arguments of those who recommended such a course of action (20:20–26). They are insidious, because they are couched in a way calculated to arouse Roman suspicion and punishment. To begin with, they say that Jesus is "perverting our nation." If they had said that Jesus had been perverting "the people," Pilate could easily have dismissed the accusation; but perverting *the nation* carried serious political overtones. Then, they not only bear false witness, claiming that Jesus calls himself the Messiah, but they also politicize the matter by their translation: "the Messiah, a king." Finally, they say that he has been stirring up the people, and there was no crime that Rome feared more than promoting sedition.

But apparently Pilate does not wish to render judgment, and as soon as he learns that Jesus is from Galilee, he shirks responsibility, passing it on to Herod, who happens to be in Jerusalem. Even though "the chief priests and the scribes" continue accusing Jesus,

Herod's attitude is one of curiosity and contempt. He had hoped to see Jesus perform some miracle, and when he does not, Herod and his soldiers mock him, dressing him in what could be taken as kingly attire, and returning him to Pilate.

Luke's note, that Pilate and Herod "became friends," has been interpreted as a sign of the reconciling power of Jesus. But most likely Luke's purpose is to show that Roman and Jewish authorities—political and religious—were all equally involved in the contempt, cruelty, and injustice perpetrated against Jesus. This point is underscored when Pilate calls together "the chief priests, the leaders, *and the people*" (23:13). Up to this point, Luke has consistently presented the social and religious elite of Jerusalem as the ones opposing Jesus, and "the people" as either following him or at least not ready to see him arrested and accused—hence the need for Judas's betrayal. Luke refers to those present when Jesus first appeared before Pilate as "the assembly [that] rose as a body" (23:1), or as "the chief priests and the crowds" (23:4). But now, without any explanation, "the people" have changed sides. This is parallel to what we find in Acts, where every reference to "the people" is positive, until we come to Acts 6:12: "they stirred up the people as well as the elders and the scribes." The implication is that, while they accuse Jesus of stirring up the people and perverting them, it is the chief priests and their entourage who have actually perverted the people. One could suggest that this would not be difficult. If Jesus was accused of claiming to be a king, and of commanding people not to pay taxes to the emperor, anyone defending him could easily be tarred with the same brush. Therefore, seeing that the chief priests, the elders, and other members of the council were accusing Jesus of such claims, the people would be inclined to dissociate themselves from Jesus as strongly as possible.

Luke makes abundantly clear that there was no legal reason for the crucifixion of Jesus. Neither Herod nor Pilate found him guilty of any charges. Herod simply mocked him, and Pilate sought a compromise through the double route of flogging Jesus and offering to release him instead of Barabbas. Textual evidence suggests that verse 17, indicating that Pilate was expected to release someone on the occasion of the festival, is an interpolation. All that Luke says is that the crowd asked to have Barabbas released. At the end, a tragically ironic injustice results: Barabbas, who actually was in prison "for an insurrection that had taken place in the city, and for murder," is released, and Jesus is handed over for punishment. To compound the irony, the criminal who is released bears the name of Barabbas, which means "son of the father."

There has been much inspirational fiction written on Barabbas, the first person for whom Jesus died. The dominant thrust of that fiction is that Barabbas was overwhelmed by the gross injustice that had been committed in freeing him and crucifying Jesus, and this led to his conversion. There is nothing in any of the Gospels to warrant this. But still such literature has proven popular, because this is often the experience of those who come to the conviction that Jesus has died for their sins. The famous phrase, "there, but for the grace of God, go I," applies first and foremost as Jesus is led away to be crucified.

Pilate's reluctance to condemn Jesus (although there is no washing of hands in Luke) and Herod's finding no guilt in him have been interpreted as signs that Luke's writing had an apologetic purpose, trying to tell Roman authorities that there was no reason to crucify Jesus or to persecute his followers. But the truth is that Luke does not present Roman justice in a very favorable light. Twice Pontius Pilate offers to flog Jesus and then let him go—a punishment too harsh if he was innocent, and too lenient if he was guilty. The final result of the entire episode is that the wrong man is crucified, even from the point of view of Roman law and interests.

A very different message is drawn if we read the passage within the context of what was said above about conquering violence through suffering and the cross. Injustice is a form of violence. The best way to conquer it is to unmask it, to show it for what it is. In going to prison in Alabama, Martin Luther King Jr. laid bare the injustice of the law and laid the foundation for a new and more just order. In laying bare the council's prevarication and Pilate's timorousness, as well as the malleability of so-called justice, Jesus validated his call and his promise of a kingdom of peace and true justice.

## 23:26–54 *Death and Burial*

### 23:26–31 *The Way to the Cross*

The verses that follow stand at the center of the long-cherished Christian tradition of the *via crucis*, "the way of the cross." The "stages on the way to the cross" are a series of scenes or events, some taken from the Gospels and some the result of popular tradition, often depicted on the walls of churches, or along paths in monasteries and retreat centers, at which believers stop and meditate on the sufferings of Jesus and their own spiritual life.

Verse 26 says that "they" led him away, and then "they" seized Simon of Cyrene. Who are "they"? In Greek the subject is often implicit in the verb, and such is the case here. Are these "they" who now lead Jesus away the same who led him away after the arrest (22:54)? If so, the story line seems to be that it was still "the chief priests, the officers of the temple police, and the elders," as well as the mob of henchmen they had brought with them to arrest Jesus, who now lead Jesus to the cross. Or is it the assembly that had earlier risen "as a body and brought Jesus before Pilate" (23:1)? (The verb in 22:54 is the same as in 23:1, and similar to the verb in 23:26.) Or is it the "they" in the previous paragraph, where "they" are "the chief priests, the leaders, *and the people*" (23:13)? The point is important, because it bears on the question of the participation of the Jewish people in the death of Jesus. Except in 23:13 and its context, "the people" do not participate actively in the opposition, conspiracy, and trials that lead Jesus to the cross. When we get to the actual crucifixion, Luke is careful to distinguish between "the people" and its supposed leaders: "the people stood by, watching; but the leaders scoffed at him" (23:35). If we follow Luke's account into the book of Acts, we find that almost at the very beginning Peter tells "the whole house of Israel" that they have crucified the Lord and Messiah (Acts 2:36). But "they" immediately repent, and from that point on, up to Acts 6:12, "the people" are generally on the side of the followers of Jesus and against the leadership that opposes them. Luke places the blame for the death of Jesus or of his early followers not on the people of Israel at large but on their leaders, who fear that Jesus and his movement will both undercut their authority and bring about the wrath of Rome, and on the Roman powers of occupation.

Simon of Cyrene is a tantalizing figure. He appears in all three Synoptic Gospels. Mark 15:21 tells us that he was "the father of Alexander and Rufus," which implies that Mark expected his readers to know who these two were. Both Matthew and Luke omit this detail. Had something happened between the writing of Mark and the writing of the other two Gospels, leading the latter to omit all reference to Alexander and Rufus? To complicate matters, Acts tells us that among the leaders of the church in Antioch were "Simeon who was called Niger" and "Lucius of Cyrene" (Acts 13:1). Was this Simeon called "Niger" because, coming from Cyrene, he was dark-skinned? Could he have been the same person who carried the cross of Jesus? In Acts 19:33 a certain Alexander suddenly appears, with no explanation as to who he is—certainly a Jew, and apparently a Christian, although even this is not clear in the text. In Romans 16:13 Paul greets "Rufus." All of these bits of information can be woven into several different plots. But the truth is that all these names— Simon, Alexander, and Rufus—were common in the first century, and we have little basis to identify different people bearing them. All that can be said is that Mark's readers were familiar with the names of Rufus and Alexander, and that a few decades later both Matthew and Luke saw fit to exclude them. By the second century, the gnostic Basilides claimed that Jesus exchanged places with Simon, so that it was the latter who was crucified, while Jesus, in the form of Simon, stood by laughing![4]

All of this points to the danger of reading too much into the text, as if it were possible for us to decipher all that stood behind it. This is particularly true when interpreting narrative texts originally addressed to readers who knew people and circumstances that we cannot now recover. All that we know or can know about Simon of Cyrene is what the text itself says, with the added datum in Mark that he was the father of Alexander and Rufus, whoever they may have been. The text always remains "other," with mysteries that we wish we could unravel but cannot.

---

4. Irenaeus, *Against Heresies* 1.24.4, my trans.

Having said all that, one is still tempted to reflect on the two men whom Luke has just brought into the narrative, with no introduction and no follow-up: Barabbas and Simon of Cyrene, respectively, the first person for whom Jesus dies, and the first to bear his cross. Throughout the last chapters of Luke, Jesus has repeatedly told his disciples of his death for them, and of the need for them to take up their cross. Now the first one for whom Jesus dies is an otherwise unknown criminal, and the first to bear his cross an apparent bystander. (Luke's wording here on carrying the cross is similar to Jesus' invitation to his disciples to "take up the cross" in 9:23.) One is tempted to follow this line of thought, wondering where Jesus might be at work beyond the confines of what we tend to think are his followers and believers. But one must take care, lest one allow such reflections to go far astray from what the text actually says, and into allegorical flights of fantasy.

The NRSV correctly refers to those who followed Jesus on the way to the cross as "a great number of *the* people." What Luke means is not simply many people, but many from among the people of

"Daughters of Jerusalem, do not weep for me. Weep for yourselves
    and for your children"
Those tears over those
who condemned Jesus
cannot be tears of compassion.
They are tears of unconsolable sadness
over the hardness of heart
that continually gives rise to fresh crimes.
They are a cry to heaven,
pleading for mercy
and for that heavenly strength
that can induce conversion
and thus halt the spiral of violence.
The weeping of the daughters of Jerusalem
was heard by the heart of God.
Jesus redeemed all.
To all he offers the opportunity to live a liberated life,
which will not call for weeping or lamentation ever again.
—Leonardo Boff

*Way of the Cross—Way of Justice*, trans. John Drury (Maryknoll, NY: Orbis, 1980), 61–62.

Israel. Once again, the people are not mocking Jesus, nor rejoicing in his death. On the contrary, Luke's use of the verb "followed" has connotations of discipleship. In particular, he tells us that some women from among the people were "beating their breasts and wailing for him." The reference to these women once again brings to the foreground Luke's emphasis on the role of women in the life of Jesus and of the early church. In these last two chapters of his Gospel, it will be women who wail for him on the way to his crucifixion, women whom Luke will single out as standing among the crowd (23:49), women who will accompany his body to the tomb (23:55), women who will first learn of his resurrection (24:1–7), and women who will first carry the news to the apostles (24:8–10).

The words of Jesus to the women may well bear two levels of significance. On the one hand, they appear to be an announcement of the evil that would befall Jerusalem less than forty years later—and before Luke wrote his Gospel. On the other, they are an eschatological warning of the evil to come upon the world. The phrase "daughters of Jerusalem" has a long history in biblical literature, and by the time of Jesus had come to signify the entire city of Jerusalem. In addressing these women Jesus is in a way addressing the entire city. Great evil will come over the land, to the point that what was earlier considered a blessing (having children) will now be seen as a curse, and people will be clamoring for destruction, even calling on the mountains to fall on them. All of this will be the result of the evil that these women now witness, for if "they" (the Romans, the religious leaders, or humankind in general?) can do this to Jesus "when the wood is green"—when the power of evil has not been entirely unleashed—it will be much worse "when the wood is dry."

> On the Cross there hangs the Lord
> Of heaven and earth
> And amid the stress of war
> Peace comes to birth.
> —St. Teresa
>
> E. Allison Peers, trans. and ed., *The Complete Works of Saint Teresa of Jesus*, 3 vols. (London: Sheed & Ward, 1946), 3:298.

### 23:32–49 The Cross

Although there is no other passage in the Gospels that has proven more fruitful in Christian literature, art, and theological reflection,

Luke's account is rather sparse. His report on the trials before the Sanhedrin, Pilate, and Herod is longer than his report on the crucifixion. Much of the passage seems to be constructed in sets of three: three crosses, three groups around the cross (the people, the leaders, and the soldiers), three sayings of Jesus from the cross, and three responses to his death (the centurion, the women, and his acquaintances, among whom the women are singled out).

The first saying of Jesus (v. 34) is absent from some manuscripts, thus leading some scholars to declare that it is not part of Luke's original text, while others argue that it fits so well within the framework of Luke's theology and within the tripartite structure of the narrative that it must be considered part of the original text. There is no doubt that the saying is consistent with Luke's understanding of the gospel. Jesus' petition that his tormentors be forgiven is parallel to Stephen's in Acts 7:60. As to the theme of ignorance, in Acts 3:17 Peter declares that those who crucified Jesus "acted in ignorance," while Paul says as much in Acts 13:27.

In most of the sentences describing the early proceedings at the "place that is called The Skull," it is not clear who is the subject of the action. For reasons of English grammar, the NRSV and other English translations supply the pronoun "they": "they crucified Jesus . . . they cast lots." The ambiguity leaves open the question of who "they" are. Presumably, they are the soldiers entrusted with the task of applying the death penalty; but the lack of a subject in these sentences gives the impression that there is enough guilt to go around, and has also provided the basis on which later Christians have often declared, "It was I who crucified Jesus." However, the lack of an explicit subject in

> How shall I express my delight on thee, O cross? By you has hell been despoiled, and its gates are now closed whom you have ransomed. By you the demons are terrified, repressed, conquered and crushed. By you the world has been renewed and beautified. . . . By you human nature, being sinful, has been justified; being damned, has been saved; being enslaved to sin and to hell, has been freed; being dead, has been resurrected.
>
> —St. Anselm
>
> *Prayer Before the Holy Cross* 3, my trans.

these actions is also an indication that the enmity that was unleashed against Jesus was not mere human animosity. At the cross, Jesus is confronting an evil reality that goes far beyond any human activity, plan, or conspiracy. Jesus is confronting the very structures of evil. In more traditional terms, Jesus is confronting the evil one himself, and all the powers he can muster, including the power of Rome and the subordinate power of the leadership in Jerusalem.

When we come to verses 35–36, the subjects of the sentences become explicit: "the people" (v. 35a), "the leaders" (v. 35b), and "the soldiers" (v. 36). Significantly, while the leaders and the soldiers mock Jesus, the people stand by, watching. It is as if the people were caught between their sympathy for Jesus on the one hand, and their fear of Rome and their own leaders on the other, and were therefore unable to do anything but watch. Clearly, Luke has no wish to blame the Jewish people for the death of Jesus, which results from the connivance of the imperial power of Rome with those local figures whose own power depends on Rome's approval. The inscription, "This is the King of the Jews," makes this clear. Neither Rome nor the Jewish ruling elite could countenance such a claim. Rome had to quash any hint of rebellion; and the local authorities who needed Rome's support had to make certain that they were in no way connected to any form of sedition. Once again, evil manifests its structural nature as it is incarnate in political and colonial reality.

The scoffing presents a subtle but piercing irony: both the leaders and the soldiers call on Jesus to save himself. Particularly the leaders say: "He saved others; let him save himself." Luke's intended readers (presumably all Christian) would know that Jesus cannot save himself because he is actually saving others.

Following the tripartite structure of the passage, in verse 39 a third scoffer joins the leaders and the soldiers: one of the two who are being crucified with Jesus. Here the same irony appears once more: "Save yourself and save us." The response of the other criminal is the first of a series of three indications that the one who is about to die on the cross is no ordinary criminal. First of all, he declares Jesus to be innocent—a verdict later reaffirmed by the centurion. He then acknowledges what all the mockers have rejected, and what the inscription says about Jesus being a king: "remember me when you come into your kingdom." The leaders and the soldiers laughed at Jesus as a pretended king; this man pleads before him as one pleads before a king.

Significantly, before those who mock him Jesus has remained silent. But now he addresses the one who pleads before him, uttering what in Luke's account is his second saying from the cross: "Truly I tell you, today you will be with me in Paradise." This saying of Jesus has often been used as a proof text to argue that immediately upon death the soul of the believer goes to heaven, against those who say that the soul has to await the final resurrection.

> His tragedy is that his introduction to paradise came so late. . . . And his glory is that he found him in time. . . . His tragedy and his glory are not unlike yours and mine. And Good Friday is the opportunity to redeem tragedy into glory. For what is our tragedy but our failure to grasp what Christ can do for our lives here and now? And what is our glory but to discover with him how to live in heaven even while we live on earth?
> —Howard G. Hageman
>
> *We Call This Friday Good* (Philadelphia: Muhlenberg, 1961), 29.

Without entering into such a debate, one can at least see that this is a rather flimsy argument. Indeed, were one to take this text in that literal and doctrinal fashion, one could similarly quote other texts to claim that immediately after his death Jesus was not in paradise, but rather in the place of the dead, or, as the Apostles' Creed says, "he descended into hell" (Eph. 4:9; 1 Pet. 3:18–20).

Such a debate obscures the text itself as a response to the irony that has permeated the earlier part of the narrative. Jesus, who has saved others, will not save himself. But even now, as he is about to die, and as he undergoes the torments of the cross, he is able to save the repentant criminal.

The story of the repentant thief is one of three signs before the death of Jesus indicating that this is no common execution, nor only the death of an innocent man. It is followed by the response of nature to what is taking place. The sun fades and darkness covers the earth. The darkness may be a sign of mourning on the part of all of creation.[5] Or it may be a sign that this is the time of "the power of

---

5. For instance, it is thus that Cyril of Alexandria interpreted the passage in the fifth century: *Commentary on Luke, Hom.* 153.

darkness" of which Jesus spoke on the occasion of his arrest (22:53). This became the standard interpretation during the Middle Ages, and in some cases into Roman Catholicism in the nineteenth and twentieth centuries, in which popular piety held that at this time on Good Friday "the devil is loose," and one should take no risk. To this day, in some regions of Spain and Latin America, children are not allowed to play on Good Friday for fear of what the devil, who is loose on that day, might do to them. In early Christian literature, the three hours of darkness were sometimes interpreted as a typological sign of the three days Jesus would remain in the tomb (see pp. 24–25, "Further Reflections: Typology").

> Created beings suffered with him in his suffering. The sun hid its face so as not to see him when he was crucified. It retracted its light back into itself to die with him. There was darkness for three hours. The sun shined again, proclaiming that the Lord would rise from Sheol on the third day.
>
> —Ephrem the Syrian
>
> *Commentary on Tatian's Diatessaron* 21.5. Quoted in Just, ed., *Luke*, 368.

The fading of the sun and the reigning darkness point to the cosmic significance of what is taking place. As the fall had implicated all of creation—"cursed is the ground because of you," Genesis 3:17—now the struggle of Jesus with the powers of evil, and his eventual victory, also impact all of creation.

The third sign, the veil of the temple being rent in two, has also been interpreted in various ways. Already during the patristic period some took this as a rejection of Israel and its faith.[6] Most commonly, it is seen as a sign that now the way is open for all to enter into the Holy of Holies, that God is no longer hidden behind the veil. In Hebrews it is a sign that we now have "a hope that enters the inner shrine behind the curtain, where Jesus, a forerunner on our behalf, has entered" (Heb. 6:19b–20a; cf. Heb. 9:1–14; 10:19–21). Thus, while Hebrews affirms that the rending of the veil means that the way to the Holy of Holies is now open, it also connects this with Jesus' role as the forerunner, as the one who by going ahead has opened the way.

---

6. Such was Ambrose's interpretation; see Arthur A. Just Jr., ed., *Luke*, Ancient Christian Commentary on Scripture: New Testament 3 (Downers Grove, IL: InterVarsity Press, 2003), 368.

After the significance of his crucifixion has been acknowledged and announced among humans (the thief), in creation (the darkness), and in the religious and spiritual sphere (the rending of the veil), Jesus utters his last saying from the cross, and dies. His last words, "Father, into your hands . . . ," close a ministry in which he had repeatedly announced God's paternal love, and the need to trust in the love of God.

Immediately after the death of Jesus, Luke once again refers to three reactions. First, the centurion agrees with what the thief has proclaimed from his cross: "Certainly this man was innocent." Second, the crowds return home, "beating their breasts" in a sign of grief and even repentance (see 18:13). Finally, Jesus' acquaintances, among whom the women are singled out, stand at a distance, watching—and Luke says nothing about their reactions or feelings. It is useless to speculate, as some interpreters have done, that their reaction was one of numbness, or of fear, or of expectation. What Luke makes clear is that these people witnessed the death of Jesus. This is important, because soon they would be witnesses to his resurrection.

> Mother Jesus . . . carries us within him in love and travail, until the full time when he wanted to suffer the sharpest thorns and cruel pains that ever were or will be, and at the last he died. And when he had finished, and had borne us so for bliss, still all this could not satisfy his wonderful love.
> —Julian of Norwich
>
> *Showings,* trans. Edmund Colledge and James Walsh, Classics of Western Spirituality (Toronto: Paulist Press, 1978), 298.

From the earliest times, Christians spoke of Jesus as their Savior. The very early Christian symbol of the fish was a way of referring to Jesus as "Jesus Christ, Son of God, Savior." There is no doubt that in the story of the crucifixion the theme of Jesus as Savior appears repeatedly. Yet the text does not answer the question, How is it that Jesus saves? Luke tells us that Jesus had to suffer (9:22; 17:25; 24:26, 46), but he gives little indication as to the connection between his sufferings and the believer's salvation. He does not even include the explanation that Jesus was to "give his life a ransom for many," which the other two Synoptic Gospels include (Matt. 20:28; Mark 10:45). He is writing from a perspective of belief and to an audience of believers; but while he tells the story, he does not say much by way of doctrinal interpretation. Clearly, his readers would know that Jesus was their Savior, and would see in Luke's writing the narrative of how this came about. But Luke would not tell them exactly how they ought to understand it.

This is not surprising. Although we tend to think that we express our theology in our worship, what actually takes place is most often the opposite: it is worship that shapes theology and doctrine. The early church was worshiping Jesus long before it asked the question, How is Jesus God? And it was celebrating the power of Jesus' work of salvation long before it sought to express it in a doctrine or theory of atonement.

Living twenty centuries later, it is difficult for us to see this. The course of history has shaped our understanding of the biblical text, so that we now read it through the lens of later doctrinal developments. This is particularly true of how we understand Jesus' work of salvation. One of the five "fundamentals" that gave its name to fundamentalism was the substitutionary view of atonement—that Christ died in our place, as payment for our sins. This view of atonement has become so prevalent that even those of us who are not fundamentalists often think that in departing from it we are also departing from Scripture. Just how far we are shaped by a tradition of interpretation is shown in the irony that the fundamentalist movement, which prided itself on being purely biblical and rejecting all innovations, declared that the scriptural view of atonement was one that was not fully formulated until the eleventh century, and even then was seen by many as an innovation!

As we look at the early church and the writings from that time that have survived, it appears that Christians tried to express their experience and conviction of salvation in Jesus Christ by means of a series of images or metaphors. It is best to call them such, because these were not competing doctrines or "theories of atonement," but rather alternative and often complementary ways to express a work of salvation celebrated in worship and lived in experience. While it is true that there were different emphases and emerging theological traditions, it is also true that these did not usually see one another as mutually exclusive. Therefore, when it comes to metaphors or images by which to express and seek to understand the saving work of Christ, there was little argument as to which were correct and which were wrong. As long as these various metaphors did not deny the physical life, death, and resurrection of Jesus, they were all acceptable and mutually enriching. One of these that has prevailed for the last thousand years is the image of substitutionary atonement: Jesus died in payment for our sins. Yet not one ancient Christian writer takes this to be the only, or even the main, way to understand Christ's saving work.[7] Other metaphors are Christ as our example, as the victor over death and sin (he "made captivity itself a captive," Eph. 4:8), and as the head of a new humanity (1 Cor. 15:22). This last image is significant also for the importance it gives to the church and the sacraments. The church is crucial to salvation, for it is the body of the new head. It is in the life of the new head, Jesus Christ, that the church has life, and in the resurrection of its head that the church awaits its own resurrection. And, just as branches must be grafted into a vine, and then nourished by it, in order to live, so must Christians be grafted into Christ though baptism, and be constantly nourished through the Eucharist. While all these metaphors are helpful, no one of them—nor even all

> If Christ be the Saviour of the world in any sense, the thing He did must be at least as great as the world. And if it is as great, then no less manifold. . . . It is only a poor Christ that can be housed in a poor creed, and a feeble prophet that is canonised when a sentimentalized ethic is offered as religion.
>
> —P. T. Forsyth
>
> *The Work of Christ* (1910; repr. London: Independent Press, 1958), 234–35.

of them together—fully explains how it is that Christians and the church owe our life and salvation to Jesus, even though they do help us reflect on and express the wonder of redemption through Jesus Christ.

---

7. Tertullian is the first to use the term *satisfactio* in connection with payment for sin; but in so doing he is usually referring to penance (*On Modesty* 13; *On Patience* 13). The one passage in which he seems to come closest to a substitutionary view of atonement (*On Modesty* 22) can also be understood in terms of Christ as the liberator and conqueror. It is not until the fourth century that one begins to find abundant texts that explicitly and undeniably interpret the death of Christ as a substitutionary payment for sin.

> But our Lord was trampled on by Death; and in his turn trod out a way over Death. This is He Who made Himself subject to and endured Death of His own will, that He might cast down death against his will. . . . Death slew and was slain. Death slew the natural life; and the supernatural life slew Him.
>
> —Ephrem the Syrian
>
> *On Our Lord* 3, trans. A. Edward Johnston, in *Nicene and Post-Nicene Fathers*, 2nd series (repr. Grand Rapids: Eerdmans, 1956), 13:306.

Nor does Luke support any one of these metaphors in particular. As we look back at all that Jesus has said about himself and his relationship with his disciples, and forward to the end of the Gospel account, it would seem that the emphasis falls on following Jesus, not just in acts of worship but in the very path to the cross and to victory through it. Those who follow him become participants in his sufferings and his cross, as well as in his new life and resurrection. As the story of Jesus becomes also the story of his disciples, they partake both in his cross and in his victory.

### 23:50–54 *The Burial*

All four Gospels stress the burial of Jesus, mentioning witnesses to that event. In the Synoptics, those witnesses are Joseph of Arimathea and the women. In John, they are Joseph of Arimathea and Nicodemus. The burial was important to early Christians because it precluded any notion that Jesus only appeared to be dead, and thus made clear that the resurrection was much more than an illusion or a conjurer's trick. To say that Jesus was buried, and that there were witnesses to his burial, was a way of saying that he had indeed been dead, and had risen from among the dead. For similar reasons, in the second century the Old Roman Symbol, the forerunner of our Apostles' Creed, affirmed that Jesus was "crucified, dead, and *buried.*"

Joseph of Arimathea makes the arrangements for the burial. The women are unnamed in Luke's account but are presumably the same as are listed in 8:2–3 and 24:10; they seem to be passive witnesses of the burial. Joseph of Arimathea is not mentioned in the New Testament in any other connection. Like Simon of Cyrene, he appears briefly toward the end of the Gospel narrative with little introduction, in order later to reappear in countless legends and traditions.

His role in the burial of Jesus serves first of all as a reminder that the Romans, not the Jews, were legally responsible for the crucifixion. Joseph has to ask Pontius Pilate for the body of Jesus. Also, being a member of the council or Sanhedrin, Joseph stands as a sign that, in spite of the impression Luke may have given earlier (23:1), the council was not unanimous in its rejection of Jesus. According to Luke, Joseph "had not agreed to their plan of action," and "was waiting expectantly for the kingdom of God"—which may be taken to mean that, unlike others in the council, he was unwilling to bend uncritically before the power of Rome. Finally, we are told that he was from a town in Judea, which contrasts with the women, "who had come with him [Jesus] from Galilee." The conflict between Judeans and Galileans may have played an important role in the rejection of Jesus; but this is not the entire story. In Judea, and even in the council, there were people such as Joseph of Arimathea.

The presence of the women in this passage prepares the reader for the crucial role they will have in the story of the resurrection itself. They are depicted as not taking part in the burial itself, but simply "following" and "seeing" where and how Jesus was buried. This apparently passive role will give greater credence to their witness after the resurrection. They had no part in the burial, and would be entirely surprised by the resurrection. They will be going to the tomb on the first day of the week simply expecting to anoint the dead body of Jesus with herbs and spices, which was usually done before the burial, but apparently in this case was postponed because the Friday sun was setting, and the burial must take place before the beginning of the Sabbath at sunset.

While all three Synoptic Gospels refer to the Sabbath between the crucifixion and the resurrection (Matt. 28:1; Mark 16:1), Luke explicitly says that the women rested on the Sabbath "according to the commandment" (23:56b). This may be interpreted in various ways. First, it may be seen as the ultimate tragic irony in the events surrounding the death of Jesus. Luke has repeatedly told of cases in which Jesus placed compassion above blind obedience to the laws of the Sabbath. Indeed, this was one of the early causes of his conflicts with the religious authorities of his people. Now his body has to wait while his disciples, ready to anoint him, observe the Sabbath.

Second, we may see in this sentence (23:56b) an instance of Luke's interest in showing that Jesus and his followers did not despise or reject the Law. The burial of Jesus took place in haste before the beginning of the Sabbath out of respect for that day, and out of the same respect the women waited until the end of the Sabbath to anoint the body of Jesus. Finally, it may be a way of pointing out that Jesus lay in the tomb on the same day on which God rested after creation—that Jesus' rest in the tomb, like God's rest in creation, points to a new beginning in history. (There was a tradition within Judaism that one blessed morning, after the Sabbath, the world would awaken and discover that, rather than simply another first day after the Sabbath, it was the eighth day, the fulfillment of all of creation, the end of the endless cycles of weeks and years. When celebrating the resurrection on the first day of the week, Christians were also celebrating the advent of the new, the end of history, the eighth day of creation! It is for this reason that many ancient baptistries are octagonal in form.)

## 23:55–24:53

### The Resurrection

### 23:55–24:12 The Women and the Other Disciples

The narrative connection between the burial and the resurrection is practically seamless. In 23:55 Luke directed our attention to the women who were present at the burial, and now he continues telling us about the activities of these women once the Sabbath rest had passed. It is interesting to note that here again Luke will tell parallel but different stories about the women disciples and the men. In this particular case, however, the story about the women comes first. These women have been present, but have remained mostly in the background of the story, ever since Luke introduced them in 8:2–3. In the narrative of the passion and burial, even while others deny Jesus or flee, these women stand firm, although at a distance. Now they come to the foreground as the first witnesses to the resurrection. They, no less than the rest, believe that in the cross all has come to an end. It is time to return home to their more traditional lives. But before they do that, they must perform one last act of love for their dead Master: they must anoint his body.

As one reads this passage jointly with those that follow, there is a marked contrast between these women and the other disciples. The women do not see the resurrected Jesus. The two figures at the tomb (presumably angels) simply tell them that he has risen just as he had foretold, and they believe. Luke does not even say, as do Matthew and Mark (Matt. 28:7; Mark 16:7), that they are instructed to tell the rest of the disciples (an injunction they follow in Matthew, but not in Mark). They simply hear the witness of the two men at the tomb, and apparently on their own initiative go and tell the others. In contrast, these others do not believe them, and all except Peter pay no attention. Peter himself, even though he runs to the tomb and finds it empty, and even though he is amazed, simply returns home and does not seem to do anything about it—not even tell the others. Even when Jesus appears to these other disciples and shows them his hands and his feet, they are still not quite ready to believe (24:40–41). The contrast is such that one cannot avoid the conclusion that it is purposeful, and that Luke is stressing the faith of these women who have traveled with Jesus from Galilee, and who were the only ones who remained true throughout the entire story of the betrayal. Even though the later course of church history, with its expectation of entirely male leadership, would lead us to think otherwise, it is they who bring the message of the resurrection to the eleven, and not vice versa.

While all of this is important, it should not overshadow or obscure the significance of the resurrection itself. Although Luke's accounts of the appearances of the risen Jesus are more extensive than those of the other Gospels, even in Luke they are brief when compared with the length of the Gospel itself. While such brevity might give the impression that the resurrection is not very important, probably the opposite is true: the evangelists are underscoring that the culmination of the story is the resurrection itself. The resurrection brings about a new reality, a new order. Things do not continue as before, and precisely for that reason there is no need to continue the story after the appearances of the risen Lord. Even Luke, who gives three such stories, mentions in passing that Jesus had also appeared to Simon, but says no more about it (24:34). The resurrection is not the continuation of the story. Nor is it just its happy ending. It is the beginning of a new story, of a new age in history. As we shall see in commenting on the story of the ascension, Luke is the only Gospel writer who says a word about what happened after the resurrection appearances. Later, he would continue that story in Acts. But even he knows that in a sense the story has actually ended with the resurrection. The victory is won. What now remain are no more than skirmishes in a battle that has already been won.

> From now [the resurrection of Jesus] on, all books on geography will have to be different; for it is here, and not elsewhere, that the center of the earth is found, the navel of the universe, the white post from which all kilometers and light-years will be measured.
> —José María Cabodevilla
>
> *32 de diciembre: La muerte y después de la muerte* (Madrid: Biblioteca de Autores Católicos, 1982), 175.

Although the resurrection was at the heart of the early Christian message and of the worship of the early church, the message of the resurrection slowly receded into the background; and Christian worship, piety, and preaching tended to focus on the death of Jesus rather than on his victory. Eventually, many preachers found it quite difficult to preach on Easter, for all they could say was either that Easter proves that Jesus was the Son of God, or that it proves that there is life after death. In this entire process, the resurrection of Jesus was displaced from its earlier role as the center of Christian piety and worship.

In the twentieth century, and even more in the twenty-first, great changes took place in the life of the church that began bringing the resurrection of Jesus back to the center of Christian piety and worship. In the traditionally Christian countries, Christianity began receding both in numbers and in social influence. This awakened a renewed interest among Christian leaders and theologians in the time when Christianity found itself in a similar situation, namely the time up to the fourth century. One of the many results of this interest (as well as of some interesting discoveries of ancient texts) was a liturgical renewal that to a large measure restored and adapted many of the worship practices of the early church. Among the resulting changes, some of the most notable were in the new Communion rituals developed by several major denominations, Protestants as well as Catholics. These new rituals focused once again on the connection between Communion on the one hand and the resurrection and final victory of Jesus on the other. They did not do this by downplaying the cross and Good Friday, but, on the contrary, by emphasizing how great is the victory of Easter after the great evils unleashed on Good Friday.

Meanwhile, Christianity was growing by leaps and bounds in countries where until then it had been only a small minority. This growth, coupled with the decline in traditionally Christian lands, meant that the numeric center of Christianity—and much of its creative strength—shifted from the North Atlantic to the South and the East. In many cases, in these lands Christianity is taking forms that are quite different from those that have become familiar to us in the West. Indeed, much of its growth has been not in denominations transplanted through the missionary enterprise, but in native churches deeply rooted in their own culture. Looking anew at the gospel story, these younger churches are often rediscovering elements in the Christian faith that had been obscured over the centuries of the history of Christendom. Much of this has to do with their contexts, which are seldom supportive and quite often hostile. In such hostile environments, the message of radical opposition, political conspiracy, painful death, and victorious resurrection truly becomes good news to believers. Quite often, these believers come from oppressed and marginalized groups, and therefore for them the victory of the resurrection is a sign of victory both over the oppressive powers of sin and of the devil, and the equally oppressive powers of politics, economics, caste, and ethnic prejudice.

Thus, in the areas that were part of Christendom as well as in the rest of the world, Christians have been rediscovering the significance of the resurrection as victory over the powers of the old age, and as the beginning of a new order and a new history pointing to the final establishment of the reign of God.

This sounds very positive, but is not always all that easy. Guatemalan Presbyterian poet Julia Esquivel has written a poem entitled

"Threatened by Resurrection." This may seem strange to us, that the message of Easter may be threatening. But the truth is that the resurrection of Jesus, and the dawning of the new with him, poses a threat to any who would rather continue living as if the cross were the end of the story. The women on their way to the tomb were planning to perform one last act of love for Jesus, and then would probably just return home to their former lives. Peter and the rest would eventually return to their boats, their nets, and their various occupations. But now the empty tomb opens new possibilities. Now there is no way back to the former life in Galilee. Even though Luke tells us that Peter simply went home after seeing the empty tomb, we will soon learn that this was not the end of it: Peter himself would eventually die on his own cross. The resurrection is a joyous event; but it also means that Jesus' call for his disciples to take up their cross and follow him is still valid. The road to the old ways in Galilee is now barred. The resurrection of Jesus impels them forward to their own crosses, and indeed, we know that several of the disciples suffered violent death as the result of their following and proclaiming the Risen One.

When Esquivel wrote her poem, part of what she had in mind was that faithful discipleship in her native Guatemala was a very risky enterprise, that things would be much simpler and safer if one were not impelled by the resurrection to oppose injustice, oppression, and all forms of evil. The full message of Easter is both of joy and of challenge. It is the announcement of unequaled and final victory, and the call to radical, dangerous, and even painful discipleship.

### 24:13–35 *On the Way to Emmaus*

All that Luke says about the resurrection of Jesus and his appearance to his followers takes place on the Sunday after his crucifixion. This second story takes place "that same day" on the road to Emmaus, a village otherwise unknown. It has three main components: the conversation of the disciples with Jesus on the way to Emmaus (vv. 13–27), the meal at Emmaus (vv. 28–32), and the subsequent actions of the two disciples (vv. 33–35).

In the conversation, Jesus remains incognito. Some have employed this story to claim that the resurrected body is so different from the previous body as to be unrecognizable. But this is not what Luke says. It is not the body of Jesus but the eyes of the disciples that prevent them from recognizing him. Furthermore, when appearing to the disciples later on he is fully recognizable by them. At any rate, this is not the main thrust of the passage, and should not prevent us from focusing on that main thrust, which is the relationship between Jesus and the entire history of God's revelation to Israel. At the beginning of his Gospel, Luke offered a genealogy linking Jesus to the history of Israel and of all humankind since the times of Adam. Now at the end he presents Jesus explaining how he fulfills Scripture, "beginning with Moses." We tend to read the story of the road to Emmaus as one more appearance of the risen Jesus; and it certainly is that. But it is much more than that. Note that these two disciples, although they have already heard the news of the resurrection (vv. 22–24), are still "looking sad" (v. 17). The resurrection by itself is not enough to wipe away their sadness. They are disappointed because they expected certain things from Jesus, in fulfillment of the ancient promises made to Israel (v. 21), but these things had not come about. On the contrary, the one whom they expected to be the liberator of Israel had been handed over to Rome by the chief priests and leaders of Israel (v. 20). Apparently they are sad not just because Jesus has died but also because he

> O Thou who this mysterious bread
> didst in Emmaus break,
> return, herewith our souls to feed,
> and to thy followers speak.
> —Charles Wesley (1745)

has not met their expectations. It is for this reason that Jesus shows them that it was "necessary that the Messiah should suffer these things and then enter into his glory" (v. 26).

Thus at the end of his Gospel Luke returns to a theme that he presented from the very beginning: Jesus is the fulfillment of the promises made to Israel. The good news is not only that he is risen, but also that Scripture has been fulfilled. The joy of the resurrection—as well as the entire life, teachings, and death—of Jesus is not only that death has been conquered, but also that this is the fulfillment of the eternal plans and the work of the God. The "road to Emmaus" that Christians and the church must always tread is the continuation of the road that Abraham took when he left the land of his parents.

The second section of the passage is the meal itself (vv. 28–32). It has been said that Jesus seems to eat his way through the Gospel of Luke, for he is frequently depicted at a meal. Significantly, the last thing Jesus does with his disciples before his passion is to share a meal with them, and the first thing he does when appearing again to them is to share a meal with them. This is no ordinary meal. It is a revelatory meal. It is a meal in which things fall in place for the disciples. Now they understand why their hearts were burning as he talked to them along the road. All the scriptural and theological explanations that Jesus gave them on the road now gain new meaning. Because he has been explaining these things to them, the meal becomes particularly significant. The scriptural teaching and the meal go together; they illumine and enrich each other. Without the one, the other loses something important. The Word and the Sacrament stand together: the Word explains the Sacrament, and the Sacrament enacts the Word and makes it a reality for the disciples. He is made known to them in the breaking of the bread; but it is because along the road he has explained Scripture to him that they know who it is that they know!

The two disciples now act on the basis of what they have heard and seen (vv. 33–35): they return to Jerusalem in haste, "that same hour," although they had earlier told Jesus that it was too late to be on the road. There they find "the eleven and their companions," which presumably includes the women who had found the tomb empty. Apparently Peter, who earlier had simply returned home after finding the empty tomb, has now had a direct encounter with the risen Jesus, and the disciples are commenting on it. To this is now added the witness of these two arriving from Emmaus, who tell them of the two events we have just discussed: "what had happened on the road, and how he had been made known to them in the breaking of the bread."

In this third section of the Emmaus narrative, the Word and the Sacrament lead to witness. Having understood the meaning of Scripture "beginning with Moses," and having seen the risen Lord in the breaking of the bread, they cannot simply remain where they are. They must bear witness, tell others. And so they hasten to Jerusalem, there to tell the eleven and their companions. The spoken Word and the enacted Sacrament are incomplete without witness; and witness itself involves both word and action.

> . . . the Word of God is not mere words, nor even ideas. It is always an action in which someone acts in self-revelation and self-giving. The Word of God is this Someone, the Christ, the living Word of God.
>
> —Louis Bouyer
>
> *Introduction à la vie spirituelle* (Paris: Desclée & Cie., 1969), 108, my trans.

### 24:36–49 *The Disciples*

"While they were talking about this . . .": Again, what we read as separate episodes Luke presents as a seamless narrative. The Emmaus episode took place on the same day in which the women went to the tomb. The two disciples returned to Jerusalem at the same hour. And now, "while they were talking about this, Jesus himself stood among them." As elsewhere throughout the Gospel of Luke, they are first terrified (v. 37), and then their joy is such that they cannot even believe it (v. 41).

The theological emphasis of this passage lies on the true, physical resurrection of Jesus. The disciples think that what they are seeing may be his ghost, a story parallel to the reaction of other disciples in Acts when Peter returns to them unexpectedly (Acts 12:12–16). Jesus seeks to convince them that he is truly risen from the dead, and that what they see is his physical body, showing him his hands and feet—presumably wounded—and inviting them to touch him. Then, in order further to prove the point, he asks for food and eats a piece of fish. The Jesus who repeatedly ate with his disciples, with sinners, with publicans, and with Pharisees now eats his last meal before leaving his disciples in the ascension. He does this in order to prove that he is not just a vision or a ghost, that he has really conquered death.

The one whose life the church shares in Word and Sacrament is not a ghost or a disembodied spirit. He is the risen Lord. Those who serve him do not serve a general moral or religious principle, nor just the natural spiritual urges of humankind; they serve one like themselves, yet Lord of all. And, because his resurrection is not a merely spiritual matter, they cannot limit their service to purely spiritual matters. The Lord who showed his resurrection to his disciples by eating with them invites his followers to show his resurrection to the world by feeding the hungry. The Lord who broke the bonds of death calls his followers to break the bonds of injustice and oppression.

In this passage, the order of word and act are reversed. The disciples on the way to Emmaus first heard the words and then partook of the act, the breaking of the bread. First came the hearing, then the bread. Here the disciples first see the act—Jesus eats the fish—and then are given the words—the teachings about Jesus as the fulfillment of what is written. Act and word are connected by promise. The resurrection itself is the fulfillment of the promises of Scripture. But then that fulfillment leads to a new promise: "see, I am sending upon you what my Father promised." Whether at the point of closing his Gospel Luke was already planning to write his second treatise to Theophilus, there is no doubt that these words, and the narrative of the ascension that follows, set the tone for that other book, Acts. Here, almost at the very end of his Gospel, Luke—who has emphasized the work of the Holy Spirit throughout his narrative—has Jesus promising his disciples that they will receive the Spirit, and that they will be his witnesses "to all nations, beginning from Jerusalem." Then, almost at the very beginning of Acts, he presents Jesus telling his disciples: "you will receive power when the Holy Spirit has come upon you, and you will be my witnesses in Jerusalem, in all Judea and Samaria, and to the ends of the earth" (Acts 1:8). Although Jesus' work on earth is now completed, God will still be present in the Spirit. The history that has come to an end in the resurrection of Jesus still goes on in the life of the church, until the final day of victory. After writing about "all that Jesus did and taught from the beginning" (Acts 1:1), Luke will write about all that the Spirit did in his disciples after the ascension and Pentecost.

## 24:50–53 *The Ascension*

Luke closes his Gospel with a very brief account of the ascension of Jesus, which he will expand at the beginning of Acts. The ascension of Jesus is both a literary bridge to Luke's next treatise and the theological culmination of the entire gospel story. As a bridge, it is repeated at the beginning of Acts, with some differences that need not detain us here. It is as the theological culmination of all that Luke has been narrating that the story of the ascension interests us here. Unfortunately, the ascension of Jesus has often been given short theological shrift. It would seem as if for many it is little more than a nice way to conclude the story, or a convenient way of explaining what happened to the body of Jesus after his resurrection: obviously, he could not die, and he is not here now; ergo, he must have gone to heaven.

But the ascension is much more than that. The ascension of Jesus to the right hand of God, as the Creed of the Apostles declares, is no less than the culmination of the gospel story and the beginning of

> O thou who in thy glorious Ascension madest divine the flesh assumed by thee and didst honour it by thy throne at the Father's right hand, make me worthy, by partaking of thy holy Mysteries, of a place at thy right hand with the saved.
>
> —Simeon Metaphrastes
>
> In *A Manual of Eastern Orthodox Prayers* (London: SPCK, 1945), 67.

the fulfillment of that for which humankind was created. As many early Christian theologians saw it (Irenaeus and Clement of Alexandria, among others), when God created humankind after the divine image, this "image" of God that was the model for humans was no less than the Word incarnate (see Col. 1:15: "He is the image of the invisible God"). Adam and Eve were made after the image of Jesus! Thus the incarnation is the fulfillment of God's plan to be united with the human creature. But the ascension is the moment at which that union comes to fruition, for now there is "one of us" where we shall all be—where from the very point of creation we were intended to be. It is to this that Paul refers in Colossians 3:3, when he declares that our life is "hidden with Christ in God": our life is in this Jesus Christ, one of us, who is now with God, and is thus hidden "in God."

> Our great High Priest hath
>     gone before,
> now on his church his grace
>     to pour;
> and still his love he giveth.
> O may our hearts to him
>     ascend;
> may all within us upward tend
> to him who ever liveth.
> —Arthur T. Russell
> (1806–1874)

The book of Hebrews makes this even clearer when, early in its first chapter, it declares that it is speaking of the Lord who is the image of God and who has risen and ascended to God: "He is the reflection of God's glory and the exact imprint of God's very being, and he sustains all things by his powerful word. When he had made purification for sins, he sat down at the right hand of the Majesty on high, having become as much superior to angels as the name he has inherited is more excellent than theirs" (Heb. 1:3–4). Then in its second chapter Hebrews poses the question of how it is that in Psalm 8 humankind is promised a power it does not have, and responds that we see this power in the ascended Jesus, for "As it is, we do not yet see everything in subjection to him [the human creature], but we do see Jesus, who for a little while was made lower than the angels, now crowned with glory and honor because of the suffering of death" (Heb. 2:8b–9a). Jesus has risen to the right hand of God as the leader or "pioneer" for those whose life is hidden with him in God, and who with him will reign when he is finally made manifest.

If so, the ascension is much more than a bridge to the rest of the story (Acts). It is the very culmination of the story Luke has been telling. This story begins with the creation of humankind (Luke

---

From this [the ascension] our faith receives many benefits. First it understands that the Lord by his ascent to heaven opened the way into the Heavenly Kingdom, which had been closed through Adam. Since he entered heaven in our flesh, as if in our name, it follows, as the apostle says, that in a sense we already "sit with God in the heavenly places in him," so that we do not await heaven with a bare hope, but in our Head already possess it.

—John Calvin

John Calvin, *Institutes of the Christian Religion* 2.16.16, ed. John T. McNeill, trans. Ford Lewis Battles, 2 vols., Library of Christian Classics 20–21 (Philadelphia: Westminster, 1960), 1:524.

3:38), leads to the incarnation, and is fulfilled in the resurrection and ascension of Jesus. The rest—the story that Luke will narrate in Acts, the story in which we still live, and the final consummation of all things—is the process whereby what we now see in Jesus will be true of the rest of us. It is this Jesus who from the right hand of God sends the Spirit he has promised, who clothes the followers of Jesus with "power from on high" (24:49) until we see him again in glory—meaning both in his glory and in ours!

# An Unconcluding Postscript

After some time of fairly continuous work, the manuscript is finally finished and ready (or as ready as it will ever be) to go off to the publishers. As I look back at the entire task, my immediate feeling is one of relief. But the truth is that I will also miss the time spent in the company of Luke and his many interpreters, who have addressed me in unexpected and not always welcome ways. This has been a time of challenge, refreshment, and often sheer joy. In the midst of a culture that is constantly telling us that "fun" is equivalent to being boisterous, being entertained, and spending money, I have had great fun sitting apparently by myself, but actually in conversation with Luke and with a host of others who are part of the same conversation: Irenaeus, Ambrose, Augustine, Anselm, Luther, Calvin, Wesley, Barth, and the lady in a church in Puerto Rico who asked me a few weeks ago about the meaning of taking up one's cross. . . . Now the task is finished, and the conversation will recede into the background, to be overshadowed by other conversations. But its memory will always be there, and I will return to it occasionally, much as one calls up an old friend, sometimes apparently for no reason whatsoever.

In this conversation with Luke, I have come to appreciate the larger structural issues within his Gospel. We are so accustomed to reading the Bible piecemeal, a few verses at a time, that we miss the larger narrative structures. In this particular case, the need to outline the entire Gospel, and to comment on it as a whole, has forced me to focus on these larger structural issues, and thus to gain greater insight into the narrative itself. Such experiences have then led me to the further conviction that, were we to ask Luke about his theology, he would simply point to his two books and say, "This is it." For Luke, theology is not a series of doctrines or of ethical principles, but a narrative. It is not something we distill from the narrative, but is the narrative itself. This is so because the God in whom we have believed is not a transcendent principle to be discussed, but an active, loving, and purposeful being to be encountered. Just as the best way to speak about someone is to tell that person's story, so it is when we speak of God, which can best be done by means of a narrative—in this case, the central story of God's action in Jesus. As the wise and learned have often forgotten, but the children know full well, there is no better way to speak of God than to tell a story!

But this is not just any story. It is not just, as has been said, "the greatest story ever told." This is not just one more story among many. It is not even the best story. It is unique. It is The Story. Reading Luke as a whole, and trying to keep in mind its full scope, it has become clear to me that Luke's story begins with creation (that is the point of the genealogy in chap. 3) and is not yet finished (which is why Acts is an open-ended narrative). It is a story that comes to its culmination in the empty tomb and the ascension, and yet it is a story in which our own chapters are still to be written. As I said in the introduction, Luke is writing about an unfinished history and an unfinished church. Yet, as I have read and reread his writings, I see that this is a cause not for anxiety but for hope. Although history is unfinished, we know where it leads. Although the church is unfinished, we know what it is called to be—and what it will therefore be, for what God calls God does.

If we ask again, as in the introduction, "Why Luke? Why now?" part of the answer is that, at a time when the uncertainties of history lead many to anxiety and even despair, Luke presents a history that, although certainly unfinished, leads not into an abyss of anxiety, but into a hope that cannot be undone.

During these months of writing, Luke has repeatedly reminded me that following Jesus is no easy matter. His message may be good news; but I do not always perceive it as such. This is particularly true as I have come to see to what extent the "great reversal" of which I spoke in the introduction pervades the entire story. As I began my study for this commentary, I knew—because many others had told me—that this great reversal was an important element in the Gospel of Luke. I expected to find it here and there: in Mary's Magnificat, in some of the parables, in the words of Jesus when his disciples debate about their own greatness. But I have found that this theme is so pervasive that without it the entire Gospel of Luke is unintelligible. Were we to delete from Luke all the passages that speak of such a reversal, we would have very little left indeed!

But that is not what has disturbed me the most. What disturbs me is that in so many instances I find it difficult to rejoice over the "good news" of the great reversal. On too many counts I find myself on the wrong side of the equation. How can I rejoice in the promise that the hungry will be filled and the rich will be sent empty away, when I know that, even though I would like not to think so, I am richer than the vast majority of humankind? How can I rejoice in all my privileges and my good fortune, when there is a possibility that all this may be no more than so much manure poured on an otherwise fruitless tree? How can I claim to do Christian theology on the basis of my studies and my degrees, when the deepest things of God have been hidden from the wise and the learned, and revealed to babes? I could probably use my own academic training in order to offer a glib solution to all of this; but then I would be denying the very Gospel I seek to interpret, and even the very Lord I seek to follow.

Luke thus leaves me completely disarmed. My education, my writings, my savings, my prestige, my resumé, count for nothing before this Lord of the great reversal. And I do not like it! I would much rather have a God who would reward my study of theology, my work in the church, my meager contributions to charity; but this is not the God whom I meet in Luke. This is a God on whom I can have no claim save the claim of grace. And, surprisingly, that is more than enough!

But something else disturbs me when I think about the theme of the great reversal in Luke. Why is it that this was never mentioned as I was growing up in the church, hearing sermons about the prodigal son, and about the rich man and Lazarus? Why is it that I never heard about this in seminary, as we studied the "Synoptic Problem," and the particular theology of Luke–Acts? How can it be that I repeated the Magnificat a thousand times, and for so long I read the Gospel of Luke, without noticing how central this theme is to the entire book? Could it be that over centuries of interpretation the church had so long read Luke from a position of privilege that the great reversal became one of those inconvenient truths we simply ignore? If that is the case, could it be that God's great gift to the worldwide church today is the growing church of the poor, who are teaching us to read the Bible anew? Could it be that God is using the last, the least, the poor, and the excluded to speak once again to the church of the first and the greatest? Could it be that the poor do have a "hermeneutical advantage," and that those of us who stand at the wrong side of the great reversal need the voice of the poor in order to renew and recover the joy of the gospel?

The task of writing this commentary may be finished. But my task is not complete. The writing is finished, because I believe I have done what was asked of me to the best of my ability—and deadlines mean that at some point we have to let go of manuscripts! But most certainly my wider task of interpreting Luke is not complete, because a conversation is never complete. In this particular case, it is not complete for a further reason: because the biblical text will continue confronting myself, my readers, and all generations to come, with its inexhaustible reserve of meaning. Interpreters today like to speak of this in terms of the "polysemous" character of the text. But I prefer to say simply that what I have found in Luke is the Word of a God whose truth, whose goodness, and whose beauty go far beyond anything we might conceive or imagine. The God who through the centuries has spoken to the church in the words of Luke, and who in these past few months has spoken to me in the same words, continues addressing creation in ever renewed ways, and calling God's people to ever renewed obedience. Ultimately, this is the reason why the biblical text is inexhaustible. The meaning of the text cannot be exhausted because God continues speaking through it to succeeding generations in ever-changing conditions and constantly facing unprecedented challenges.

Come, dear reader! Join the conversation!

# Selected Bibliography

Bartholomew, Craig, Joel B. Green, and Anthony C. Thiselton, eds. *Reading Luke: Interpretation, Reflection, Formation.* Scripture and Hermeneutic Series 6. Grand Rapids: Zondervan, 2005. A collection of 17 articles, several of them focusing on Luke's theology.

Bovon, François. *Luke 1: A Commentary on the Gospel of Luke 1:1– 9:50.* Trans. Christine M. Thomas. Hermeneia. Minneapolis: Fortress, 2002.
A detailed commentary, with particular attention to textual matters, literary genres, and the history of traditions.

Calvin, John. *A Harmony of the Gospels: Matthew, Mark and Luke.* Eds. David W. Torrance and Thomas F. Torrance. Trans. A. W. Morrison. Calvin's New Testament Commentaries. 12 vols. Grand Rapids: Eerdmans, 1972.

Craddock, Fred B. *Luke.* Interpretation. Louisville: John Knox, 1990.
Particularly helpful for preachers and others seeking the relevance of the text for today. Easily readable.

Culpepper, R. Alan. "The Gospel of Luke." In *The New Interpreter's Bible.* Ed. Leander E. Keck. 9:1–490. Nashville: Abingdon, 1995.
An excellent combination of exegesis and commentary, with particular attention to the possible implications of the text for our day.

Fitzmyer, J. A. *The Gospel according to Luke.* 2 vols. Anchor Bible 28 and 28A. Garden City, NY: Doubleday, 1981–1985. Probably the most thorough introduction and commentary on Luke available in English. Does not have as much sociological analysis as later commentaries.

Johnson, Luke Timothy. *The Gospel of Luke.* Sacra Pagina 3. Collegeville, MN: Liturgical Press, 1991. One of the best commentaries available in English, taking into consideration sociological and literary approaches to the text.

Just, Arthur A., Jr., ed. *Luke.* Ancient Christian Commentary on Scripture: New Testament 3. Downers Grove, IL: InterVarsity Press, 2003. A collection of quotations from patristic commentaries, often giving witness to alternative ways in which a given text has been interpreted in the past.

Talbert, C. H. *Reading Luke: A Literary and Theological Commentary on the Third Gospel.* New York: Crossroads, 1989. Particular emphasis on the literary and rhetorical analysis of the text, and how this impacts its interpretation.

Tannehill, Robert C. *Luke.* Abingdon New Testament Commentaries. Nashville: Abingdon, 1996. A commentary focusing on compositional analysis and on the particularities of Luke's theology.

www.wabashcenter.wabash.edu/resources/article2.aspx? Contains a well-selected bibliography on Luke.

# Index of Ancient Sources

# Index of Subjects

absence, metaphor of, 166–67
abundance, reasons for, 172–73
academics, remembering to make
    room for the needy, 80–82
Acts, book of. *See also* Luke–Acts
    connected to Luke, 2
    as the Gospel of the Spirit, 11
    parallels with Luke, 2
Adam
    linked to Jesus, 55–57, 59–60
    temptation of, 56–61
adoptionists, 53
Alexander the Great, entering
    Jerusalem, 226–27, 228
Alexandrine Christology, 45–47
Ambrose of Milan
    comparing Adam and Christ,
    59
    on Jesus' birth, 41
annunciation, 17, 20–21, 35
anointed, meaning of, 39
Anselm, Saint, 263
Antiochene Christology, 45–47
antiquity, little room in, for physical
    sciences, 82
anxiety, 160–62
apostles
    naming of, 90
    role of, as agents of Jesus' mission,
    117–18
Aquinas, Thomas. *See* Thomas
    Aquinas
ascension, 281–83
asceticism, 161
atheism, practical, 188

Augustine
    on the births of John the Baptist and
    Jesus, 29
    on Christ's birth, 20
    on the multiplication of the loaves,
    115
    on Peter's repentance, 253
    on Zechariah's silence, 28
authority, questions of, 229–30

Bailey, Kenneth E., 185
banquets
    importance of, 84–85
    as theme in Luke, 9–10, 116–17
baptism
    with fire, 51, 52
    with the Holy Spirit, 51, 52
    of infants, 215
    of Jesus, 53
    of proselytes, 50
    of repentance, 49–50, 51–52
    with water, 51, 246
Barabbas, 258, 261
barren woman, theme of, 19, 25–26, 58
Barth, Karl
    on continuity and discontinuity,
    30–31
    describing Christians as honorary
    Jews, 90
    on the virgin birth, 22
Beatitudes, 92
Becket, Thomas, 170
Beelzebul, Jesus' power coming from,
    146–47
Benedictus, 29